Emoji Speak

Also Available from Bloomsbury

Facebook and Conversation Analysis, Matteo Farina
Discourse and Identity on Facebook, Mariza Georgalou
The Semiotics of Emoji, Marcel Danesi

Emoji Speak

Communication and Behaviours on Social Media

Jieun Kiaer

BLOOMSBURY ACADEMIC
LONDON • NEW YORK • OXFORD • NEW DELHI • SYDNEY

BLOOMSBURY ACADEMIC
Bloomsbury Publishing Plc
50 Bedford Square, London, WC1B 3DP, UK
1385 Broadway, New York, NY 10018, USA
29 Earlsfort Terrace, Dublin 2, Ireland

BLOOMSBURY, BLOOMSBURY ACADEMIC and the Diana logo are trademarks of
Bloomsbury Publishing Plc

First published in Great Britain 2023
Paperback edition published 2024

Copyright © Jieun Kiaer, 2023, 2024

Jieun Kiaer has asserted her right under the Copyright, Designs and
Patents Act, 1988, to be identified as Author of this work.

For legal purposes the Acknowledgements on p. xi constitute an extension
of this copyright page.

Cover illustration and design: Jess Stevens

All rights reserved. No part of this publication may be reproduced or transmitted
in any form or by any means, electronic or mechanical, including photocopying,
recording, or any information storage or retrieval system, without prior
permission in writing from the publishers.

Bloomsbury Publishing Plc does not have any control over, or responsibility for, any third-party websites referred to or in this book. All internet addresses given in this book were correct at the time of going to press. The author and publisher regret any inconvenience caused if addresses have changed or sites have ceased to exist, but can accept no responsibility for any such changes.

A catalogue record for this book is available from the British Library.

A catalog record for this book is available from the Library of Congress.

ISBN: HB: 978-1-3501-3511-6
PB: 978-1-3503-7150-7
ePDF: 978-1-3501-3512-3
eBook: 978-1-3501-3513-0

Typeset by Deanta Global Publishing Services, Chennai, India

To find out more about our authors and books visit www.bloomsbury.com and
sign up for our newsletters.

Contents

List of figures	vi
Preface	viii
Acknowledgements	xi
Notes on Images of Emojis	xii
1 Introduction	1
2 Emoji Speak	7
3 Emoji Evolution	23
4 Emojing: How and Why?	45
5 Emoji Diversity	65
6 Emoji Power	91
7 Emoji Emotions	105
8 Emoji Sensitivity	121
9 Emoji Stylistics	149
10 Vision for the Future	169
Notes	177
Bibliography	189
Index	197

Figures

2.1	How emojis and punctuation can change the tone of a sentence	17
2.2	Examples of emoticons read vertically	19
2.3	A selection of the type of emojis used in China	21
3.1	Web 1.0 and Web 2.0 comparison	29
3.2	Face with tears of joy emoji	31
3.3	An example of the kind of 'fairy comment' you might see on TikTok	33
3.4	Redesign of the face with medical mask emoji to feature a happier face	35
4.1	Top 10 most used emojis on Twitter in 2021	47
4.2	Confetti effect when one sends a congratulations message	52
4.3	Sample message exchange that eight-year-olds might send	53
5.1	Responses from a Google Jamboard session	66
5.2	Pinched fingers emoji	75
5.3	Unicode emojis at the time of iOS 4, featuring mainly light-skinned person emojis	77
5.4	Person wearing turban and person with skullcap	78
5.5	Generic yellow emoji alongside five tones inspired by the Fitzpatrick scale	78
5.6	Combine two emojis to create a new one	81
5.7	Representation of the types of emojis on the WeChat keyboard	83
5.8	Alternative hugging emoji	85
5.9	An interpretation of Douyin emojis	87
6.1	Emojis used in a text to a landlord	101
6.2	Different versions of the gun emoji	103
7.1	Interpretation of the grinning face with smiling eyes emoji across platforms	111
7.2	Emojis and their typical interpretations in a Chinese context	114
7.3	A likeness of a real image sticker pack	116
7.4	Jjalbang	117
8.1	Rose, sun and coffee	123
8.2	Emoji Interpretations	125
8.3	Cute sheep sticker pack	129

8.4	Emoji diversity across genders	132
8.5	Conversation between two female participants	134
8.6	Table summarizing findings	138
8.7	Safe and sensitive emojis	139
8.8	Emojis that are okay to send to your seniors (Chinese)	139
8.9	Love hotel or hospital	146
9.1	WeChat 'custom sticker' feature	155
9.2	A style of comment used on TikTok, whereby each word is punctuated by an emoji	157
9.3	Conversation in a Buddhist group chat	158
9.4	A finger heart emoji and the real-life gesture	161
9.5	A sample reaction image used by a fan	163

Preface

My interest in emoji was inspired by my daughter. At the age of two or three, just as she was about to start talking, she was already able to hold a phone, scroll and select emojis[1] to express what she was feeling. As a linguist, I was amazed that a form of communication that didn't even exist when I was her age had in some ways taken the place of her first words.

These days, generations of children are growing up with digital media. A huge number of the world's children now have internet access at home or at school – although the Covid-19 pandemic has also exposed digital inequality as a very real problem, even in the richest societies.[2] Digital competence is now considered a core skill; children learn using tablets and other devices from as early as primary school. While some are concerned by the increasing role of the digital in our children's lives, our mass migration to virtual spaces during Covid-19 revealed some of the potential advantages to starting young with digital skills.

Being born into an age in which digital media is part of everyday life has allowed Millennials and Generation Z to develop fluent digital linguistic competence. What may seem as confusing as a foreign language to some is easily interpreted by many teens and young adults. Although many adults have adapted to the digital landscape – we all have that older relative who comments with strangely specific gifs – few have the instinctive knack for emojis and online communication possessed by younger generations. Understanding and using emojis is an essential part of communication for young people, who develop this competence from an early age. As more and more of their lives are mediated through digital technology, especially during the Covid-19 pandemic, they naturally keep pace with the development and ongoing cultural formation of this language.

This book looks at different ways of using and understanding emojis and visual forms of digital communication. How do our individual ways of using emojis manifest when we converse with others? And, of particular interest for this book, how can the language of emojis facilitate cross-cultural and cross-linguistic communication?

A few years ago, my daughter, now nine, surprised me once again: I realised that despite not being able to write in Korean, she was communicating with her cousin, who doesn't speak English, through social media. The cousins had found ways to communicate cross-culturally and cross-linguistically by sharing emojis, links, videos and photos. This goes to show that although English is the lingua franca of the internet, fluency in English is not a prerequisite for sharing and connecting online.

Those familiar with social media can express a great deal using a digital visual language that takes images and videos as linguistic resources, with recourse to English or other traditional written languages. Younger generations who participate online pick up a shared understanding of the grammar of this language, much of which transcends cultural boundaries, allowing them to communicate cross-culturally in ways their parents cannot fathom.

However, this is not to say the meanings of these digital modes of communication are shared universally. There is great diversity in how different people use emojis based on their cultural heritage, interests and age, as well as the context of a given interaction. All cultures and languages have their own forms of visual imagery that may not be understood by others. For example, many Korean stickers and *jjalbang* (both of which will be defined in due course) incorporate letters of the Korean alphabet, and many Chinese emoji equivalents rely on an in-depth understanding of the cultural context, certain inside jokes, and Chinese characters. Some can be understood even without knowledge of that language, but others are more complex and highly specific to that culture.

Emojis are now used in a diverse range of ways. Digital media is not just about connecting with friends; we now have businesses that operate entirely online, non-profits that use social media for advocacy purposes and whole social networks dedicated to finding work and advertising yourself professionally. Even if certain users do not use emojis in their posts, the visual imagery is still present through various reactions available to other users. For instance, Facebook provides a selection of emoji-based 'reactions' that one can use to respond to posts. Even the professional social network LinkedIn has a similar feature, allowing users to respond with a selection of emojis.

Different cultures may have differing views on when it is appropriate to use emojis. For example, in a Western context, it may be thought inappropriate to use emojis in a professional setting, such as in an email to one's boss. However, in China, where a lot of communication takes place through the multifunctional messaging app WeChat, emojis are common in work-related messages. For example, the red rose (🌹) emoji, indicating gratitude, appears frequently in Chinese work-related chats. This can be used between colleagues regardless of seniority, however, many other stickers and emojis would be deemed inappropriate to send to a superior. This shows how some cultures have integrated emojis into their registers of formality.

Different generations of people may also interpret emojis differently. Those who have not grown up with emojis tend to take them at face value or struggle to understand their nuances in a specific context, whereas younger generations and people who are highly online are more fluent in the various meanings of emojis. Many gifs and memes are tied to cultural moments or trends. But interestingly, many of these trends have emerged from a transnationally shared youth internet culture, allowing them to be understood cross-culturally and cross-linguistically. For example, many young people may understand a particular meme even if they live in different countries and speak different languages, whereas older generations may not grasp the meaning of a meme created within the context of their own language and culture.

Even the most basic emoji, the smiley face (☺), has different meanings depending on the context. Older generations tend to take this emoji at face value, assuming it means a simple smile, yet for younger generations, this emoji can also indicate passive-aggressive frustration in some contexts. This latter meaning is strengthened in its upside-down form (🙃). Given that there is so much nuance for even the simplest emoji, I am excited to present this deep dive into the ways emojis are used to communicate around the world, across languages, cultures, and generations.

Acknowledgements

This book would not have been born without the inspiration from my family, colleagues and my own students. I am very grateful to those who have provided valuable help at the different stages of the project.

Simon Barnes-Sadler, Benjamin Cagan, Niamh Calway, Frank Davey, Jiyeon Sheo, Yao Sun, Edward Voet, Zeying Wang and Marc Yeo helped me collect data from different languages and provided invaluable comments. Huge thanks to Loli Kim for helping me with the images in the book.

I am especially grateful to Louise Hossien and Alfred Weng Tat Lo, who helped me at every stage of this project and provided excellent editorial assistance and inspirational feedback.

A special thanks to Loli Kim for helping me collect data and for digitally drawing some of the images featured in this book.

I am also thankful to Morwenna Scott and Laura Gallon for their patience and encouragement throughout this project.

Last but not least, this project would not have been born or finished without the love and support from my family and friends – whom I dearly love. I want to thank my two daughters who always make me laugh with their use of emojis. I want to dedicate this book to my late Dad Taehon Joe and Stanley Kiaer, whom I dearly miss.

Every effort has been made to trace copyright holders and obtain their permission for the use of copyright material. However, if any have been inadvertently overlooked, the publishers will be pleased, if notified of any omissions, to make the necessary arrangement at the first opportunity.

Notes on Images of Emojis

Social media spaces are almost entirely copyright free. They do not follow the same rules as the offline world. For example, on Twitter you can retweet any tweet and add your own opinion. On Instagram, you can share any post and add stickers or text. On TikTok, you can even 'duet' a video to add your own video next to a pre-existing one. As much as each platform has its own rules and regulations, people are able to use and change existing material as they wish. Thinking about copyright brings to light the barriers that exist between the online and offline worlds. You can use any emoji in your texts, tweets, posts and videos, but if you want to use them in the offline world, you may encounter a plethora of copyright issues. In writing this book, I have learnt that online and offline worlds exist upon two very different foundations. I originally planned to have plenty of images of emojis, stickers, and other multi-modal resources featured throughout this book, but I have been unable to for copyright reasons. In this moment, I realized how difficult it is to move emojis from the online world into the offline world. Even though I am writing this book about emojis and their significance in our lives, I cannot use images of them in even an academic book. Were I writing a tweet or Instagram post, however, I would likely have no problem. Throughout this book, I stress that emoji speak in online spaces is a grassroots movement in which there are no linguistic authorities and corporations have little power to influence which emojis we use. Comparatively, in offline spaces, big corporations take ownership of our emoji speak, much like linguistic authorities dictate how we should write and speak properly. This sounds like something out of a science fiction story, but it is an important fact of which to be aware. While the boundaries between our online and offline words may be blurring, barriers do still exist between them. For this reason, I have had to use an artist's interpretation of the images that I originally had in mind for this book. Links to the original images have been provided as endnotes, in case readers would like to see them.

The emojis used throughout this book are either:

a. NotoColorEmoji © 2021 Google Inc, OFL License.
b. Twemoji © 2020 Twitter, Inc and other contributors, CC BY 4.0.
c. Openmoji © 2022 Openmoji, CC-BY 4.0.
d. Drawings by Loli Kim that evoke a likeness of the emojis that are being discussed.

1
Introduction

Emojis have come a long way. Beginning life as a basic set of pixelated symbols designed for an early Japanese web browser for mobile, they have evolved into an essential tool used by billions of people around the world every day in private messages, online comments sections and sometimes even work emails! At surface level, emojis are very simple to use and understand. The internet can often be a confusing place for newcomers, but try handing your smartphone's emoji keyboard to a toddler and they'll instantly be right at home with the charming little symbols. Looking more closely, emojis are so much more nuanced and complex than they may first appear.

The easy-to-use nature of emojis is probably the key to their success. Sure, we have been able to manually type out little smileys like :-) for decades now, but they're a little too time-consuming and lacklustre for widespread use. In contrast, you can adorn a text message with a colourful, eye-catching emoji with a simple tap and modern autocorrect will even suggest emojis relevant to your message to save you having to scroll through the entire list. To some, the simplicity of emoji is cause for concern. If emojis are so convenient and so efficient at expressing what we mean, will we eventually forget how to communicate effectively with words, dumbing down our language in the process?

Emoji is often known as a noun, but I propose it as a verb too. *Text* or *texting* is a letter-driven or character-driven term. Nowadays, we don't text; we *emoji*. Think of all the online communication you have sent today. How many emojis have you used? To our on-screen lives, emojis are essential. Our youngsters grow up as emoji natives. *To emoji*, thus, becomes a quintessential aspect of human communication. Emojis help us to understand others with different linguistic backgrounds and build solidarity between us. When facing difficulties, one simple emoji can speak a thousand words and seems far more sincere. Emoji imagery is powerful. For many social movements across the world, emojis are without equal. Emoji speak shows how letter words and emoji words are living together in a symbiotic manner. Every time we communicate online, we deliberate as to whether a letter word or emoji would be best to express and connect on screen.

To many, emojis might only refer to a pre-set collection of yellow faces, in this book, I show that emojis are so much more. Did you know that a sound or moving image can be an emoji too? And what about an avatar? There are all sorts of emojis when we look at the broader sense of the term. They open up a new array of potential avenues for human communication. Emojis make our communication colourful. We once lived in a world of black-and-white text, but in the emoji era, colour matters as much as any other visual or audio resource.

On the smartphone screen, letter words and punctuation markers take on another life loaded with emoji meanings. The borders between letters and emojis are often broken. *Emoji speak* is a term that I have coined to demarcate the arrival of a new speak that is by nature multi-modal and borderless. On computer screens, however, our emoji life is limited. For instance, even in writing this book using Microsoft Word, I have been unable to 'type' many emojis, as they are not compatible with the platform. I predict that this will change in the future, as emoji words are gaining more power.

Emojis do not live in one language. They are free from belonging to one culture or nation. Emoji speak liberates us from the rules of grammar and other apparatus that limits our communication. One of the first questions that I had to tackle in writing this book was the grammar of the word *emoji*. Is the plural form *emoji* or *emojis*? The *Oxford English Dictionary* asserts that either is fine, which wasn't surprising as most borrowed words in English are in the same grey area – for example, you can say *dim sum* or *dim sums*. Emoji speak reflects how our linguistic practices have changed and reached a point where individuals and subcultural communities play the major role in shaping our languages. Along with social media, emoji speak shows the changing of the times, in which ordinary people's communication matters just as much, if not more, than the elites who once set the rules.

One might say that understanding emoji is intuitive, but grasping the whole meaning and subtext may not be so easy. There is no dictionary that can include all the meanings of emoji in a context-sensitive and register-sensitive manner. The forms and meanings of emoji are constantly changing, as online communicators navigate and negotiate on-screen talks. Emoji meanings have to be carefully considered in accordance with the context. A red heart may mean nothing to some, but to others in, say, a strictly conservative Arabic culture, it could have serious consequences. In black-and-white print, there would be no possibility of using a red heart, but on screen, the colour of emojis brings out different meanings. For example, a red heart could seem more romantic than a blue one. One can also express politeness through emojis. This is particularly true in Asian cultures, where respect can be indicated using non-verbal gestures in real-life interactions. Emojis fill this gap, allowing for gestures to be replicated pictorially on screen. As such, there will be a difference in emojing styles in Asian and European communities.

Emojis help us to be super-quick and efficient when responding. Yet, this also raises a question: is this actually a good thing? This kind of rapid response is closely linked to the development of the smartphone. Our communication is now so directly influenced by technology that the two cannot be separated. Technology has increased our efficiency and productivity, but it is a double-edged sword. We may end up less human than we ever wanted. As we adapt to rapidity and hyper-productivity, our conversation may become like fast food, and we may lose the ability to produce and enjoy slow talk. Before the arrival of the smartphone, we were able to wait a couple of days for an answer to an email, and for urgent matters, we made a call. We knew the division between these two forms of communication. In the smartphone era, we cannot and do not wait. We expect an immediate answer for everything. Is this actually good for us?

This brings us to the plethora of questions with which this book engages, ranging from matters of pragmatics, ethics and legality. Another key issue is affordability. Whether you can afford an up-to-date smartphone or not can have a profound impact on your on-screen communication. Those who are not so keen to immerse themselves in on-screen life may become minorities in this super-digital era, too.

To many, *to emoji* means to use the pre-set emojis that their smartphone provides, though their representation is lacking. Using these pre-set emojis can have a direct impact on the way we think, both for children and adults. The dystopian futures that we have seen in sci-fi movies may be closer than we ever thought. Emojis make us express ourselves, but whether this is a positive or not is another matter. Emojis may look like manga or anime on the surface, but the reality is that they literally allow us to see into a sender's intentions. Sending an emoji is no light matter. There is no sense in saying, 'Oh well, it's just an emoji...'

Structure

I aim to provide insight into an emerging field of linguistics for which I coin the term *emoji linguistics*. This is a new field and one that is not always accepted without reservation under the linguistics umbrella. I hope to show the reader that emojis are more than a frivolous fad and have changed how internet users of all generations communicate online. As explained earlier, we will take a broader view of image-based methods of communication online, and use the word *emoji* as a verb (as in *to emoji* or *emojing*) to describe the act of using emojis to communicate.

In Chapter 2, 'Emoji speak', we will consider what the terms *emoji* and *emoji speak* actually mean. We will look at some key forms of emojis, including emoticons, memes and GIFs. The concepts of emoji native, digital divide, emoji expressives and emoji divide will also be expounded upon, as well as the power structures that influence our emojing habits.

In Chapter 3, 'Emoji evolution', we will take a look at the birth of emojis and how their meaning is negotiated rather than given. We will consider making our own emojis and the roles of avatars, and emoji ethics. Emojis are constantly evolving to meet demand.

In Chapter 4, 'Emojing: How and why', we explore speakers' motivations for using emojis in their communication, using my 'Three S' model to help explain the function of emojis. We will present various case studies, and look at how emojis live across the borders of languages and cultures. Emoji speak is a global hybrid form of communication that has become the norm in our daily lives. We are always developing and updating our own emoji speak idiolects and emoji speak as a whole develops in accordance.

Chapter 5, 'Emoji diversity', examines the relationship between emojis and cultural diversity around the world, and how the limited Unicode emoji collection struggles to meet varied demands. We will look at how Asian countries tend to use the emojis provided by specific platforms to fill the void that Western-centric Unicode emojis cannot fill. I pay special attention to emoji use on WeChat and Douyin by Chinese demographics.

Chapter 6, 'Emoji power', explores some of the ways that emojis can have a real impact on us and the world around us. As a part of speech, emojis can take on real significance in legal cases, in much the same way as standard speech. Emojis are also affected by censorship, social movements and marketing drives. As such, they are much more powerful than we know.

In Chapter 7, 'Emoji emotions', we take a closer look at how emojis are used to represent our emotions. Emojis often function similarly to facial expressions and gestures in face-to-face communication, bringing our online communication closer to our offline communication. However, a crying emoji is not semantically equivalent to actually crying; in fact, one might avoid emojis entirely when describing a real tragedy to convey the gravity of the situation. Where are the limits of emojis for conveying emotion, and how do they compare to real facial expressions and gestures? In this chapter, we also examine how these emotional expressions are acquired as part of our digital linguistic competence.

Chapter 8, 'Emojing sensitivity', deals with the role of interpersonal relations in the selection and use of emojis in non-English contexts, where factors such as the age, gender, and social status of both speaker and addressee often play a critical role in determining the grammaticality of a given utterance. It also considers how the general interpretations of emojis differ from culture to culture. Just as the same hand gesture might be friendly in one culture but rude in another, emojis are the same. Cross-cultural emoji misunderstandings illustrate how emojis occupy a space somewhere between global linguistic capital and regional language.

Chapter 9, 'Emoji stylistics', explores how we style our emojis to suit our pragmatic needs. We see how emojis are used in various subcultures to build new friendships and relationships and to maintain and strengthen our existing relationships. Like body language, emojis are essential to properly convey tone in our online communications, helping us avoid misunderstandings and convey a sense of friendliness and warmth in an online space that could otherwise be a cold and impersonal space. Emojis make the internet a warmer, more welcoming place!

Chapter 10, 'Vision for the future', is the conclusion, which will provide a summary of what we have covered up to this point and some ideas about what the future of our online communication might look like. It will also look at the linguistics field, and how studies of emoji can and should be integrated more into it.

2

Emoji Speak

Emojis are everywhere. Everyone uses emojis every day. So, what are *emojis*? Even though the word is used all the time, people are still not quite sure what the term means, nor how we should use them. Even the word *emoji* itself is tricky to deal with: is the plural of *emoji* just *emoji* or *emojis*? Were you to ask my ten-year-old daughter, however, she would say that emojis are used to let someone know whether you are happy or sad and that they help to avoid awkwardness. To some people emojis make a message sincere, to some they do the opposite. Ultimately, *emoji* refers to multi-modal speak. *Emoji* has a close link to pictures, but this includes letters that are interpreted as pictures, and even sounds too.

Defining emoji

The term *emoji* was added to the Oxford English Dictionary (OED) in December 2013, where it is defined as follows:

> **Etymology:** < Japanese *emoji* pictograph (1928 or earlier, perhaps after English PICTOGRAPH *n.*), small digital image or icon used to express an idea, emotion, etc. in electronic communications (1990s) < *e* picture (formerly *ye*; 8th cent. as *we*; < Middle Chinese) + *moji* letter, character (10th cent.; contraction of *mon* character, word + *ji* character, letter (see KANJI *n.*), based on a Middle Chinese compound; compare Chinese *wénzì* writing).
>
> The resemblance in form and meaning to EMOTICON *n.* is probably coincidental.
>
> A small digital image or icon used to express an idea, emotion, etc., in electronic communications.

Emoji is a relatively new addition to the English language. Yet, with less than ten years of history, the term is at the very heart of not only the English language but all world languages. Indeed, just as the word *emoji* is not bound to one language, emojis themselves do not live in one language. Emojis are translingual and transnational by nature. What *emoji* actually means is not clear. There are no grammatical conventions or rules that dictate how we should use emojis. Should it be *emoji* or *emojis*? The OED allows both forms, but in this book, I will use both depending on the context: when I want to emphasize the plurality of emojis, I will use *emojis*. Because of its English pronunciation being close to *emoticon*, *emoji* is considered as representing emotion. Etymologically speaking, *emoji* refers to pictorial words. As given in the OED definition, the word *emoji* is originally derived from Japanese. The Japanese term 絵文字 (emoji) is made up of three kanji (Chinese characters adapted for writing Japanese) that can be glossed as follows: 絵 (*e*) means 'picture' and 文字 (*moji*) refers to written characters or script. Emoji, therefore, can be roughly translated as something like 'picture characters'.

Emojis tend to appear at the end of texting chunks to show the sender's attitude. Emojis play an important role in creating emotional meanings. Emojis set the tone, but that isn't all. The emoji world is constantly evolving. Any pictorial resource used to communicate online can become an emoji. As such, the number, types and functions of emoji are growing rapidly. Of course, pictorial resources are used in our communication both online and offline, but what makes a pictorial resource an emoji is that emojis are found in our communication on our smartphone screens, and sometimes computer screens too. Emojis are found in different habitats to the other images in our world. Though emojis are often considered as adjuncts or appendices to written text, in this book, I propose emoji speak as a 'newspeak', which highlights that our communication goes beyond letter-driven texting, becoming multi-modal and multilingual.

Together, we will look at how emojis are used across varying regions and languages. These regions and languages have not previously been paid significant attention, and thus, we will see how the mysterious nature of emojis only becomes more mysterious when we consider how usage in other communities adds greater variation to the already complex English idea of *emoji*.

Sound and moving images are emojis too

Originally, emoji meant picture word but even sounds and moving images can be emoji too. I use the term *emoji speak* as a generic term for communication on screen that crosses the boundaries of language, cultures and nation states. Emoji can mean different things to different people. There are other terms for the various non-verbal signs used in computer-mediated communication (CMC), such as *emoticons*, *stickers*, *memes* and *image macros*, *GIFs* and so on, and this is made more complex as terms differ cross-culturally and interculturally. Their diversity reflects the flexibility and multi-faceted nature of the emoji world. Emoji is the most generic term that people use, hence, I will use the word *emoji* in a manner closer to its etymology of 'picture words', although the term can also include 'sound words', letters and punctuation markers. Primarily, however, emoji will refer more broadly to the use of all images (and even moving images) within electronic communications. Greater detail on all these types of visual communication will follow in due course. Instead of limiting our study to the emojis included on the emoji keyboard, we will look at the wider network of imagery used alongside textual communication on digital platforms as a complex and evolving system.

To emoji

I would also like to propose the addition of a *v.* to the *n.* in the OED definition quoted earlier. In other words, I wish to propose that *emoji* be used not only as a noun but also as a verb, as in '*to emoji*'. This is consistent with the use of 'text' as both a noun and a verb, which is linked heavily to letters. 'To emoji' reflects the evolution of online communication moving from letter-based texting to image-based *emojing*. I believe that terms such as *write*, *talk*, or even *text* struggle to capture the full scope of modern emojing behaviour. Emojis to the screen are what a pen is to paper. *To emoji* as a verb encompasses the use of a whole host of online messaging features: the emoji keyboard, stickers, soundmojis, memes, GIFs, emoticons, avatars and Animojis. Users can design and personalize many of these features, and as such, *to emoji* refers to an ever-expanding, ever-evolving practice. The word *texting* simply cannot convey the complexity of emojing. The way in which we engage in communication on our hand-held devices is entirely different to any other form of communication. Thus, *to emoji*, as a verb, is much needed.

Emojis for everyone

Never before has our human communication been so enmeshed with technology. Our communication evolution is directly linked to the computers, tablets and smartphones that we own. There are now over 6.378 billion smartphone users in the world.[1] That means over 80 per cent of the world's population owns a device capable of using emojis – and even more if we include tablets and computers in our estimate. The pandemic has catalysed our virtual immigration. Our lives have played out on Zoom and Teams since 2020. As we have discovered the holes in online communication, our emojis and memes have exploded in number and variation to fill the gaps, as we simply had no choice. Emoji speak has really evolved in recent years.

More than half of the world uses social media (54.8 per cent), and on average we spend two hours and twenty-seven minutes on social media every day.[2] This equals a record 12.5 trillion hours spent online in 2021. On Facebook Messenger alone, 900 million emojis are sent without text each day, and around 700 million are used in Facebook posts. Emojis are now a part of the mainstream and are used across generations, cultures and linguistic backgrounds. Even literacy is not a barrier to using emojis; they are extremely accessible. Thus, emojis are entirely ubiquitous.

The modern Web 2.0 is characterized by more active participation than Web 1.0, in which a limited pool of authors created content that was accessed but not influenced by other users, to Web 2.0, a user-generated social model in which users can easily engage with each other through a range of online platforms (including dedicated social networking sites and also forums, blogs, vlogs, microblogs etc.).[3] It is also characterized by the invention and widespread availability of the smartphone. Web 3.0 is on the way, with the arrival of decentralized blockchains and machine learning.

CMC is a very recent development within the much longer history of human language. Accordingly, it is perhaps not surprising that our traditional linguistic models sometimes struggle to account for phenomena in online communication. This can bias our view of new elements not found in pre-CMC language, such as emoticons and emojis, leading us to interpret them as paralinguistic or non-linguistic or to interpret novel vocabulary, punctuation and grammar as aberrant. Indeed, much of the existing writing on emoticons and emojis tends to view them in terms of how they relate to pre-CMC. For instance, some have interpreted emojis as if they are compensating for non-verbal information that would be available in face-to-face oral communication but is absent in online communication.[4] In our present study, however, we prefer to approach CMC on its own terms, rather than grounding ourselves in the linguistic models of the past. In this book, I show that emoji speak deserves to be understood in its own right as a new form of communication that shows the climax of human–computer interaction. Emoji speak that we discuss in this book is slightly different from other forms of CMC. In fact, computer screens and smartphone screens are not the same. The emoji's natural habitat is hand-held smartphones, which are much smaller than computer screens and yet much more friendly for non-text information. We are used to typing letters on computers, so computer screens are a less natural home for emojis. Emojis are not easy to use on computers. On the smartphone screen, however, the letter words and emoji words co-exist symbiotically. Colour starts to matter on screen. Emojis are part of the creative nature of human communication that transcends language barriers. Emoji speak includes a huge repertoire of multi-modal resources. Only by looking at their use, intentions and impact can we begin to understand this new form of communication that is developing so rapidly all around us.

What is emoji speak?

In this book, I propose a new term, *emoji speak*. The wording of the term is inspired by George Orwell's 'Newspeak' in *1984*. Newspeak, a combination of 'new' and 'speak', is a simplified version of the English language, which was supposed to become so reduced conceptually that it would only allow for positive discussion of the authorities' ideologies. Of course, emoji speak has no such sinister undertone, but it does bear similarities in the sense that emojis present a highly simplified and abstract form of language. Emoji speak is formed of 'emoji words', which stand in contrast to 'letter words'. The relationship between *emoji words* and *letter words* is not antagonistic; however, the two have a symbiotic relationship. As this book will demonstrate, emoji speak is not a peripheral part of communication, but a hugely important part of the computer-mediated communication that permeates every part of our lives in the modern day. Emoji speak liberates our writing from the linguistic authorities of grammar or borders of languages and cultures. It allows us to use all sorts of multi-modal resources to enrich the meaning and nuance of our online communication. It will open a new era of language where nation-state languages and their prescriptive rules may be less significant as the norms of language use come to be more determined by and seen as sets of idiolects and community practices.

The pandemic has injected online environments into every part of our lives, and online space is no longer peripheral to our world. In the past, any form of written communication was limited to cold hard text. Emojis liberate our writing from the linguistic authorities of grammar, allowing us to use all sorts of additional visual and auditory resources to enrich the meaning and nuance of our online communication. Emoji speak is a generic term that encompasses the use of emojis on the emoji keyboard, stickers, memes, sounds avatars, Animoji, emoticons and more. Texting is purely driven by letters and so we need emoji speak to balance it out. In the past, we relied on words to convey our emotions, but now we are dependent on emojis to convey our feelings. In online spaces, our feelings are literally intertwined with emojis. We simply don't know how to express attitudinal meanings without hearts, smiley faces and so on – so much so that we even use emoticons in handwritten communication, such as adding a :) to the end of a handwritten note or card. Emojis in all their various forms are just so quintessential to our communication in the modern day.

Emojis are neither written nor verbal communication. Broadly speaking, emojis to online language are what gestures are to verbal communication. Text alone seems cold and emotionless online, emojis add attitudinal meanings to online communication, much like body language does to speech. It does not stop there, however. Emoji speak is not as simple as adding a few smiley faces to a text message. It is a form of communication in which one is required to gain fluency, but it is a lifelong endeavour, as emojis evolve so quickly. Whereas one can learn a language in a set amount of time, emoji speak requires constant acquisition. It is very difficult to define the exact meaning and attitude of any emoji, and it is an awareness of the emojing community around you, personally, regionally and internationally, that allows one to gain an understanding of an emoji and all its potential connotations. One can even make their own emojis, so the dynamism is tremendous. On the one hand, emoji speak and one's emojing style is highly individualized: they depend on the unique way one has or has not seen emojis circulated and reproduced online, and one's own preferences for online communication. A two-year-old will emoji differently from a teenager who will emoji differently from a middle-aged adult. On the other hand, emoji speak varies from culture to culture and shows great regional and inter-regional variation.

This book will take you on a journey through the complexities, nuances and varieties of emoji speak that exist around the world in various international and regional communities. Emoji speak is neither a replica of written communication nor of verbal communication. It is a point of intersection between the two. Without it, our online communication would be lacklustre. It stems from the online grassroots culture that smartphones and social media have empowered. Emoji speak is an innovative practice that we can no longer communicate without. It is a creative assembly of visual multi-modal devices that is border crossing in an irreplaceable manner. Emoji speak attests to human creativity at its peak. We imaginatively adapt emojis to suit our needs in this multicultural, multilingual world. We use emoji speak to cross borders and interact on an international scale. And yet, despite this, doubts creep in as to whether huge corporations, big data and social media platforms are manipulating our creativity.

Of the people, for the people

Emojis do not live within any language. They are free entities that we share all around the globe, regardless of which language we speak or where we live. Online communication is uniquely characterized by international interaction and millions of global users all using the same platforms. As such, there is no linguistic authority that can tell us the definitions of emojis or when they are most appropriate to use. In other words, there is no OED or equivalent for emoji speak. It is entirely unlimited by traditional forms of linguistic authority. It is the people that shape the meanings of emojis. The grassroots movement holds the most power in emoji speak.

Emoji speak does show a lot of regional variation, but on the other hand, its pictographic nature creates a basis of mutual comprehension that crosses borders. At the peak of multiculturalism, emojis are exactly what we need. Although there are unique regional and cultural connotations among different groups of people, emojis generally help to display our sentiments to those with whom we are communicating. Emojis are less prone to having meaning lost in translation. Take, for example, the use of the *raised fist with dark skin tone* for the Black Lives Matter (BLM) movement or the use of yellow and blue hearts to show solidarity with Ukraine during its conflict with Russia. These are symbols that have become ubiquitous all over the world that unite us for a common cause. Could words have done the same thing? Emojis are a bridging tool that lowers the language boundaries between all of us, regardless of where one lives. They empower the grassroots and allow their voices to be heard, and movements to gain traction.

Alternative authority

Although there is no official authority over emoji speak, there are several factors that we must be aware of that influence our emoji speak. The leaders of emoji speak are the youth. Outside of digital spaces, it is parents, grandparents and other adults who help their children to learn how to communicate. In the digital world, it is the youth that are pioneers of emoji speak, and it is the youth that often teach adults how to communicate online. As such, emoji speak has revolutionized the direction of learning. It is no longer just top to bottom, old to young, now the young teach their elders, from the bottom to the top.

It is not only the youth that have authority over our online communication. At the peak of technology, our lives are enmeshed with technology. In the past, we used pen and paper to write, and as such, we communicated in a relatively autonomous way. Now, our communication is so heavily reliant on technology that communication and technology are simply inseparable. What that means is that technology is the alternative authority for emoji speak. AI, such as predictive text, and other big data collections subtly influence our online communication. We could view ourselves as being trained by software and big data, meaning our emotions and reactions are being manipulated by an invisible force. Whether we use iOS or Android is also impactful. Whether one has access to a smartphone, laptop or tablet makes a difference, as do the platforms that we use. What is available to us greatly affects our emoji-speak behaviour. Even though the emoji repertoire seems boundless and entirely unlimited, there are powers that may subtly manipulate the development of emoji speak over time.

The 'emoji native'

The term *digital native* was introduced by Marc Prensky to refer to people growing up with access to digital systems, and who are accordingly 'native speakers' of digital language(s), as opposed to those who have been introduced to digital systems as adults, who are therefore 'digital immigrants'.[5] In line with the term *digital native*, I would like to propose the term *emoji native*. Emoji natives are those who have grown up using emojis in texting and instant messaging. In doing so, they have acquired what I would call 'emoji literacy'. The meanings of each emoji are not obviously defined, and thus their definitions must be learnt and acquired over time. Much like learning to write, we must learn which emojis are appropriate and when, and also develop our own style of emojing. This is a lifelong process, as emojis are constantly evolving. Emoji natives are those who are passionately engaged in learning at all times. Thus, they are comfortable with using a range of emojis and use emojis spontaneously with little thought. As such, they are fluent in emoji speak. This is not to say that older adults do not use emojis, they certainly do, but, as we will observe in the later chapters of this book, they do not use them so liberally or so innovatively. Emoji natives are really the ones who set the tone for emoji use and its significance. Emoji natives are also sensitive to the fact that they may be talking to someone who is not an emoji native, and as such, they change their emojing behaviours accordingly. This kind of fluency is not found in those who have grown up without emojis.

Digital and emoji divide

The digital divide is expressed in the emoji divide too. Where we emoji or not is not so much about age, but about accessibility of technology, internet connection and platforms. It is estimated that around 4.5 billion people are connected to the internet worldwide, as of 2021. Meanwhile, 1.4 billion people live in internet poverty.[6] Internet poverty is measured by the affordability, quantity and quality of internet connection available. World Data Lab estimates that 93 million people in China are experiencing internet poverty. About 54 per cent of those living in sub-Saharan Africa were not subscribed to mobile services, as of 2020.[7] In the United States, only 57 per cent of low-income users have home broadband, as opposed to 93 per cent of the highest earners.[8] Our communication has capitalism at its centre. Those who are not benefiting from the capitalist system are also left out of online communication developments. In the past, linguistic authorities were made up of people, but now capitalism has gained power over our linguistic evolution. Affordability very literally impacts human communication.

There is also another side to the digital divide: those who choose not to participate in online communication. In my department at Oxford University, there are many who choose not to have a smartphone and not to use social media, even though they can afford to have the newest devices. Though it is relatively rare, there are people who prefer not to engage in digital spaces. It should be noted that this also opens up a digital divide that is different to the internet poverty divide. There is also a divide between the digitally keen and digitally disinterested.

Emoji expressives

Broadly speaking, for the last four decades, since Grice, semanticists and pragmatists have mainly been concerned with models of meaning that focus on the logical, factual or truth value of statements.[9] However, this has left certain aspects of meaning comparatively under-studied. For instance, until recently there has been relatively little research on how a speaker's attitude towards the topic affects the meaning of the utterance. Meaning is not one-dimensional; it is multi-layered, and we must consider all potential sources of meaning.

Potts was an early proponent of non-propositional meaning, arguing for the necessity of also considering the expressive dimensions of meaning.[10] Potts proposed that there are two types of meaning, namely, (i) *at-issue* (inherently lexical) meaning, and (ii) *commitment* (inherently pragmatic) meaning. Potts argued that although commitment meaning had often been dismissed as peripheral, commitment meanings are actually at the very centre of linguistic meaning. In fact, commitment meanings – particularly those of expressives – are often so powerful that speakers cannot use these expressions at all without wholly committing themselves to the expressive content. Consider the following example from Potts:

That bastard Kresge is famous.

(a) Descriptive meaning: 'Kresge is famous.'
(b) Expressive meaning: 'Kresge is a {bastard/bad in the speaker's opinion.}'

The expression *bastard* contributes to a dimension of meaning separate from the descriptive meaning. That is, regardless of whether the descriptive meaning of the statement is true or false, the expressive meaning projected by the word *bastard*, which reveals the speaker's attitude toward *Kresge*, remains constant. In this way, Potts argued that commitment meanings are just as crucial as lexical meanings. It is almost impossible for us to speak without revealing something about our attitude toward what we are describing. Therefore, it is not only impossible but misguided, to attempt to study lexical meaning in isolation from commitment meanings. Speaker-commitment meaning does not only provide an independent meaning to the whole proposition but also surpasses other meanings. For instance, if I say, '*Amazingly, John gave all his money to a charity*', the whole proposition sits under the scope of amazement.

We can apply this framework to how we use emojis online, too. Emojis seem just as powerful as verbal expressives, in that they can also alter the meaning of a whole proposition. Emojis create another layer of meaning that is mostly attitudinal. Just as Potts showed how we cannot analyse lexical meaning separate to commitment meanings; we also cannot study the language we use online without paying close attention to emojis. For instance, just by adding or changing

> Hey, can you cover for me on Saturday?
> Reply (a) Okay ☺
> Reply (b) Okay 🙃
> Reply (c) Okay.

Figure 2.1 How emojis and punctuation can change the tone of a sentence. Source: Emoji from NotoColorEmoji © 2021 Google Inc, OFL License.

an emoji in a sentence, the tone of the sentence might change from a friendly tone to one indicating reluctance or frustration (see Figure 2.1).

In the earlier example, the descriptive meaning of all three replies is the same: the person is agreeing to cover for the other person at work. However, the difference in tone between reply (a), (b) and (c) is drastic: reply (a) seems friendly, while (b) seems openly annoyed or reluctant, and reply (c) seems clipped and angry, although there is room for individual interpretation. In this way, analysing emoji use is essential for properly understanding the meaning of online communications; a great deal of important meaning would be lost by focusing on lexical meaning alone. Emojis have come to be a courtesy at this point. We present our attitude in a message clearly by using emojis to be considerate to those to whom we are talking. To emoji or not to emoji, that is the question.

What emojis mean for our lives is not such a simple question to answer. They are not just simple devices to make our online communication nice and friendly. It is simply not possible to express oneself appropriately without at least some emojis in our exchanges on smartphones. Instead of being a softening device, emojis are increasingly becoming mandatory elements of online communication. The level of (in)appropriateness of one's emoji use can either strengthen a relationship or damage it. For emoji migrants, it can be hard to attune to which emojis are appropriate in which contexts. This is further exacerbated by the fact that we are living in a time where an absence of emojis is not an act of neutrality. Rather, emoji-less communication looks incomplete and could even have non-positive implications, as demonstrated earlier.

Emoji repertoire

Before launching into further discussion and analysis, I should set the scene with a brief overview of some of the 'emoji words' that exist. The boundaries of what counts as an emoticon, emoji, sticker, letter, punctuation marker or meme are all very vague. The meanings of these terms differ between different subcultural communities. In the following, we look at some of the well-known meanings of these terms, but it is impossible to include all the variation that exists across different regions and cultures. All multi-modal communicative resources are included in our definition of *emojis* for the purposes of this book.

Emoticons

The OED defines *emoticon* as 'a representation of a facial expression formed by a short sequence of keyboard characters (usually to be viewed sideways) and used in electronic mail, etc., to convey the sender's feelings or intended tone'.[11] The word *emoticon* is a compound of two English words, *emotion* and *icon*. What differentiates an *emoticon* from an *emoji* is that the former was generated by combining ASCII symbols typed on a standard keyboard, while emojis must be typed using a special emoji keyboard on a smartphone or other device. The first emoticons were the smiley sign :-) and the frowny sign :-(, which were first used in a message posted on an electronic bulletin board by Dr Scott Fahlman in 1982.[12] Dr Fahlman and his colleagues at Carnegie Melon University had been discussing options for use as a marker to distinguish a humorous joke from a serious notification when writing on the bulletin board. Keyboard symbols such as %, *, # and & were considered, but eventually it was the smiley and frowny signs that won the day. Emoticons are still used today despite the popularity of emojis due to the ease with which one can type them on a standard keyboard and their intuitiveness.

The range of potential emoticon faces typable on a standard keyboard is surprisingly wide. In the Western world, emoticons are usually read sideways, for example :-). 'Asian-style emoticons' are read vertically and are not captured by Zappavigna's system network, as she points out. Literature dealing with emoticons and emojis in English sometimes cites the limited expressivity of (Western style) emoticons as creating the space that would ultimately be filled by emojis.[13] However, even a cursory glance at the expressivity of emoticons (or *kaomoji*) used by Japanese speakers and Chinese speakers (see Figure 2.2) casts doubt on such a line of reasoning, given the impressive amount of detail, expressivity and nuance expressed through various characters such as letters, punctuation or other systems of notation.

The repertoire of these emojis varies between languages. The emoticons make use of different orthographies, notably including mathematical language (∇),

(*^.^*)　　　(⌒‿⌒)
(ᴛ◇ᴛ)　　　(≧‿≦) ♡
(ó﹏ò｡)　　　(oﾞ‿ﾞo)
^ⓞ🞄ⓞ^　　　(ඊ˙̫ඊ)ɔ
(⌒‿⌒)　　　(눈_눈)
(o˙꒳˙o)　　　┌(ಠ_ಠ)┘
('益')　　　(o•ω•o)

Figure 2.2 Examples of emoticons read vertically.

Greek letters (ω), Chinese characters (益) and even Korean characters (눈_눈). The interpretation of these emoticons may also vary more than one might assume; in later chapters we will return to the issue of variation in interpretation of emoticons and emojis.

Emojis

We have already taken a brief look at the etymology and meaning of this word as identified by the OED. The first set of emojis, which comprised 176 characters, was developed in 1999 by a Japanese artist, Shigetaka Kurita.[14] His main goal was to introduce a simple way to send information for the interface of a mobile internet platform from the Japanese mobile carrier DOCOMO. The use of emojis was gradually accepted in Japan as a useful way to convey information in mobile communication. Eventually, the popularity of emojis in Japan led to their integration and adoption worldwide: when Apple launched its iPhone 3G in Japan, in June of 2008, Masayoshi Son, the CEO of SoftBank Group, requested that Apple integrate the set of emojis available to Japanese mobile users, claiming that Japanese users – who were used to emojis being available on Japanese mobile phones – wouldn't be able to go without them. As a result, SoftBank's emoji system was incorporated into iOS 2.2. Apple was not the only company to recognize the potential of these characters. In the same year, Google's Gmail also enabled emoji functionality.

The full integration of emojis into Unicode was a slow process. Unicode is a universal character encoding standard, designed to display characters in a consistent manner on all devices. Since different languages have different writing systems, a standardized system is necessary to ensure that characters in different languages can be typed and displayed correctly. Many scripts around the globe, including emojis, are encoded with unique values in the Unicode system. The first proposal to add emojis to Unicode was made in 2000, but it was rejected at the time.[15] Emojis would gradually be added to Unicode in the late 2000s with the backing of Google and Apple. In 2009, Unicode 5.2 added 114 emoji characters, and Unicode officially adopted emojis the following year with Unicode 6.0, which included an additional 608 emojis, bringing the total to 722. Smartphone users outside of Japan could still only type emojis using dedicated apps, however; it was not until the following year, 2011, when Apple would finally integrate the emoji keyboard for users outside of Japan. Unicode has been adding more and more emojis ever since, and at the time of writing there are now over 3,600 official emojis.[16]

In this narrower sense, an emoji is a type of pictograph that computers associate with a predefined code. These codes mean that when sending emojis, devices can send short text codes telling the other device what emoji to display, rather than sending large image files that require more bandwidth – especially important on mobile devices. However, although Unicode's handling of emojis has made them compatible with a wide range of devices and platforms, the actual appearance of emojis still varies across platforms because individual emoji designs are trademarked. Google cannot use Apple's emoji designs on their Android phones, meaning that the same emojis appear differently on an iPhone as compared to an Android phone. Each device interprets the same Unicode reference code as a different image. Websites such as emojipedia.org and unicode.org provide full lists of the emojis that have been adopted into Unicode, with illustrations of how each emoji varies in appearance across platforms.

Some platforms provide their own emoji keyboards. For example, WeChat, the most popular social media service in China, has its own emoji keyboard that is used more often than the Apple emoji keyboard on the platform. WeChat emojis are very different to those of the emoji keyboard, and their meanings will not be immediately apparent to users who are not familiar with the platform. Take a look at these emojis and guess what they mean:

Nope, (a) isn't a smirking face, (b) isn't just a blank-faced person, (c) is more than a handshake, (d) isn't a greeting before a martial arts fight, (e) isn't just a knife and (f) isn't just a happy person wearing shades. (a) actually means cool, as 666 is a slang term for 'cool' in Chinese; (b) is actually a hug emoji; (c) is used to show respect; (d) is used to thank and acknowledge that the other person has something that they can teach you or help you with; (e) is used as a comeback when someone makes fun of you; and (f) is an expression of pride.

a)  b) c)  d)  e)  f)

Figure 2.3 A selection of the type of emojis used in China. Source: design by Loli Kim, reproduced with permission.

These emojis are not even available to type in any platform other than WeChat. This demonstrates how much the platforms that we use matter. The emojis that are available on each platform influence our communication habits. This creates mutual feelings of solidarity between users, and also a divide between those who do and do not use a certain platform. This also reminds us that emojis do not exist within one language. The emojis just seen are WeChat emojis, not Chinese emojis. Emojis are borderless. Our individual emoji repertoires come from the platforms that we use and our devices. We are not limited by region at all.

Stickers

A sticker is a bespoke image available for use through a particular messaging service, or downloadable for general use through a particular app. Unlike emojis, stickers have not been adopted into Unicode. Many messaging services provide their own stickers as part of their strategies for brand differentiation. The range of stickers available is immense, and spans all imaginable topics and themes, from cartoon characters and celebrities to faces from paintings by European master painters. Stickers often feature brands or trademarked characters, and some apps, such as LINE (an instant messaging app similar to Whatsapp that is widely used in South Korea and Japan) and WeChat, feature a sticker marketplace where creators can sell sticker packs featuring their original characters for real money.

Image macros and memes

Image macros are easily recognizable images that are often posted and reposted across the internet. The term *image macro* was coined on the Something Awful forums in 2004, when the forum added the ability for users to easily add popular images to their comments by using simple text commands (in computer terminology, 'macro' refers to a command used to make a computer perform a sequence of tasks – useful for automating repetitive tasks). For instance, Something Awful users could type [img-blownaway] to 'summon an image containing "I'm blown away!" in pale turquoise all caps'.[17] This is similar to how emojis use Unicode codes to avoid having to upload the same image every time.

Early image macros often featured block capital text in Impact font at the top and bottom of the image, usually with a setup for a joke on the top and the punchline below. Eventually, the term *image macro* came to be used interchangeably with the term *meme*, and nowadays the term *image macro* is reminiscent of the internet in the latter half of the 2000s, sounding somewhat dated.

The term *meme* was first used by Richard Dawkins to refer to self-replicating units carrying cultural meaning (essentially a cultural version of the concept of genes).[18] Dawkins's use of the term *meme*, of course, has a much wider scope of application than images shared on the internet. Most image macros are intended to be humorous, and often the same image is captioned with a variety of captions to create different jokes along a similar theme. Ordinary netizens make memes with reference to popular culture or classic art. Unlike emojis, memes are not centrally created. Memes are uncensored, flexible and available to all.

An example of an image that became extremely productive in terms of image macro creation is a screenshot from a scene in Peter Jackson's film adaptation of Tolkien's *The Lord of the Rings* trilogy, in which Boromir (played by Sean Bean) states, 'One does not simply walk into Mordor'. This image has been used to create countless image macros with variations on the line, expressing the sentiment that a particular task or activity is not as simple as one might think or suggest.

GIFs

The acronym GIF refers to Graphics Interchange Format, an image format that can be used to present animations by allowing image frames to be displayed with time delays. Although GIFs are not always animated, the term *GIF* is commonly used to refer to animated GIFs. The acronym GIF is often written in lowercase online, reflecting the term's shift in perception from an acronym to a fully fledged word in its own right. Indeed, from this point on I will refer to gifs in lowercase. Many current messaging apps and platforms feature a 'gif keyboard' function or similar, allowing users to search by keywords to find popular gifs to insert into conversations.

3

Emoji Evolution

Emojis are constantly changing and evolving, as is emoji speak. As emojis are created, their forms and meanings are contested and negotiated by users across the globe. Over time, some emojis thrive and survive, while others become less visible. Not all emojis are visible or available to all. Some are limited to particular subcultural groups or platform users. For instance, pre-set emojis differ from platform to platform. The Unicode-approved emojis are limited in their inclusivity and are not able to make our on-screen lives amply diverse. Hence, people make their own emojis, using images and sometimes audio too. The arrival of virtual reality (VR) and avatars require us to start thinking seriously about the ethical issues of emojis too. Should avatars and emojis be true to ourselves? Can we use them to create our dream selves, rather than real selves?

I'm not the first to write about emoji from the perspective of linguistics or semiotics. Books like Philip Seargeant's *The Emoji Revolution* (2019), Marcel Danesi's *The Semiotics of Emoji* (2017), Vyvyan Evans's *The Emoji Code* (2017), and Gretchen McCullough's *Because Internet* (2019) all feature serious discussions on how emoji are used in our communication. The world of emojis moves fast, and while 2019 may not sound like very long ago, it is a long time in emoji years. The 2020 pandemic forced our work and social lives into online spaces, accelerating an existing trend towards spending more of our time online to an unprecedented degree. For many of us, our social lives took place almost entirely through screens. Emoji provided a small but significant method of making the otherwise cold online world feel a little bit friendlier.

The social media landscape has also changed significantly since 2019, most notably with TikTok's explosion in popularity around 2020. TikTok only became available worldwide in 2018, but by 2020 it had already become the most downloaded app worldwide. It now rivals social media juggernauts like Instagram, Twitter, Snapchat and Facebook, particularly among Gen Z audiences. TikTok's enormous popularity, coupled with its unique video-centric format, has made it a hotbed for language innovation, spawning countless new memes, slang terms and ways of using emoji. No current discussion of emoji would be complete without a thorough discussion of TikTok's role in emoji innovation, yet few, if any, books on the market have discussed this up till now.

At the heart of emoji development, which is always in line with technology and data collection by big tech companies, people are worried about how the emoji world may be being censored, controlled and manipulated by central data systems. While we do not have AI developed to the extent of *I, Robot* (2004), it is not too absurd to liken the film to our current reality. Our digital, Web 2.0 world is controlled by a range of corporations who could very easily manipulate us. Just like VIKI, these corporations give us freedom of expression, but they also hold a lot of power over us. In the midst of exciting emoji evolutions, we must pause and think about the influence of big data, and its effect ethically, legally, educationally and psychologically. This problem may be in the process of resolution anyway with the coming of Web 3.0. Perhaps Web 3.0 makes the future of emoji brighter, allowing for more uncensored diversity and inclusivity.

Adapting to limitations

People want smaller phones that they can express a lot with. That's both a challenge and the driving force for colourful emoji speak! Most smartphones are between 5 and 5.6 inches. The iPhone 13 models come in 5.4 and 6.1-inch sizes, with the 5.4-inch iPhone 13 Pro positioned as Apple's smallest iPhone. There are no linguistic authorities for emoji speak. Nonetheless, the platforms that we use may impose limitations that we have to creatively overcome. Creativity is at the centre of humanity, and we tend to find novel ways to push against the limits of our technology to express ourselves to our maximum potential. When the only way to message each other on mobile phones was to pay for each 160-character SMS text, we didn't limit ourselves to only the most basic messages to save money – we created 'text speak' and emoticons to convey complex messages with as few characters as possible. Likewise, Twitter's character limit hasn't stopped users from uploading longer pieces of writing; they simply upload screenshots of paragraphs written on the iPhone Notes app (or equivalent) instead – so much so that a 'notes app apology' has become a cliché whenever a celebrity becomes embroiled in controversy[1]. The technology we use imposes certain limits and rules on how we can communicate – but we are experts at finding loopholes to do things our own way.

As such, online communication is highly flexible, and we are adept at innovating new methods to suit our ever-evolving linguistic needs. Just like words, the meanings of individual emojis, gifs, stickers and memes are not static; they have their own lives and trajectories, and often evolve or change in meaning over time. This can make emoji speak rather difficult to interpret for those who do not keep up with every new development, as these ways of communication can be highly context-dependent. This can often lead to miscommunication – especially between different generations, who may interpret the same message within different cultural frameworks.

Smart phones, platforms and more

Emoji development is closely intertwined with smartphone development. The smartphone era has well and truly arrived. People all around the world text with their family and friends, as well as post messages, photos and videos on various social media platforms. A study from the Pew Research Centre found that 76 per cent of adults in eighteen countries designated as advanced economies and 45 per cent of adults in emerging economies own smartphones.[2] In advanced economies, 90 per cent of adults use the internet and 67 per cent use social media, while these figures are 60 per cent and 49 per cent, respectively, in emerging economies. The study found that across all countries, younger people are more connected to the internet, use more social media and own more smartphones than older generations. For example, in the UK in 2018, 93 per cent of adults aged 18–34 owned smartphones, compared to 60 per cent in the 50+ age bracket.

Smartphones have also changed the way we text. Texts from the pre-smartphone era looked more like telegrams: there was a character limit, and they could only contain numbers and letters. Crystal notes that when the first smartphones were released, messages sent with smartphones often employed emojis, pictures and videos in conjunction with traditional letters and numbers.[3] Since their arrival, smartphones have developed into an inseparable part of many of our lives, and they have become the principal form of communication for the current generation. Our styles of communication have also changed to suit the medium, and smartphone users today, especially 'digital natives' who have grown up using these technologies, have innovated countless ways of squeezing expressive potential out of text-based online communication.

The way that people use language on social media platforms, otherwise known as social networking services (SNS), is similarly creative and multimodal. The language used on platforms like Instagram, Facebook and Twitter is not a simple replica of its offline counterparts. Emoji language is neither a transliteration of spoken language nor a duplication of handwritten messages. It doesn't even look like other online communication forms, such as email. Each platform, then, influences users to develop platform-specific emoji styles. The way that Gen Z use emojis on TikTok is far different to how a broader range of generations use emojis on WhatsApp. Facebook Messenger prompts users to use the thumbs-up emoji, whereas Instagram displays a selection of eight of a user's most used emojis in the comments sections. WeChat has its own emoji keyboard, and KakaoTalk (popular in South Korea) has a rich array of sticker packs that its users commonly use. As such, platforms directly influence our communication.

Platform specifics: Snapchat

Snapchat is a messaging application with image and video functions that was launched in 2011. It is highly popular, with more than 290 million active users as of 2021. It is the eleventh most used mobile application in the world.[4] US and European users make up 95 million and 78 million users respectively. The countries with the highest numbers of users consist not only of the United States (second largest) and European countries, like France (third largest) and the United Kingdom (fourth largest), but also many Asian and Middle Eastern countries, like India (the largest), Saudi Arabia (fifth largest), Pakistan (sixth largest) and Iraq (ninth largest).[5] Snapchat emojis operate a little differently from other platforms: rather than just expressing emotions and/or concepts, Snapchat uses emojis to indicate the degree of social interaction between users and their friends on the application. Snapchat introduced emojis to replace the previous 'Best Friends' feature that displayed who users most frequently interacted with, which was removed due to certain breaches in privacy. These emojis are termed as 'friend emojis' and appear beside the usernames of friends to help users monitor their relationships with these friends on the platform. Which emoji appears depends on the timing, frequency and pattern of one's interactions with a friend on Snapchat. For example, the emoji with sunglasses signifies you share a mutual best friend with another user – that is to say both of you send a lot of 'snaps' (picture messages) to this common friend. This differs from how the same emoji might be used typically on any other social media platform. For example, when we are messaging on WhatsApp or commenting on someone's post on Facebook, the emoji with sunglasses often means 'cool' or expresses a confident attitude. A user with a smiling face with smiling eyes emoji next to their name is one of your best friends on Snapchat, but not your number one best friend, as this is signified by a yellow heart. On any other platform, these emojis would simply represent a smile and a heart. Thus, Snapchat is able to creatively repurpose existing and common emojis to fulfil a brand-new function, that is, representing social relationships.

Another unique emoji feature of Snapchat is the ability to use a Bitmoji. A Bitmoji is an avatar that users can customize to resemble themselves, which generally can either be used as an emoji (whereby one's custom avatar will appear on an emoji template), inserted into comic strips or overlaid on 'snaps'. In 2021, Bitmojis were given a 3-D upgrade, following the trend of increased interaction in virtual environments like the Metaverse. Facebook also has a similar customizable avatar function, although the degree of customization is more limited as compared with Snapchat. Facebook users cannot customize the specific clothing that their avatars wear, rather one can only choose from a preselected list. In comparison, Bitmojis allow for infinite possibilities in the creation of new meanings through personalized emojis that can be tailored to suit individual needs. This kind of customizable feature suggests that we may see a rapid development of new emojis that are unrecognizable or easily misinterpreted outside of their local contexts. Alternatively, these customized emojis may leave less room for misunderstanding and could possibly take on less ambiguous meanings even if used across different cultures, as they can are more personalized to the sender.

Online and offline spaces

Just as online language is becoming more like face-to-face communication in some ways, so too is online activity becoming more and more a normal part of our interactions with the physical world. The boundaries between the online and offline worlds are blurring as more services are being moved online. A concrete example of this is business 'change of address' posters. Generally, when shops move, they change premises, so provide information about their new physical address, to enable customers to find their new location. Now, it is not uncommon for a business to move from physical premises to an online-only business, and to create posters which matter-of-factly state that they have moved online, as if their new online location were just as tangible as a brick-and-mortar storefront. In other words, they treat online spaces just like physical, real-world spaces, showing just how much the online world has now become part of our daily lives.

Similarly, online banking has made 24/7 banking possible, although people can still opt to go to the physical bank if they so need or so wish. Online and offline banks form a mutually informed space, where the two work in tandem for a better banking experience. Their functions are both distinct in some respects but blurred in others. The same can be said of online shopping: though one can go to physical stores, there are certain circumstances where online shopping can be more beneficial or may cater to certain issues of time, distance or money.

As such, it is also important to remember the interplay between online and offline environments, and that communication takes place in and across both spaces. Barton and Lee, in their book *Language Online*, warn against creating viewing online and offline spaces as completely separate:

> When we say online and offline, we are merely referring to different situational contexts where communication takes place. We are not suggesting, however, that people's lives are either carried out online or offline, nor are we implying that the online is replacing the offline. Many contemporary social practices seamlessly intertwine online and offline activities, and they cannot be separated.[6]

Online and offline spaces are intrinsically linked and both spaces influence each other. However, no matter what channel we use to communicate, our communication is sensitive to register and domain. Online language is not the same as offline communication, such as speech and (physical) writing. One characteristic that tends to distinguish much CMC text, for instance, is the absence of the full stop (period). One of my informants described the presence of a full stop in mobile-texting space as unfriendly and rude. Interpretational freedom is another characteristic of mobile language. Some people use a lot of emojis in highly nuanced ways, while others use emojis rarely or not at all.

Web 2.0 culture: Active participation

After the release of the Apple iPhone in 2007, the market experienced a surge of touchscreen smartphones with advanced operating systems. With the use of multi-touch gestures, a relatively larger screen and the removal of the physical keyboard, touchscreen smartphones have provided more flexibility for the development of third-party software for mobile devices, known as applications or apps since the late 2000s. As the hardware and overall performance of smartphones have improved, a larger number of more sophisticated applications has been developed. Tasks that once required desktop or laptop computers are now possible on mobile devices. Making or receiving a phone call is now merely one function among many. That the 'phone call' function was assigned with the same open/close UI and was treated as one of the 'apps' on the first iPhone is symbolic. The function of making or receiving a phone call is, of course, prioritized in the operating system, but users can temporarily disable all notifications, including phone calls, if they do not want their ongoing task on the device to be interrupted. In the latest versions of operating systems like iOS and Android, the phone call 'app' also works as a hub for all the calling functions of other applications. The importance of the traditional phone call has arguably decreased in the smartphone era when compared to the pre-smartphone world. Various alternatives to phone calls and SMS texting have also appeared. Many of the messenger programs that were initially developed only for desktop and laptop computers have been ported to mobile platforms. Some of the most widely used online messenger programs are even exclusively available on mobile devices. Many of these messenger programs also provide their own calling and messaging services.

As internet culture has developed, there have been some shifts from informational networks towards interpersonal resources.[7] This shift can be described in terms of a movement from Web 1.0 to Web 2.0, and their differences are outlined in Figure 3.1.

The shift towards Web 2.0 is par for the course with the spread of smartphones. The smartphone is a multi-functional portable device. It is not only a miniaturized computer but also an effective mobile communicator. Each and every smartphone that a person uses works as a hub for most types of online communication. However, the use of a smartphone remains a personal experience. It is not surprising to see more and more active contributions and communications performed by ordinary users as the mobile device industry grows.

	Web 1.0	Web 2.0
Mode of usage	Read	Write and contribute
Unit of content	Page	Record
State	Static	Dynamic
How content is viewed	Web browser	Browsers, RSS (Really Simple Syndication) readers, mobile devices, etc.
Creation of content	By website authors	By everyone
Domain of	Web designers and geeks	A new culture of public research?

Figure 3.1 Web 1.0 and Web 2.0 comparison.

Arrival of Web 3.0: Decentralized platforms

Web 3.0, also known as Semantic Web, aims to transform the internet service for websites and applications through the use of blockchain technology to facilitate the processing, transformation and assembly of data and content.[8] Different from the previous Web 1.0 and 2.0 where data is mostly stored in centralized mega-platforms and corporations, Web 3.0 aims to interconnect data in a decentralized way by converting display-only information to meaningful, highly tailored content through the interaction between computers and humans. Web 3.0 is more focused on the use of machine learning to provide near-human-like intelligent content for each internet user through the power of AI to achieve real-world human communication. It is hoped that Web 3.0 can create a more secure, intelligent and connected space of data for users and decentralize the influence of large technology companies in controlling the data.[9]

More than meets the eye

Emoji speak is often dismissed as trivial or not 'real' language; however, emoji speak is ubiquitous in CMC so it is essential for properly understanding most online communication. It is no longer surprising to see every, or almost every, chunk of text scattered with emojis. Typically, emojis have been seen as having an adjunct-like role, added to the end of a message from time to time. Their importance is much greater, however. The Oxford English Dictionary's 2015 Word of the Year was the face with tears of joy emoji, demonstrating the significance of emojis in our communication currently. Interestingly, an *emoji* is not a word that can be looked up in a dictionary. You could not flick through a dictionary and find an *emoji* easily. What is even more important, however, is that you cannot define an *emoji*. The grassroots in online communities decide the meaning of emojis, and so having the face with tears of joy in the Oxford Dictionary seems somewhat nonsensical. In the UK, this emoji can simply be used to signify that you found something very funny. Whereas in China, it is often used when a user does not want to send a message without any emojis, as it could be perceived as impolite or rude. This would likely not happen in the UK. As such, emojis are so contextual that there is far more to them than meets the eye (Figure 3.2).

Figure 3.2 Face with tears of joy emoji. Source: NotoColorEmoji © 2021 Google Inc, OFL License.

Making emojis

Although when it comes to 'in-message' emojis, users tend to use preset emojis, like the Apple or Android emoji keyboards, memes provide an interesting example of users creating their own emojis. Memes spread and evolve in meaning, much like words. Part of the reason that certain memes spread and grow in popularity to such an extent is that they provide a recognizable template which can easily be altered, allowing users to change the meaning of the original image to craft their own joke. For instance, one meme that became popular in 2020 began with a screenshot from the TV series *Glee* captioned, 'I am going to create an environment that is so toxic'. This particular meme is distinct from many image macros in that the text that accompanies the image was unedited from the English-language subtitles on the screen; that is to say, this was simply a screenshot taken from the relevant episode of *Glee*.

After the original tweet became popular, however, other users began blacking out parts of the caption to alter the meaning of the original image. Popular memes often spread because they actively encourage participation, with users competing to make the most creative interpretations of the original template. There are online meme generators that provide templates, like the picture of Sue Sylvester earlier, that allow users to change the picture or the text.

In other cases, memes spread as they are, without the need for this kind of creative participation. For instance, many users simply save amusing memes to a folder on their device in order to build up a collection of images that they can repost later. On sites like Twitter, users will often tell the original poster that they have downloaded their meme by replying to the original poster's tweet telling them that they are 'stealing' their meme to repost elsewhere, often communicating this fact using a meme.

Memes also have a significant impact on verbal communication online more generally. For example, one image of a cute shiba inu dog, nicknamed 'doge', inspired users to caption images of the dog with intentionally ungrammatical text akin to babytalk, imagining how the somewhat silly-looking dog in the image might speak or view the world. These images helped to popularize phrases and words that are now ubiquitous online. For instance, perhaps the most common trope of the 'doge' meme is the incorrect use of modifiers, as in 'much art' or 'very wow'. These types of constructions are now very common online.

The popularity and forms of image-based communication depend on technological trends and advances. Earlier computers, with a limited ability to display images, forced users to come up with creative ways of expressing tone using only the ASCII set of characters; this resulted in innovative emoticons such as :-) and ^_^. Similarly, GIFs only became popular in texting once it became possible for smartphone users to access large amounts of mobile data for a reasonable price. It was not so long ago that sending even a single image via SMS was prohibitively expensive for many. We will explore the lives of these image-based forms of communication online.

As with emojis, the visual, representational nature of many memes may lead one to assume that their meanings are universal. Indeed, for some memes and gifs, this is more or less true; responding to a joke posted on Twitter with a gif of somebody laughing would be a fairly unambiguous way of showing your appreciation for the joke. In a sense, memes and gifs used in this way are less prone to misinterpretation than some emojis as they are more detailed and often come with additional context (for instance, many gifs are made from short clips of TV shows, which supplies concrete context for what is happening in the gif). It is also no coincidence that many of the most popular memes and gifs are taken from some of the most popular TV series and films; *SpongeBob SquarePants*, *The Simpsons*, *Futurama*, *The Office* and *Shrek* have all spawned a huge number of popular memes and gifs. The wide familiarity with the source material enables other users to easily grasp their meaning, enabling complex ideas to be expressed through a single image (or sequence of images, in the case of a gif).

Although the visual nature of memes (combined with the more widely known cultural backgrounds in some cases) can lead to more universal meaning in some cases, the opposite is also often true; internet culture is frequently highly self-referential, with some memes requiring knowledge of several earlier memes, niche news events, or current or past trending topics on sites like Twitter. Rather than communicating meaning universally, such the sky is the limit 🧚 ✨ 🌸   stay on the ground 💫 🦋

Figure 3.3 An example of the kind of 'fairy comment' you might see on TikTok. Source: Emoji from NotoColorEmoji © 2021 Google Inc.

memes often serve to create or reinforce in-group solidarity, as they are only comprehensible to a niche audience of people who are aware of the callbacks and references alluded to in the meme. Additionally, the rapid speed at which the internet creates and discards new trending topics and memes means that one must spend a significant time online in order to keep up with the most current memes. This may point to there being linguistic variation in online language dependent on how much time one spends online, and on which platforms, which warrants further study.

The meanings of an emoji can also differ for different groups of users, much as certain words acquire slang meanings within different subcultures. These innovative meanings will often seem opaque to those outside of a particular group or subculture. For instance, in 2020, 'fairy comments' became a popular method of conveying sarcasm among teen users of the social video-sharing app TikTok. These comments are characterized by 'soft' emojis such as fairies, butterflies and sparkles, used alongside extremely sarcastic text. The humour of these comments comes from the mismatch between the soft, positive emojis and the harsh, sarcastic content of the message (Figure 3.3).

The examples earlier illustrate how although non-verbal methods of communication such as emojis may initially seem universal and borderless, their lives and trajectories are in fact much more complex. A single emoji can have multiple meanings across different groups of users. Additionally, phenomena such as fairy comments remind us that users have a highly active role in shaping the meanings of emojis, constantly innovating new ways of utilizing the fixed set of characters despite their lack of agency in the actual creation of new emojis.

Making meanings

The process by which the meaning of an emoji is negotiated is a strange one. Unlike a standard verbal language, emoji users cannot innovate their own emojis (although they can create novel combinations). Instead, new emojis are decided by the Unicode Consortium, meaning most emoji users have little say in which emojis are added to the lexicon. However, once Unicode introduces a new emoji, its meaning awaits negotiation by emoji users. Unicode provides little guidance on what the intended meaning or usage of a new emoji is, providing only a matter-of-fact description such as 'grinning face with one large and one small eye'. This means that although the addition of new emojis is a top-down process that users have little control over, the *meaning* of new emojis is negotiated from the ground-up by users of emojis. For instance, when Unicode introduced the aubergine emoji, it was unlikely that they intended it to be used primarily as a phallic symbol, yet now the latter meaning is so ubiquitous that Instagram and Facebook have taken steps to ban some uses of the emoji on their platforms.[10]

Indeed, while some emojis mimic established gestures or expressions, such as the thumbs-up emoji or frown, others are decidedly more abstract, evoking a certain feeling without having a real-life analogue. For instance, the 'upside down face' is rather abstract and does not correspond to any existing expression or gesture. Despite the range of possible interpretations of this emoji, however, users have successfully negotiated its meaning so that it is now widely interpreted as a marker of sarcasm or annoyance, as if one is smiling to cover up one's true annoyance with the situation.

Emoji fashion

Emojis are constantly going in and out of fashion This is not only because the meanings of emojis and other image-based communication methods are always changing, but also because the systems themselves are always changing. Technology is always developing, and even the software we rely on every day can become obsolete with little warning. Ways of communicating that once seemed common sense can quickly fall out of use: we no longer send each other faxes or send 'winks' on the now-defunct MSN Messenger.

Emoji speak adapts fluidly to our communicative needs. The use of emojis can adapt to current events in several ways. First, an existing emoji might take on a new meaning or become more frequently used. Second, new emojis might be created in response to current demand. We will look more closely at how the meanings of existing emojis can vary from place to place and at the demand for new emojis in certain cultures later on in this book.

The language we use reflects what is important in our lives, and sometimes changes in our lives can transform a niche or unpopular emoji into a staple of our daily emoji lexicon. For instance, according to Emojipedia, uses of the microorganism and face with medical mask emojis soared in March 2020. This is when the response to Covid-19 ramped up in many countries around the world. As the severity of the pandemic became clear and lockdowns continued, Apple also took the step of redesigning the expression of the masked face emoji in its iOS 14.2 update, changing the emoji from a neutral or negative expression to a smile. This change reflected a shift in our perception of mask wearing; the original design was created to symbolize illness, but, during the pandemic, we began wearing masks to prevent Covid-19 from spreading, even if we were not ill ourselves. In this new context, wearing a mask became part of the daily reality of even healthy people, not just a momentary bout of illness (Figure 3.4).

The raised fist with dark skin tone emoji saw a similar spike in usage in June of 2020, when it was used in association with the Black Lives Matter movement, and frequently collocated with hashtags such as #blacklivesmatter or #BLM. The raised fist has been used as a symbol by many groups and movements, but its association (particularly for the variants of the emoji featuring darker skin tones) with movements that call for Black pride and social justice for people of colour have been widely known since Tommie Smith and John Carlos raised their fists on the winners' podium after the 200 m race at the 1968 Summer Olympics.

Another example tied to social justice issues is Twitter's implementation of a new emoji for use in association with the MeToo movement in 2017. This emoji was frequently a collocate of the hashtag #MeToo. This movement saw women around the world publicly declaring via social media platforms that they had been the victims of sexual assault or harassment, in order to demonstrate how common sexual violence really is. The emoji incorporates three raised hands of different skin tones, reinforcing the idea that sexual violence is a problem affecting people of all races.

More recently, on 8 April 2021, Twitter released an emoji for use by the Milk Tea Alliance movement, celebrating the alliance's first anniversary. The Milk Tea Alliance is an online movement comprising netizens principally from Hong Kong, Taiwan, Thailand, and Myanmar (although with strong support in India and some

Figure 3.4 Redesign of the face with medical mask emoji to feature a happier face. Source: Twemoji © 2020 Twitter, Inc and other contributors, CC BY 4.0.

other countries) that developed in response to Chinese nationalist commentators online. Later, the alliance evolved into a movement against authoritarianism across Southeast Asia and was also influential during the coup in Myanmar. The name of the movement is derived from the fact that drinking tea with milk is a practice in the countries where the movement developed. The emoji, which appears on Twitter when a user types one of the various hashtags associated with the movement (in a range of languages), is composed of a cup of milk tea against a background of three colours, which represent the colours of milk tea in regions where the alliance was formed online. According to the Twitter Public Policy account, there were over 11 million tweets featuring the hashtag in the one-year period from April 2020. The creation of this emoji demonstrates Twitter's efforts to keep up with social trends as well as the ever-evolving internet language.

Not all groups, however, find easy representation in emoji speak. If one's cause is not 'in fashion', then a representative emoji may never come into existence. Even if there is a symbolic emoji, its meaning may not spread to a wide enough audience. As such, even though emojis unite us at times, they also divide us. Emojis are yet to cater to all demands, and as such, the digital divide becomes more severe.

Avatar evolution

The early internet was not a very visual place. The first incarnation of the internet was a US military project called ARPAnet (ARPA standing for Advanced Research Projects Agency), which began development in 1969. By 1971, an email function had been developed for the network.[11] At this point, computers were mostly limited to displaying ASCII characters and text, and one had to type commands to the computer to operate it. The graphical user interfaces (GUIs) that we are now familiar with would not be commercially available until the early 1980s with Apple's Lisa computer. Because of this, early communication online took place almost entirely through text alone. Users had no way of knowing what the person they were talking to looked like and had no access to the information we might usually infer from someone's appearance in real life such as gender, age or ethnicity. Body language and non-verbal communication were also impossible to convey without explicitly explaining them through text, making it difficult to communicate tone.

Many in the 1980s and 1990s predicted that we would solve these problems of communicating gestures and facial expressions by entering hi-tech VR worlds, where 3D representations of ourselves, or 'avatars', would mimic our movements and allow us to communicate online just as we do face-to-face. While recent software like VRChat does deliver somewhat on this promise, allowing users to chat in a virtual reality space, controlling custom avatars using sensors that track head and body movements, VR equipment remains expensive and difficult to set up, and this is still a niche form of online communication. Even if most of us are not jacking into cyberspace in the way sci-fi writers like William Gibson envisaged in the 1980s and 1990s, digital representations of ourselves still permeate much of the digital landscape in more subtle ways; avatars are still a big part of how we communicate online. For example, Hana Bank in South Korea announced in July 2021 that it had set up its employee training institute on Zepeto, an application in which users interact through customizable avatars that are initially automatically generated from a photograph of the user.

Avatars are digital representations of people or bots.[12] These can range from display pictures or profile pictures on social media platforms, like Facebook or Twitter, to 3D models rigged up to mimic one's movements in real time on platforms like VRChat. The word *avatar* itself comes from a Sanskrit word meaning 'descent', which typically referred to the descent of a deity like Vishnu to the earth. This meaning became broader over time, however, coming to refer to embodiment of something in general, including one's 'embodiment' in an electronic medium.[13]

Emoji ethics

Avatars on social media raise questions about emoji ethics. Should people be able to remain anonymous? Should we ensure our avatars look like us? Or should avatars allow us to create an idealized version of ourselves online? Most social media platforms encourage users to upload an avatar to be displayed on their profile and alongside comments or posts one makes. In this section, I will be limiting the discussion to this kind of avatar (also often called 'display picture' or 'profile picture' in this context). Although many platforms expect users to upload a real photo of themselves (especially on platforms like LinkedIn, where one's profile is expected to look professional) many users choose to use illustrated depictions of themselves, photos of pets, memes, or other popular images, or even a photo of somebody else (particularly if the user is a bot or scammer!).

A user's choice of avatar will usually depend on the platform and on the purpose of the account. For example, a corporate brand account may use the company's logo for the display picture, while a politician is more likely to use a professional headshot. Someone who wishes to partake in online discussions anonymously may use a picture of a fictional character they like, while bots and troll accounts may simply stick with the default placeholder avatar; in fact, a blog post from Twitter developers in 2017 announced that they were changing the design of the default Twitter avatar because it had become so strongly associated with trolls, making the default design grey rather than brightly coloured to make the default avatar less prominent and to encourage users to view it as a placeholder.[14]

Indeed, there is evidence to suggest that avatars shape how we perceive others online and that we use them as 'a means of identifying, recognizing, and evaluating others' in mediated communications like those taking place online.[15] We tend to transfer the evaluations and assumptions that we make of another user's avatar to the user behind the avatar, in much the same way as we form judgements and assumptions about others based on their physical appearance in unmediated face-to-face interactions. Users themselves are aware that their choice of avatar or display picture may influence how others perceive them online and may make conscious choices to influence their perception by others, as in the real world.[16] One's online avatar need not resemble one's physical appearance, however, and users are free to represent themselves with avatars that do not match their real-life gender, build, style or race – however problematic some of these choices may be – and can incorporate fantasy elements into their avatar's appearance. Of course, users are also not required to choose an avatar that resembles a person or creature, and many take a more anonymous or abstract route, using artwork, landscapes, memes, photos of their pets and so on.

The total malleability of users' avatars can also present problems in online discussions, however. In political discussions, for instance, one's lived experiences and identity may factor into how others weight one's opinion on a matter – particularly when discussing issues specific to a certain group of people. For example, one might be inclined to view a billionaire's opinion on whether the minimum wage is sufficient to live on as less relevant or informed than the opinion of somebody who actually works for the minimum wage. Similarly, slur words against a marginalized group may be used in a 'reclaimed' sense by people within the group targeted by the slur, but still viewed as offensive when used by somebody outside of that group. In this way, a speaker's own identity may impact on how the content of their speech is interpreted or received.

This can quickly become problematic in online discussions, however, where users are free to take part in discussions anonymously, or even lie about their identity when it is convenient. Users can set their avatar as a stock image found online, for instance, to attempt to speak for other groups or to strawman political opponents. This may explain the following tweet, where a former Republican congressional candidate in Pennsylvania in the United States, Dean Browning, made the odd claim that he is a 'Black gay guy' – a claim undermined by his avatar, which clearly depicts a white man.

Other users quickly began speculating that the politician did not mean to tweet this message from his main account, but that he had accidentally forgotten to sign into a fake 'burner' account where he presumably pretended to be a Trump-supporting gay Black man – something that would be politically useful given the former president's reputation as racist[17] and homophobic.[18] Washington Post journalist Phillip Bump investigated, attempting to find the fake account Dean was trying to post the tweet from and found an account under the name 'Dan Purdy' that was created about a month prior, which also claims to be a gay Black man and who frequently responds to Dean's tweets. The account uses a cartoon avatar of a Black man generated using Apple's Memoji feature and had a history of making sexist and racist tweets.[19]

Dean Browning later claimed that he had not been trying to post from a side account but had been 'quoting a message that I received earlier this week from a follower'. Irrespective of the dubious credibility of this claim, however, this case shows how using an avatar to impersonate those of other groups in order to score political points is one way that avatars can potentially be abused online. Despite this risk, the customization of avatars to individual user's specifications comes with many positives, as we will see in the following sections.

Avatars for exploring identity

Assuming another identity online need not always be this problematic. Avatars can also be an avenue for exploring one's identity or having fun role playing with others. Avatars can allow us to represent ourselves as we wish, free from the constraints of our physical appearance in real life. Users are therefore free to experiment with the creation of alternate or idealized selves to represent themselves in online spaces.

Video games are excellent spaces for this kind of exploration. Many video games allow users to customize their avatar, which they can then control, moving through the virtual world and interacting with its inhabitants and other players. One of the most immersive types of video games to emerge has been the

MMORPG (massively multiplayer online role-playing game) where hundreds or thousands of players may be playing simultaneously in the same virtual world. Examples of these include *World of Warcraft* and *Final Fantasy XIV*, and these games typically feature highly detailed character creation tools, allowing players to customize almost every aspect of their avatar's physical appearance.

Players are given free rein to design their character as they see fit, and the fantasy settings of many of these games encourage users to use their imagination rather than simply trying to mimic their real-life appearances. Some players may choose to flesh out the history of their character by writing a detailed backstory and may role-play as their character, interacting with other users from their character's perspective.

For many people, these virtual worlds can be useful platforms for experimenting and exploring one's identity, free from the restrictions of the physical world. Kai Baldwin's 2018 study asked transgender gamers about their experiences using avatars in games and their relationships with said avatars.[20] Baldwin found that of the thirty participants interviewed, more than two-thirds 'explicitly stated they have used video game avatars to experiment with their ideal physical presentation'.[21] Many stated that they designed their avatars to have characteristics 'they wished they could possess in their physical bodies', with one participant describing his avatar as 'an inner me' and another describing it as 'an extension of [himself]'.[22] One participant, a trans man identified pseudonymously as James, recounts that creating his main World of Warcraft avatar, a male blood elf[23], helped him through his transition, writing:

> I made my main character when I was coming out, and through him I was able to stabilize myself. All of my worries, fears, questions, insecurities, and overall depression were quelled when I played my blood elf. Discovering him and his history, and writing his story, helped me discover my own story as well . . .[24]

Baldwin also notes that James's avatar had the name James before the real-life James changed his name following transition. Baldwin writes that 'James changed his name to match the avatar he views as part of himself'.[25]

Some participants also found that playing as their idealized avatar helped with their feelings of gender dysphoria (discomfort caused by a mismatch between one's gender identity and the physical characteristics of one's body); James wrote, 'whenever I'm experiencing dysphoria, I always imagine that I am James and in James's body instead of my own, and it often helps [heart emoji]'.[26] Another participant, Nathan, found that the experience of 'total immersion' when playing also extended beyond the game, writing, 'In my mind I'm him. Even after I come off the game, I feel more masculine for a while'. The participant Zane, however, reported that although playing the game could help with feelings of dysphoria, it was easy to become reliant on the feeling of escape it provided, stating that some days, '[he] wouldn't want to quit playing because [he] couldn't handle the dysphoria any other way'.

In conclusion, therefore, Baldwin's study shows that virtual worlds and the avatars players use to inhabit them can be valuable spaces for exploring identity and gender, allowing players to inhabit a virtual body completely unrelated to their physical one. Baldwin writes that the customizable avatars offered by some video games offer players the chance to 'construct a virtual body completely independent from the limitations imposed by physical existence', where the virtual world becomes 'a site for identity construction, where users are free to experiment with and perform idealized or alternative selves'.[27]

The vtuber phenomenon

In addition to allowing people to express their identity, avatars may also allow people with public personas to protect or their private identity and image. For example, some entertainers have begun streaming or making YouTube videos through a persona represented by a virtual avatar. These entertainers hide their real identity, completely assuming the persona of their virtual avatar, which usually takes the appearance of a cute anime-style character. These avatars can be controlled using head-tracking and body-tracking software similar to that used by virtual reality headsets, allowing the avatar to mimic the real-life movements of the user in real time – a crucial point considering that live streams on sites like YouTube or Twitch usually make up a huge part of these entertainers' content. These entertainers are often referred to as *virtual YouTubers* or *vtubers*.

Although the first vtuber is often credited as UK vlogger Ami Yamato, who started her YouTube channel in late 2011, the trend did not catch on until Kizuna Ai began uploading videos in December 2016.[28] Kizuna Ai also coined the term *virtual YouTuber*, which later became shortened to *vtuber*.[29] Soon after her debut, Kizuna Ai became a viral phenomenon, spawning huge numbers of imitators, and by the end of the following year the trend had become hugely popular in Japan. Ai's channel has been hugely successful: as of 2021, Kizuna Ai's main channel has nearly three million subscribers and, among other things, she has appeared on TV talk shows, appeared in commercials, performed a live music concert as a hologram, collaborated with prominent music producer Yasutaka Nakata on a pop song.

The vtuber phenomenon quickly became big business. Agencies like Hololive formed, hiring talented entertainers and designing them appealing, highly marketable avatars to use while live streaming. These organizations loosely followed the structure and model of established Japanese idol agencies, debuting different 'generations' of virtual idols to keep their roster from getting stale, and 'graduating' them when a voice actor quits. The idea of 'virtual idols' had been attempted in Japan previously, when the idol talent agency HoriPro created virtual idol Kyoko Date in 1996 to avoid the problems of idols ageing or becoming embroiled in scandals. In 1996, however, computer-generated graphics technology was much more rudimentary, and Kyoko Date's graphics had to be created manually beforehand, making live, spontaneous interactions impossible. In contrast, today's software allows a vtuber's avatar to mimic their movements in real time, allowing them to act naturally and spontaneously, interacting with their audience.

Although the trend was mainly limited to Japan at first, international fans still participated in the fandoms for these Japanese vtubers, with bilingual fans working to translate what the streamers were saying into other languages in YouTube uploads of clips from their streams. Eventually, agencies also began seeing profit in international audiences, and Hololive debuted its first generation of English-speaking vtubers in September 2020.

The growing popularity of vtubers also inspired existing streamers and content creators to join the trend, and popular Twitch streamer Pokimane debuted a vtuber avatar in September 2020. Pokimane found advantages in the vtubing model, saying during the livestream that 'no-cam streams are so comfy [. . .] Especially because, I don't know, sometimes it gets tiring to get people comment on you'.[30] When she doesn't feel like streaming with her camera on, she usually gets comments asking her to turn the camera on, and sees a decrease in viewers. By using an avatar, she can avoid having to pay attention to her appearance while still having a visual representation of herself to keep viewers entertained. Another English-speaking vtuber, 'Nyanners', also stated that 'using an avatar in this way creates a clear-cut separation between my life as a content creator and my personal life as a human behind the avatar', describing it as 'less of a mask and more of an extension of myself' that allows her to 'open up about things and express myself in ways that would otherwise feel uncomfortable.'[31] In this way, then, avatars can be useful tools for today's online entertainers. They combine the appeal and marketability of cute anime characters with the intimacy and relatability of a live streamer, while also allowing the people behind the avatar to stop worrying about looking perfect on camera and to express themselves openly.

Soundmojis: Emojis find their voices

Social media platforms are always looking for the new innovative emojing craze. By providing users with the best emojing options, companies can attract users to continue using their platforms. When users find that emojing options suit their needs, they feel as though their online communication satisfies them. One new feature that Facebook added in 2021 was the soundmoji. This is a limited selection of emojis, which when clicked on, play a related sound. For example, the rolling on the floor laughing emoji provides the sound of an audience laughing, and the violin emoji plays a short violin song – it should be noted that the emojis are not animated.

Apple's Animojis and Memojis can also be given a voice. Animojis are a range of animal emojis, and Memojis are emojis that can be customized to look like the user. Animojis and Memojis use Apple's TrueDepth camera software to mimic a user's movements and facial expressions. Users can record themselves saying something, and accordingly the Animoji or Memoji will move in the same way as the user did while speaking. Where Facebook's soundmoji's are not customizable, Apple's Animojis and Memojis are entirely personalized.

Summary: A fine line between humans and technology

Emoji speak is constantly evolving. When we think of linguistic evolution, we imagine it happening over the course of many decades, or even centuries. Emoji speak is evolving on a daily basis. New trends can take off in a matter of hours, and old trends can be forgotten within a week. Never has our communication been so dynamic and rapidly developing. I am sure by the time this book is published in 2023, there will have been many new additions to our emoji speak repertoire that were not around in 2022, when I wrote this book.

When it comes to emoji speak, we move just as fast as it develops. Read receipts have trained us to respond to messages quickly, so much so that our online communication is more reactive than responsive. If we take a step back and think about this new behaviour, then one starts to wonder where our humanness lies in the digital world. We are almost programmed to automatically use emojis. As we become more and more submerged in technology, we must ask ourselves how we can bring our humanness into digital spaces and retain our own individual identities.

4

Emojing

How and Why?

Words have limits. Think of trying to comfort or express condolences, sometimes we just cannot find the right words to say what we really feel or mean. This is particularly true in writing, where we do not have facial expressions or tone of voice to convey our sentiments. This is where emojis step in to save us. Emojis speak on our behalf and express how we feel. They save us time and help us to bond with who we are talking to. In the busy multilingual and multicultural age that we live in, emojis allow for more diversity within our communication because it is individualized and made from the bottom up. Thus, emojis promote the values of inclusivity and quality. Throughout history, there has been a precedent for sharing signs, generation to generation, culture to culture. Emoji speak is a natural extension of this sharing. It helps us to overcome language barriers and cultural differences and communicate more efficiently and effectively than ever.

Emoji motivations

Every time we speak to each other online, we make thousands of tiny decisions about how to express the meaning we want to convey. From word choice and punctuation to emoji selection and frequency, each message involves a huge number of factors that all work together to express something to the recipient. The meanings of the words we use are only part of the story; in online communication, the way we use capitalization, punctuation, emojis and the like also function to tell the listener something about ourselves. If there are so many decisions to be made every time we type a message, then what informs how we choose to present our messages? What factors – unconscious or conscious – help us make all these tiny decisions about how we emoji?

To tackle this question, I coin the term the *three S's*: 'speed', 'style' and 'solidarity'. *Speed* refers to both the actual speed at which we communicate (i.e. how quickly or slowly we respond to a question or text) and the clarity of the overall message (i.e. making your meaning as clear as possible to avoid misunderstandings, which slow us down). *Style* refers to our individual repertoires of emojis and non-verbal linguistic techniques, and how we use them to express ourselves. Finally, *solidarity* relates to the social functions of language: some of our emojing choices are made primarily to forge bonds with others and to express a sense of community and belonging. These three factors inform how we emoji in our online communications.

Speed matters

The speed at which we form language can carry almost as much meaning as the words we say. Silence is not neutral or meaningless. If a politician hesitates too long before responding to a difficult question in a debate, for example, we may think they are at a loss for words because of being unprepared, or that they are trying to cover something up. We might interpret an awkward silence following a confession of love as indication that the addressee does not feel the same way. Other non-verbal cues may help inform our interpretation of these silences. This is also a factor when we communicate online or via text. Most modern messaging services and apps tell us when a message has been read by its recipient, and so an uneasy type of silence can arise when we know the recipient has read our message but, for whatever reason, has not responded. This is often referred to as leaving somebody 'on read' and is generally considered rude in online communication. Compared to face-to-face silences, where one can still read the other person's expressions or body language, these online silences feel impenetrable and can be even more hurtful if sensitive or difficult topics are involved. For instance, a romantic interest leaving an invitation for a second date 'on read' might be even more disheartening than a flat-out rejection in many cases. Social media has created a new kind of anxiety for humans. Waiting for a response makes us insecure. As such, we are pressured by social media to respond quickly.

Taking too long to respond can often end up hurting the recipient's feelings, so sometimes we need snappy, efficient methods of communication to signal our acknowledgement of a message without too much thought. This is where emojis and other non-verbal methods come in handy. One can agree to a friend's suggestion with a simple thumbs-up emoji, or show you found somebody's joke funny with a gif of someone laughing, for instance, speeding up our communications.

Style matters

I hope it isn't too much of a truism to say that the way we express ourselves reveals a lot about us. This is not only true of our individual vocabularies – the pool of words each of us tends to draw from when we communicate – but also of our non-verbal linguistic techniques. In face-to-face communication, for instance, one might notice that a particular friend often tilts their head in a certain way that is unique to them during conversation or that they frequently use a particular gesture. In online communication, on the other hand, we might notice that somebody tends to favour a particular emoji, respond with gifs a lot, or never capitalize words. Just like in face-to-face communication, these types of non-verbal behaviours, whether conscious or not, often tell us something about how the other person wishes to present themselves or be viewed.

To give a very simple example, the number of emojis that someone tends to use in conversation might tell us something about their personality. For example, when someone types without using emojis, it may not be because they are in a serious situation or speaking to someone of a higher status, it may simply be because they find emojis too flamboyant, or an overcompensation in meaning. Hence, somebody who uses no emojis or gifs at all might come across as mature and confident, rather than sombre or lacklustre. Meanwhile, somebody who uses a lot of emojis may want their online writing style to seem approachable or friendly, while those who use dozens of emojis at a time may be perceived as a childish, immature writer. Many have also observed generational differences in how people tend to emoji,[1] so aspects such as our age may be revealed by our emoji use. In this way, our emojing behaviours can influence how others see us, and we may choose to use these techniques intentionally in order to project a certain image to somebody else.

Figure 4.1 Top 10 most used emojis on Twitter in 2021. Source: NotoColorEmoji: © 2021 Google Inc, OFL License.

As you can see, the majority of the most used emojis were very positive. This is not to say that everyone in the world was feeling very positive in 2021. Emojis don't always express our true feelings. Instead, online communication has made it almost automatic for us to add different smileys and positive emojis. Although emoji style is often very personalized and deliberate, we must also be aware that we have been trained to use emojis, to some extent and sometimes, we use them subconsciously.

Solidarity matters

Emojis and other non-verbal techniques can also help us forge bonds with each other and relate to one another. Words on their own can often be somewhat ambiguous when isolated from the body language and tone of voice that would usually clarify our intended meaning in face-to-face communication; emojis can help span this gap, allowing us to convey our emotions more effectively. Emojis let us soften messages that might otherwise come off as blunt or cold, providing a sense of warmth, friendliness or comradery.[2] This means that not using emojis is no longer a neutral act. Emojis have become so conjoined to the idea of friendliness that not using any emojis at all is seen in a negative light. To create solidarity, one is almost forced to use emojis. If you do not use any emojis in your talk at all, you risk becoming an online outcast.

Just as the identity of one's counterpart might influence vocabulary selection – for instance, a bilingual speaker using words from another language with a fellow bilingual speaker – we often adjust our emojing depending on the person to whom we are speaking, building solidarity through a shared understanding of the same kind of language. A teenager might exchange niche memes and inside jokes with their friends but stick to more widely understood emojis when messaging their parents, perhaps only using the standard set of facial expression emoji.

Although emojis are often framed as a type of universal language, emojis often have particular meanings within certain groups that may be inscrutable to those outside of the said group. Within K-pop fandoms, for example, emojis are often used to refer to specific K-pop idols, often to save characters on platforms like Twitter, which limits the number of characters per post. Those unfamiliar with how these emojis are interpreted within K-pop fandoms would be totally unaware that these emojis are even being used to refer to an idol, so they work almost like a code, signalling membership within the fandom. This is yet another way emojis can be used to build solidarity within a group.

The climax of borderless communication

With the widespread adoption of smartphones, many of the casual, informal chats that would previously have been limited to face-to-face conversations now take place through text. As a result, many of the quirky linguistic behaviours that were previously limited to spontaneous speech can now also be found in the fast-paced world of text messages. An interesting example of this can be seen in the text conversations of multilingual speakers. If you have ever overheard a spoken conversation between two multilinguals, you may have noticed them speaking in a mixture of languages, either sprinkling in words from their other language(s), shifting wholesale between different languages throughout the conversation, or responding to a comment in one language with a response in another. Although these behaviours are commonly seen in the spontaneous speech of multilingual speakers, formal written language, most especially in the modern age before the rise of text messages, tended to be formal and non-spontaneous; this type of language would not be accepted in an academic essay, for instance. However, in addition to helping to connect multilingual speakers, messaging apps and SNS also encourage these kinds of spontaneous, informal multilingual behaviours to deal with the rapid pace of conversations that take place on said platforms. The pictorial nature of emoji speak allows for some level of understanding to be created between speakers of different languages any time that it is used. As such, emojis lower the boundaries between people by increasing the overall intelligibility. The meaning created is of course less precise than letter words, but it is more universally comprehensible.

Communication on mobile devices also allows the freedom to navigate multiple language repertoires and orthographies within the same communicative exchange. The simplicity of switching between different keyboards means that users are not limited to using one language by their device. This allows for translanguaging to take place:

> Translanguaging simply means (i) receiving information in one language and (ii) using or applying it in the other language. It is a skill that happens naturally in everyday life, e.g. when a child receives a telephone message for his/her mother in English and conveys the message to her in Welsh. This skill needs to be developed systematically throughout the education system so that pupils are able to switch efficiently from one language to the other, thus fully utilizing their bilingual capability.[3]

Translanguaging is all about using multiple languages seamlessly and creatively, recognizing that the borders between languages are socially, culturally or politically defined, and as such have no basis in objective reality.[4] In a multilingual, multicultural society, everyone translanguages to some extent. Multilinguals translanguage all the time, naturally transitioning between languages according to the person with whom they are speaking and where they are. Translanguaging includes the verbal and non-verbal aspects of communication. Through a combination of the two, the most effective communication can be achieved. Translanguaging happens in online and digital spaces, where people engage with crossing the borders between languages using emoji speak, which has never been bound to nation-state concepts.

An example of this found in the instant messaging communication examined for this book is mutlilingual conversation between a mother and daughter. As we will discuss in more depth later, this type of multilingual communication, where information is received in one language and used or applied in another, is called 'translanguaging'. In this case, the mother wrote in Russian, while the daughter wrote back in French, adding to her words with a cute cat emoji and a photo of her dinner. Russian, French, an emoji and a picture all coexist, working together to achieve our three objectives of speed, style and solidarity.

We observed myriad such examples. To provide some flavour of their range and diversity, we provide more examples later. In one exchange between a father and daughter we saw an effective use of emojis by both parties. Emojis can be used by anyone, regardless of factors like gender or age. In an interview with the daughter, she said that they use a lot of 'stickers' (her term for emojis) when they are being playful and joking around. She said in the case of this exchange, it had been a few days since they last spoke, so they were using emojis in a jocular manner. As we mentioned before, emojis are often used to add a prosodic dimension to the exchange, and in this case, they help father and daughter convey their emotions to each other without having to explain them lexically.

Various orthographies or writing systems can also be used to convey ideas and emotions. In online translanguaging, the use of these orthographies is not limited to the languages to which they are traditionally attached. In one instance, two friends exchanging messages used not only two languages, English and Japanese, but one of them uses the kanji 笑 twice in this example to mean 'lol', as well as a Japanese-style emoticon (ˆ ˆ). In an interview about her exchanges with her Japanese friends, the interviewee noticed that most of her Japanese friends don't leave a space between words and emojis, probably because there are no spaces between words in Japanese.

This is also seen in the messaging habits of another primarily English-speaking informant chatting with her Korean friend. Although the majority of the exchange was in English, at the very end she inserted some Korean Hangeul. In the interview, she explained, 'I often use ㅎㅎ in conversation with Korean friends, even if I am typing in English, as I think it is sometimes more appropriate than "lol" or "haha" – which are often seen as sarcastic or not sincere – and it's also easier to type'. The informant's comment reveals that English expressions like 'lol', which at face value seem equivalent to the Korean 'ㅎㅎ', are not actually equivalent in this context. The English expressions leave room for interpretation, whereas the Korean expression simply signifies laughter, without the negative connotation.

In conversation between two Singaporean nationals, we saw a mixture of English, Singlish, Chinese, Hokkien and emojis, illustrating how translanguaging can flourish in online texting in creative and innovative ways.

In another example from Singapore, we observed both English-style (. . .) and Chinese-style (。。。) punctuation used within the same conversation, demonstrating the flexibility and dynamism of the online space; users are not limited to one single style or language. In certain instances, a speech bubble consists of only emojis, showing their power in electronic communication. Here, we can get a grasp of the true extent to which language is bent and stretched in texting spheres, where emojis and different languages coexist and blend to create a novel space of innovative and creative language use that transcends social and political boundaries.

Colourful conversations

Before our communication moved to our smartphone, laptop and tablet screens, we often experienced written communication in black and white. Emojis have ushered in a colourful era in which our messages are more fun and creative than ever. Communication now is audio-visual as well as textual. Newer iOS updates have allowed for balloons, confetti, sounds and even vibration effects, meaning we do not only have to communicate with words.

Smartphones now allow messaging without any typing at all. It is possible to have a voice-messaging conversation, in which multiple parties simply record short audio messages and send those to each other. This helps to get around the need for auto-correct features, and misunderstandings based on lack of prosodic features in a typed message. With the release of the iPhone 7 came a new iOS

Figure 4.2 Confetti effect when one sends a congratulations message.

that allowed even more creativity in the way people could communicate through iMessage. It became possible for users to apply various effects to their messages. Messages can now be made to stream with confetti, as in Figure 4.2 or otherwise adorned with balloons, fireworks, hearts, lasers, a shooting star, etc. You can even add gifs to your messages, or use 'invisible ink'. Many of these effects are also available in the messaging systems of other applications, like Facebook Messenger.

These various elements, when added to a message, help to compensate for the absence of prosodic features like tone, pauses, volume and so on that would be present in a spoken utterance. They can be assembled creatively to deliver an effective message. In the absence of such prosodic features or some form of compensation for them, misunderstandings could occur and communication could break down.

Much of the innovation in the use of these elements can be attributed to teenagers and young adults. However, with smartphone ownership increasingly common among children, even the very young are using emojis, videos, audio and various messaging effects to successfully communicate with their peers. In Figure 4.3, I have recreated the kind of messages that my daughter sends to her friends. She is eight years old. The emojis significantly outnumber actual words. This style of sending emojis has become popular among young children.

These message exchanges can sometimes feel like a comic strip. The combination of text, pictures and onomatopoeia brings the conversation to

Figure 4.3 Sample message exchange that eight-year-olds might send. Source: Emoji from NotoColorEmoji: © 2021 Google Inc, OFL License.

life, making it more interesting and appealing. In fact, with the popular South Korean messaging app KakaoTalk, the use of real 'cartoons' is very popular in mobile messaging among South Korean young people. These are often called *jjalbang* in Korean, an abbreviation of *jjallim bangji* 짤림 방지 ('keeping from being cut out'), which originated from an internet forum based around posting photos. Posts without a photo attached would be deleted, so users started posting unrelated pictures alongside their posts when they simply wished to chat to other users without wanting to share a picture. As a result, the amusing pictures that now often accompany messages on platforms like KakaoTalk are now referred to by the same name, *jjalbang*.

Emoji idiolects

Each person's emoji speak is a highly individualized method of communicating. Linguists no longer exclusively look at the way people communicate according to the 'static' categories of wider society, such as gender, class and ethnicity.[5] Instead, it is generally accepted that we tailor-make our own communication styles informed by the communities and subcultures of which we are part, so-called *communities of practice*. Our position in society and membership of common interest groups shape our communication behaviours into individual *idiolects*. What's more, we may also make use of particular bits of language we are aware of that are associated with other groups which we may not be part of, but whose attributes and values we wish to reference, display or appropriate. Crucially, the meaning of these bits of language is not fixed but is continually reinterpreted and recombined in different contexts by diverse interlocutors.

In this way, our use of language not only reflects our position and affiliation within wider society (and our local social networks) but allows us to creatively and contextually make meaning and communicate about ourselves, our situations or the topic at hand using all the means we have at our disposal. This is true of our online communication in general, but especially so for emoji speak. Although there are general trends in emoji use, we all balance our needs for speed, solidarity and style in our own unique way. Fashionable emojis arise from subcultural groups, rather than one big language community. Emojis that are of interest to one person, perhaps because they are in common use in a *community of practice* with which they are involved, or they associate it with a particular contextual meaning, may seem lacklustre to another. As such, the three Ss help us to build our own idiolect, which serves to make meaning in the unique contexts in which we communicate.

Emoji competence

Everyone has their own emoji idiolect, but not everyone has emoji competence. Emoji competence refers to our ability to engage in multi-modal communication using the proper register. It is about making use of the emoji repertoire and assembling the pieces together according to the person with whom you are speaking. One must 'tune in' to the situation, and decide how to employ one's idiolect accordingly. For example, Emoji absence or misuse can cause misunderstanding and the breakdown of communication:

> An example I immediately think of is how my mother tends to not use emojis often and it has led to multiple misunderstandings between us. The most common one happens on a weekly basis. I get a message from her saying 'Call me' or 'Call me later', or even 'Call me as soon as possible'. Whenever I read those messages, I instantly start panicking as the lack of emoji makes the sentence sound (or look) very hurried. I always immediately message back 'Did something happen?' or 'Is everything okay?' also not using emojis as it feels like

the situation is serious. The answer I always get from her is completely different from what I expect and goes along the lines of 'Nothing happened, why? I just want to talk'. The message does not come across as casual because of a lack of emoji. If she had written 'Call me later ☺' the intention of just wanting a casual conversation is understood. (Extract from an interview with a twenty-year-old student)

Emoji competence is also about being able to understand the multi-modal signs that we experience online. It is being able to recognize that, say, the '+' symbol on Google Drive means upload and the '↓' symbol refers to download. Such tech-driven images are very logical, and yet they need to be learnt. These images help for multilingual communication, but also create a digital divide between those that are familiar with them and those that are not. Age is not always the determining factor in whether one has the emoji competence to recognize these images. It can be to do with whether one is technologically keen or not, too. Image awareness is a key facet of emoji competence, and is one of the main reasons why there is a divide between emoji natives and emoji immigrants.

Emojis between generations

What effect does the use of emojis have on intergenerational communication? Young people tend to have very defined idiolects that are influenced by niche communities that older generations may not be part of. There is so much diversity that misunderstandings can arise. Letter words have definitions that can be searched for in dictionaries. Emoji words have no such categorization. Emoji speak is highly individualized, personal and subcultural. This can result in communication mismatches. These communication mismatches can occur between anyone, not just between the binary categories of *young* and *old*. It is so much more fine-grained than that.

Let's examine this in various cultural contexts. Generally, in Korean language and culture, differences in generation often require differences in language use (encoded into predicate morphology, for example). What role do emojis play in Korean intergenerational communication? What about internet slang in Spanish intergenerational communication? The following statements by younger online users discuss the intergenerational divide when it comes to online communication.[6]

Do emojis make intergenerational communication easier or more difficult?

Informant 1 (Korean): Through emojing, intergenerational communication becomes much easier in Korean. We can use a lot of cute emoji to replace many difficult forms of honorific and politeness. Korean is a language which is very sensitive to the speaker–hearer relationship. Politeness is an important virtue and trigger of language use. In face-to-face communication, speech, prosody and gesture can convey such meanings, also disambiguating the meanings. But in writing, such disambiguating or softening strategies can be lacking. Emoji are used to fill pragmatic gaps such as these, making the dialogue flow without misunderstanding or unnecessary conflict.

What about internet slang? Who can use it?

Informant 2 (Spanish): I think one of the biggest intergenerational issues when it comes to online communication is internet slang and abbreviations. Our parents' generation does not seem to be very acquainted with the use of expressions like 'lol', 'lmao', 'ikr' or 'cba', or their Spanish counterparts. I think older generations prefer a standard writing style, and, to an extent, it would come across as awkward for me to receive a text from my mother using internet slang, as it does not seem appropriate.

When is the conversation finished?

Informant 3 (Belgium): I have personally grown accustomed to the communication problems that come with intergenerational texting. There are a few things that bother me such as much as either wrong usage or lack of emojis that can lead to misunderstandings. But above that, one problem that I have noticed is how when I message my father, he does not feel the need to answer to my message even if I send him a question. He thinks that because he saw the message that is enough and the conversation is over. I disagree with him on this point as I always seek for a confirmation that the person I am texting received my information and has taken it into account. A simple 'okay' is enough, but is often not written until I message my father multiple times asking if he saw my message – to which he answers that he obviously has and is puzzled as to why I need a justification for it. I cannot deny the truth of that, but in contrast with real-life conversation where the facial expression of one's interlocutor shows if the information has come across or not, only a message can do so in online communication. That for me, is the main problem that I have come to face with intergenerational communication.

As with any other form of language, there is a gap when it comes to intergenerational communication online. From the earlier statements and other interviews, this generational difference may be summarized as follows:

the older generations are more likely to adhere to prescriptive or linguistic norms, whereas the younger generations, who have grown up with online communication, are more willing to be creative and innovative with the language they use in the online sphere. Older people may be willing to learn and expand their own emoji speak repertoire, but they are simply fighting against the long-entrenched habit of following prescriptive approaches to language.

Punctuation has feelings too

Traditional punctuation has started to fall away in the smartphone era. The presence or absence of punctuation, as part of the wider emoji speak repertoire, has taken on new kinds of meaning that are quite different to the meanings that punctuation typically carries in other contexts. Emoji speak liberates our punctuation from its traditional role, giving it an altogether different meaning.

Smartphones make typing so much easier than earlier mobile phones, and this has led to a qualitative shift in the way we use punctuation. Before smartphones, texts were often highly abbreviated, limited by character count and the relative difficulty of typing. With smartphones, however, there are far fewer obstacles to typing what you want to say, and therefore more complex uses of punctuation are more accessible than previously. Yet, interestingly, it seems that the meaning of punctuation has shifted from a neutral grammatical indicator to something that serves to indicate tone, attitude and emotion.

Previous work has shown that there are prosodic cues in speech to signal paralinguistic information (such as speaker attitude) in a number of languages.[7] Gunraj et al. found that interpretation of a full stop as serious was only prevalent in the context of text messages (and not in hand-written notes), and also showed that the inclusion of full stops in texting makes utterance appear more 'insincere' than those without full stops.[8] In preliminary research before the writing of this book, I took a different approach and looked into whether positive or negative feelings are associated with the use of full stops, rather than sincerity. In this way, it is concerned with the positive or negative attitude that the receiver perceives the sender to have in their use or non-use of full stops in a text. Eighty participants were provided with simulated text messages or emails, followed by a response consisting only of 'OK' and one of four punctuation or emoticon types. They were asked to grade how the responder might have felt about the original text message or email on a Likert scale. See the following for an example of a simulated testing stimulus.

This study examined both text message and email scenarios, and the results point to some interesting similarities and differences between the two. Emails are judged more negatively only when there is either no punctuation or a full stop, but those were the only major differences between text messages and email, with other stimuli showing similarities across both media. Subjects were notably more likely to judge a simulated text message or email as having a negative responder attitude when a full stop appears (as in 'OK'.), in comparison to no punctuation use. In addition, although subjects rated emails as more negative overall, the positive or negative effects of punctuation use can be seen as a consistent property of many forms of written electronic communication. This study suggested that punctuation in computer-mediated communication holds paralinguistic power in a way that is comparable to prosody in spoken language.

When people abandon conventional prescriptive grammar rules in mobile languaging, this is generally for the sake of efficiency, to achieve a desired effect, or to avoid conveying an unintentional insult. For instance, one of my informants said,

> Full-stops in texting naturally give off a bizarre feeling of animosity. Using full-stops in a text conversation seems to show that the person using them is either angry at his/her interlocutor, or is being extremely serious. In general, a full-stop in a text conversation leads to the feeling that the conversation is over and does not encourage the interlocutor to answer. I have argued once with my friend over the use of full-stops as she kept using them and I thought she was angry at me. I asked her to stop using them if she was not feeling any negative emotions, and she thankfully understood and stopped. Another use of full-stops that I have seen is the sarcastic use, which I have used myself before with my closest high school friend as a joke. Although I think that for this kind of understanding around the full-stop to work, both people should be on the same wavelength when it comes to its meaning. The same way as wrongly used emojis, full-stops or the lack of them, could lead to misunderstandings.

The absence of a full stop in online messaging seems to be common cross-linguistically. Han has built a database from KakaoTalk, South Korea's most popular SNS messenger service, and Facebook, using messages from different age groups (ranging from people in their tens to fifties), both male and female, totalling 100 people.[9] The database consists of —four to six months of dialogue logs. He found that a full stop almost never appears in young people's messages (people in their tens, twenties and thirties), but that it starts to appear in the dialogue of users in their forties and fifties. The following is an extract from an interview with a girl in her teens and a man in his fifties:

Interviewer: When I looked at the group chats of teenagers, they hardly used full stops. Why do you think they do not use them?

Teenage Girl: I think using a full stop makes your talk a bit rigid. Also, it makes one feel that the dialogue has finished.

Mr An (50s): I never intentionally drop a full stop. Using a full stop for me is like a habit. I feel it's not properly finished if a full stop is absent. I think this is the case for my generation. We are so accustomed to the grammatical conventions in writing. For me, unless I am in too much haste, I don't finish a sentence without a full stop. I think it is the same with other people in my group chat. Most of them are in their forties. If I use a full stop, then I feel I can't put an emoji afterwards. I feel some sort of inconsistency and disconnection. I need to put emoji before the full stop.

We see here a generational difference between those who are more influenced by prescriptive grammar and those who are less influenced by prescriptive grammar. Further interviews showed that despite this influence, the older generation is still open to different styles when languaging happens in a mobile space. Talking about the use of slang or abbreviations, the male speaker in his fifties said that the reason why they use those forms is because they are influenced by younger generations. In traditional written and spoken Korean, prescriptive grammar has a rather inflexible style based on criteria such as honorifics, (in)formality and (im)politeness. What we are seeing with mobile languaging is that now people, whether young or old, have created their own 'tailor-made' mobile languaging styles, which cannot be captured or explained by traditional prescriptive grammar.

There are multiple ways of expressing and communicating information and emotion, but at the same time, the ways in which people interpret them are also diverse. The interpretation can change based on various demographic characteristics like age, gender, economic status, ethnicity, nationality, language background, etc. But ultimately, just as with spoken language, two individuals will never have identical online languaging patterns; a person's online idiolect is the result of their personal background, experience, education and the sum total of their life trajectory. There are certain tendencies that overlap in conjunction with demographics, but ultimately, as with spoken language, online language is open to the interpretation of the individual. While the interpretation of online language is an individual process, there are certain patterns of interpretation that have emerged. As noted earlier, Gunraj et al. revealed that messages ending in periods/full stops are perceived as insincere,[10] and my own research ahead of writing this book showed that messages ending with a full stop tend to be interpreted as carrying negative sentiment.

Within the world of online modalities in which sentence-final punctuation determines emotional stance, the full stop bears connotations of finality, bluntness and lack of enthusiasm. For example, between peers, in response to a message reading 'want to go for dinner?', 'yes!', 'yes :)', or 'yessssss' would suggest enthusiasm and cheerful acquiescence, while 'yes.' suggests a lack of interest. 'Yes. . .', on the other hand, suggests hesitation. Outside of instantaneous back-and-forth messaging, using one or more 'x' – meaning kisses – is a useful sentence, message and exchange closer, while in back-and-forth exchanges, it is more common to finish messages simply with no punctuation, or with different smileys to convey emotional stance. Within online exchange, ellipses are also freely employed to soften assertions by mimicking pause or hesitation in speech. In general, the rules around the use of punctuation are lax, meaning that repeated exclamation or question marks may be used to nuance different stances. In fact, '!!!!!!!!!!', '??!?!', and '??' are all common and acceptable as stand-alone responses, indicating surprise or amazement, incredulousness and puzzlement, respectively.

In that the inclusion of the appropriate smiley can put the recipient of the message at ease, removing some of the emotional confusion that can arise from the lack of contextual clues in a text or online message – a message like 'see you later' risks leaving the recipient confused as to the sender's feelings – the attentive inclusion of emotional cues through emojis or creative punctuating can be seen as a practice of care within computer-mediated communication.

The rapidity of online communication can also lead to the omission of entire punctuation systems if they get in the way of rapid communication. In Spanish, for instance, exclamation points and question marks are traditionally used at both the beginning and the end of the sentence, with the initial mark being inverted. Recently, however, use of the sentence-initial punctuation is often omitted in texts and online messages, with many users opting for only the sentence-final mark. Spanish language texters have also begun to omit the accent marks over many of the vowels, used to indicate irregular stress, which often is the only way to differentiate between homonyms (e.g. 'llegó' means 'he/she arrived', and the word 'llego' means 'I arrive').

Emojis as a visual performance

Emojis work as effective gap fillers in our virtual communication. Despite the arrival of Unicode emojis, which allow users to send detailed, expressive images, many people continue to use emoticons made using standard orthographic characters (e.g., :-)). These kinds of emoticons are still very popular in Korea, for example, and the most common varieties are seen very frequently in text conversations. For instance, laughter or happiness is often expressed as 'ㅋㅋㅋ' ('kkk' – similar to *LOL*) or '^^'. 'ㅋㅋㅋ' can also fulfil the useful role of a gap filler when other emojis or emoticons are not appropriate, contributing to its survival in the lexicon even after the introduction of emojis. The '^^' emoticon represents smiling eyes. Negative emotions, on the other hand, are expressed with tears represented by the emoticon 'ㅠㅠ'. This emoticon visually expresses tears: the horizontal line on the top of each hangul character represents a closed eye, while the two vertical lines represent streaming tears. As with the smiling eyes emoticon (^^), Korean emoticons are read vertically, rather than horizontally like Western emoticons such as ':-)'.

The meaning of emojis can be sensitive to their immediate context: sometimes, the same emoji can mean different things depending on how many times it is used. For example, one of the most commonly used emoticons in Korean is the 'squiggle' (~). Using one squiggle can mean 'please', or even be perceived as a kind of nagging, but using multiple squiggles at the end of a sentence or message can be perceived as begging (as in, 'please, please, please'.) The squiggle can also soften the overall tone of communication. Of course, removing these emoticons does not hamper the delivery of the message, but it can make the conversation feel more rigid, so speakers naturally tend to use them when they feel like a given text message does not carry the desired emotional nuance. We asked a number of informants familiar with the squiggle about what the squiggle means and how they use it in conversations:

- The reason I use the squiggle is to add the message onto whichever phrase that I am using, meaning things like 'take it easy' or 'I am happy with you' or 'don't take it too serious'. In some ways the wave-like motion of this emoticon imitates the gentle waving hand gesture that is used often when using phrases like these.
- My intention for using the squiggle is as a softener – it has a cute effect. If you are making a statement about meeting at a café and I say 'ok, ill see you at five' then I'll add a squiggle. It is an ending that makes it friendly. It might have some gender component. I might feel strange using it to a male. When using it to a female I use it to be in line with a more feminine way of communicating.
- I find it weird to not use embellishments for up to two to three texts to be weird – I would never send this many messages without this kind of

softening embellishment. It is a kindness – a friendliness – a punctuation mark. I think the visual aspect is really important for me when I am texting Korean friends. It really helps the flow of the text and to make it natural.

- For me, in my experience emoji use just enhances the text. It is never essential to the meaning of the words but may be essential to the overall feel of the conversation. E.g. lack of emojis would make the conversation appear too serious or if too many emojis were used it would also diminish the seriousness of the conversation.
- I feel emojis suit Korean more. I don't really want to bring all of that to English. Hangeul symbols give a lot of flexibility and fit so well with texting. It becomes a performance – how can I craft this text to be visually stimulating, etc. You can change so many vowels around in Korean – there is so much room for playing around with hangeul. It is a dynamic texting language. The flexibility in Korean and freedom of expression comes out in texting.

As is clear from these interviews, the Korean squiggle is highly flexible in its meaning. First it is mainly used as a softener to help smooth out one's language. This can help ease our online interactions by modulating one's tone and adding a playful element to the 'visual performance' of digital communication. In this sense, using emoticons can help manage conversation by creating an amiable environment. Such emoticon use emphasizes the visual aspects of language delivery. However, the same emoticon can once again be deemed inappropriate when used without caution:

- If my sister-in-law uses squiggle in a situation that is sensitive, it can be problematic. If my Korean students use squiggles then I will feel a little bit uncomfortable, because they are younger than me.
- Like banmal can cause conflict, so can passive aggressive emoji use. Also, this can be annoying because many squiggles seem like nagging – 'It is like a nagging voice'. Also, because it isn't explicit you can say you didn't mean it.

In this way, emoticons like the squiggle are not a one-size-fits-all answer to smoothing conversations. Although they can help soften one's tone in some situations, they can also have the reverse effect in others, meaning they must be used by skilled speakers who are attuned to various kinds of contextual information.

Summary: Emoji transparency

In summary, there is a great variety in language use in the online sphere, which varies by user according to social, subcultural and other group allegiances. Emoji speak, by definition, allows for innovative hybrid communication that cannot be explained by prescriptive grammar. It allows us to cross borders without a second thought: its pictorial nature creates a general intelligibility that all can understand. We each have our own idiolect that appeases our desires for speed, style and solidarity. Our idiolects stem from the communities and subcultures that we are part of in an entirely personalized manner. Emoji competence relates to our ability to build our own idiolects to bring us closer to the communities that we are part of, and it also relates to our ability to recognize online images and their significances.

Emoji speak almost forces transparent communication. The choice to use emojis is significant and the choice to not use emojis is also significant. In online settings, emoji speak is more powerful than letter words or punctuation. If you choose not to engage with emoji speak, then you highlight yourself as the odd one out. You almost need to follow the emoji patterns of your online community to remain in a safe space. Otherwise, people may misconstrue who you are and your intentions. Not using emojis is far from neutral behaviour. Emoji-less communication has negative connotations attached. As such, emoji speak demands that you reveal your emotions or the emotions that you would like to present yourself as having at all times.

5

Emoji Diversity

Countless emojis are made and used across the borders of languages, cultures and platforms. There are emojis that are popular and even commercialized, and yet there are also emojis that are personal and subculture specific. By and large, the most frequently used emojis are the pre-set emojis that are provided by our phones and the social media platforms that we use. They are readily available and easy to access. These centrally manufactured emojis are limited in their representation of our diverse world. In this multicultural era, we need an array of emojis to reflect the diversity of our society.

Nonetheless, our emojing habits reflect our demographic diversity. Much as we live unrestrained by borders, our emoji use is unrestrained by borders too. As our virtual migration progresses, the diversification of emoji speak will only accelerate. Our individual differences, subcultural preferences, cultural differences and national identities all become visible in our emoji use, in which emojing trends are varied and nuanced.

Emoji interpretation

During a lockdown period in 2020, I hosted several interactive workshops on Google Jamboard. During these workshops, I asked the majority non-Korean participants what they thought various KakaoTalk stickers meant. As you can see in the following, I received varied responses. Although all the replies were in a similar vein, no two answers were exactly the same. This perfectly exemplifies the nature of emojis. They are pictorial, so we receive some kind of similar sentiment from them. However, our own opinions inform a more nuanced and complex understanding that is personal to each individual (Figure 5.1).

Although each person's emoji idiolect is, indeed, unique to them, it is also possible to look at emoji as both a reflection of and constituent part of the

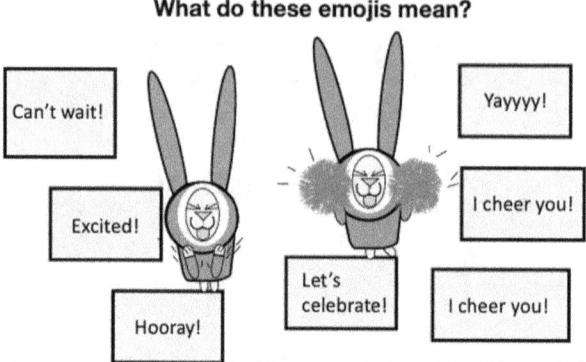

Figure 5.1 Responses from a Google Jamboard session. Design by Loli Kim, reproduced with permission.

societies in which they are used. It is not only English speakers for whom emojis have become an integral part of online communication. A major inspiration for writing this book has been the desire to explore how emojis are used in a range of other languages and cultures. Many past works on emojis have looked at usage mainly in English-speaking communities. The meanings associated with various emojis are not set in stone. Emojis sit on a spectrum of universality, with a core lexicon for which meaning varies less and a peripheral lexicon for which meaning varies more across different cultures and contexts.

Although emojis are often seen as an addition to natural language, they should also be seen as forming part of a wider verbal and non-verbal repertoire that individuals draw on when communicating. Emojis can be viewed as part of a wider repertoire belonging to a particular idiolect, rather than as one of several discrete codes that a speaker can switch between. By thinking of emojis as one part of one's overall repertoire, the variety seen in emoji use around the world becomes less surprising. The high sensitivity of emojis to sociocultural factors also strongly resembles verbal cues.[1] There are also clear parallels with loanwords, which can take on all kinds of new meanings and associations that might be surprising to speakers of the original source language.[2]

Emoji etymology

Recall that the word *emoji* is originally derived from Japanese. The Japanese term 絵文字 (*emoji*) is made up of three kanji (Chinese characters adapted for writing Japanese) that can be glossed as follows: 絵 (*e*) means 'picture' and 文字 (*moji*) refers to written characters or script. *Emoji*, therefore, can be roughly translated as something like 'picture characters', an apt description.

Loanwords often have multifaceted histories due to their complex histories within multiple languages, and the term *emoji* is no different. Although the complex history of how kanji characters are used in Japanese (and, indeed, Korean) is beyond the scope of this book, it is worth noting that the kanji used to write 絵文字 are part of a script originally imported from China over a thousand years ago and adapted to meet the needs of Japanese (including the creation of many new words not borrowed from Chinese). After its creation in Japanese, the term *emoji* was borrowed into English and officially adopted by the Unicode Consortium. The English pronunciation, however, differs significantly to the Japanese pronunciation; while the Japanese sounds closer to (ˈɛmɒdʒi), in English the word has taken on the pronunciation (iˈmoʊdʒi). It is not clear whether this is the result or cause of the common assumption that the word's etymology is related to *emotion* (or *emoticon* – see the following). As described earlier, the Japanese etymology of *emoji* is unrelated to 'emotion', however, and it is simply a happy coincidence that the very sound of the word brings the association of 'emotion' for English speakers.

Because the characters used to write 絵文字 were originally imported from China into Japanese, one might assume that the word *emoji* could have been easily exported back into Chinese. However, the word 絵文字 (pronounced as *huiwenzi* in Chinese, and meaning 'drawing letters'), or 绘文字 in simplified script, tends to be found only in limited contexts – namely, more scholarly texts such as encyclopaedias. This is because although it is written in Chinese characters, the word does not exactly make grammatical sense in contemporary Chinese. Instead, the word 表情符号 (*biaoqing fuhao*, 'facial expression symbol') is often used to refer to emojis within smartphone OSs, while the term 表情 (*biaoqing*), 'facial expressions', is commonly used to refer to emojis in Chinese, with the term 小黄脸 (*xiaohuanglian*, 'little yellow faces') also seen from time to time. As a caveat, we should note that China is perhaps a special case because Chinese platforms have their own set(s) of emoji equivalents separate to the Unicode characters.

Although the Unicode emojis are used across most of the world (that being the very point of the Unicode system), the reality is that each emoji, just like each loanword, often accrues new meanings in each new context. As I have previously discussed, a seemingly identical word will often undergo dynamic changes to its meaning, form and identity to accompany a new sociolinguistic environment.[3] Although the form of an emoji can theoretically be controlled by platform holders or Unicode, once an emoji has entered use, the meanings and associations of the emoji are much more difficult to centrally determine.

The words used to refer to emojis in other languages, and the nuances carried by said terms, have different stories for every language. For example, the Korean term 이모티콘 (*emoticon*, derived from the English portmanteau of *emotion* and *icon*) is often used as a generic term in Korean to refer to non-verbal, pictorial representations used in text, including emojis and more. In contrast, the meaning of the word *emoticon* in English is limited to representations of faces using standard typed characters and does not include emojis. We now move from questions of diversity in the conception of emoji to diversity as it is represented by emoji themselves.

Unicode: Emojis controlled and censored

We have made brief mentions of the Unicode Consortium throughout the book up to this point. Now, we introduce it in more depth. The Unicode Consortium is the organization in charge of handling the implementation of emojis into Unicode, the system that allows typed characters to appear the same across different devices, and it also selects which emojis are to be added in each update to Unicode. Because Unicode is such an integral part of how our devices send and receive information online, the Unicode set of emojis becomes available as a matter of course to a huge number of users on a wide range of platforms, explaining how the Unicode set of emojis has achieved its dominant position in the West. The same Unicode emojis are realized differently on different platforms, but it is still an incredible feat that emojis display correctly across platforms at all. The Unicode emojis form a core set that is accessible to such a wide range of people that they deserve special attention. Although anyone is free to create their own emojis, or to download independently created emojis, the amount of effort this requires is prohibitive to most users, who will likely find an appropriate emoji in the Unicode set anyway, not to mention that other sets lack the cross-device integration inherent to Unicode.

Well, the good news is that, in theory, anyone looking to create their dream emoji can write up a proposal and send it to the Unicode Consortium, where it will be assessed by the Unicode Emoji Subcommittee. If the Unicode Emoji Subcommittee likes a proposal, they will send it up to the Unicode Technical Committee, which meets quarterly, and a list of draft candidates will be submitted for public review. Emojis might then be submitted as data files for different platforms for use. The criteria for assessment are provided online.[4] Unfortunately for those who rightly point out the uneven cultural representation in the current set of emojis, it is not easy to create a successful proposal aiming to fill a cultural gap in areas such as regional foods. One criterion of a successful proposal is that the proposed emoji must demonstrate high levels of global use. In other words, the emoji must exist in some form already and be in common use on a range of platforms online, prior to being integrated into the Unicode set. Other important criteria are compatibility, distinctiveness and completeness.

It is also specifically stated that not only do petitions establishing demand for an emoji not help a proposal but such evidence also 'just detracts from the strength of your proposal'. Accordingly, Unicode actually lists 'petitions and frequent requests' as the first so-called 'selection factor for exclusion' for rejecting a proposal. Some of the other selection factors for exclusion are similarly concerning: the 'faulty comparison' criterion establishes that proposals should not be justified on the basis that the suggested emoji is more important than other existing emojis. The guidelines explain that this means one should not argue that the existence of four different mailbox emojis means there should be space for the proposed emoji, and the existence of a Tokyo Tower emoji does not justify the addition of an Eiffel Tower emoji. What is concerning about this criterion is that it can be read as arguing that if one culture is represented first in a given semantic space, there is then no room for emojis representing similar concepts from other cultures. In practice, despite these guidelines it is very difficult to figure out exactly where the lines are for accepting a new emoji. The important thing here is that the decision-making power is held centrally by the Unicode Emoji Subcommittee and the Unicode Technical Committee.

Although it is true that anyone can suggest the addition of an emoji, the success of one's proposal ultimately depends on the decision of a small group of people based on rather obscure guidelines. This is the case even when there is a clear and documented demand for adding a certain emoji. Power over the emoji lexicon, then, is concentrated in relatively few hands. As of July 2021, the Unicode Technical Committee has ten full members (Adobe, Apple, Yat, Facebook, Google, Microsoft, Netflix, SAP SE, Salesforce and the Ministry of Endowments and Religious Affairs of Oman), four institutional members (Bangladesh Computer Council, the Government of India, Tamil Virtual Academy and the University of California, Berkeley), and one supporting member (Emojipedia). Although there are other member categories, these are the only members with voting rights. Voting membership is concentrated in Western technology and software companies, and although there are some voting members from other regions (most notably the Indian subcontinent), the Unicode Technical Committee is a long way from being able to describe itself as representing the full spectrum of global users. Acquiring membership with voting rights ranges in cost from $10,000 (for institutional members that qualify for a discount) to $21,000 for full corporate membership – a prohibitively high barrier to making one's voice heard in shaping how the emoji lexicon develops. As such, although emojis allow for more expressivity online, we must be aware that large corporations have monopolies over which emojis are available to us and thus manipulate our online behaviour without us knowing.

Campaigning for inclusion

By this point, we have probably made clear that diversity is a reality of language use. But is this just coincidental, or is there value in protecting this diversity? The argument could be made that standardization is also a natural and frequently observed feature in the history of languages, resulting from the increasingly broad dissemination of recorded language in the form of writing or audio–visual material, among other reasons.

The basic principle that people around the world should be able to express themselves as they see fit can be seen in Article 19 of the United Nations Universal Declaration of Human Rights, read in conjunction with Article 2 of the same text:

> **Article 2**
>
> Everyone is entitled to all the rights and freedoms set forth in this Declaration, without distinction of any kind, such as race, colour, sex, language, religion, political or other opinion, national or social origin, property, birth or other status
>
> **Article 19**
>
> Everyone has the right to freedom of opinion and expression; this right includes freedom to hold opinions without interference and to seek, receive and impart information and ideas through any media and regardless of frontiers.

I am of course not arguing that organizations such as the Unicode Consortium, or the various technology providers that adopt Unicode, are violating human rights by not instantly providing a set of emojis that meets the needs of everyone everywhere. The right to freedom of expression should not be interpreted as meaning that everyone has a legal obligation to enable the expression of everyone else (and even if that were the case, the Unicode Consortium and other technology companies are doing a lot more than most to help this!). All the same, it would not seem controversial to say that the ideal for the international community would be for individuals to be free from discrimination towards their freedom of expression based on categories such as 'race, colour, sex, language, religion, political or other opinion'.

What is more, the impact of the availability of Unicode emojis should not be underestimated. Although people are free to search elsewhere for alternative emojis or even have a go at creating their own, in practice, most people tend to make do with the features built into social media platforms or their smartphones out of convenience. This means that the selection of emojis offered by default on popular platforms and hardware has the scope to be extremely influential on how we emoji. Just as it has been easy for linguists to write emojis off as a peripheral aspect of communication, many have dismissed the lack of representation and diversity in the emoji lexicon as a trivial issue; if emojis aren't important, why should we care how diverse the lexicon is? But maybe we should trust grassroots campaigners from marginalized groups when they tell us this is an important issue; and when people like Jeannie Suk, the first Asian-American professor to hold tenure at Harvard law school, says, 'Until dumplings have a place at the emoji table, ours cannot be a truly inclusive society', maybe we should listen.[5]

Given the importance of food and cooking in all of our everyday lives, it is unsurprising that lots of the emoji lexicon are devoted to depicting various kinds of food, drinks and cooking utensils. By looking at the various food and drink emojis and delving into their cultural origin and significance, we can understand which cultures are represented more or less in the emoji lexicon. This can tell us a lot about the awareness of a particular culture globally, as well as also serving to reinforce imbalances in awareness of certain cultures.

Despite the vast size and variety of the emoji lexicon, it is clear that some cultures are represented to a far greater extent than others. This is a more significant problem than it might at first seem. Although being able to send a small image from one's smartphone representing part of one's cultural heritage or a favourite dish from home may seem like a trivial concern, emojis are a huge part of our everyday online communication, and it can be frustrating for those from less-represented cultures to be unable to express aspects of their daily lives in the manner that those from better-represented cultures take for granted. Emojis are so visible globally that when a culture is represented in an emoji it can lead to greater visibility for that culture, as many who are curious about the meaning or origin of a new emoji might look up its meaning. Having emojis to reflect one's national and cultural symbols for people around the world to see and use in daily conversation can play a role in having a more privileged place on the world stage. Given the globalized and digital nature of today's world, it seems reasonable to suggest that those from less well-represented countries, or those visiting said countries and hoping to discuss their experiences in familiar ways, should be able to do so. However, despite the continuing expansion of the emoji catalogue and the inclusion of more and more diverse cultural references, the balance of dominant emojis is still far from ideal, with the majority of foods, drinks and other items belonging to either Western, English-speaking (generally meaning the United States) or Japanese cultural origins. While this is unsurprising given emoji's origins in Japan and its subsequent proliferation by US-owned tech corporations via the California-based Unicode Consortium, the diversity of emojis still leaves something to be desired given that they are intended for use all over the world by an increasingly globally connected population.

Let us, then, take a closer look at the available food emojis as a measure of how different cultures are represented in emojis. At the most basic level, the emoji lexicon covers a wide range of ingredients common to cultures all over the globe, such as fruits, vegetables, garlic, nuts and so on. These items are relatively innocuous and carry little 'cultural odour'; they are not particularly associated with any one culture. However, once we move into emojis representing particular dishes we find that preferences for certain cultures become more common, as we will see.

Perhaps unsurprisingly, given the development of emojis laid out above, the dominant cultural origins of food emojis representing specific dishes (across Apple, Android, and other platforms) are Western, American and Japanese. For example, stereotypical US-style junk foods are notably over-represented, with six distinct emojis: bacon, a hamburger, French fries, a hotdog, pizza and a chicken drumstick. Even the icon for the 'food and drink' category draws from American imagery; the icon for this section on the Apple emoji keyboard is a soda cup and burger, while Android's is a burger, demonstrating the heavy Western influence exerted by the two most common smartphone software providers in the world. With the exception of bacon, which was added to Emoji 3.0 in 2016, these fast-food items have all been included in the emoji lexicon since 2015, when Emoji 1.0 – the first emoji documentation from Unicode which includes all emojis approved between 2010 and 2015 – was released. As such, these images hold pride of place as foundational parts of the emoji library.

Next up are emojis representing Japanese cuisine. Emojis in this vein include a wide variety of food items, covering a broad range of highly recognizable Japanese dishes and culinary items. These include rice balls, curry rice, sushi, shrimp tempura and a bento box. Given that emojis were invented and first reached mainstream popularity in Japan, it is no surprise that there is disproportionate representation of recognizable Japanese foodstuffs in the global emoji library.

However, in addition to these globally recognizable items, there are numerous food items which may not be familiar to those living outside of Japan or those who are less aware of the finer details of Japanese life and culture. These emojis depict items such as *oden* (a collection of various items that are skewered and cooked in broth), *kamaboko* (a chewy fish cake often included in dishes such as ramen, here depicted in the form of *narutomaki*, which has a typical pink and white swirl pattern) and *dango* (slightly sweetened small dumplings made from various kinds of flour and often coloured pink, white and green). These emojis, which have long been part of the emoji lexicon, shine a spotlight on the finer details of Japanese cuisine, fleshing out the portion of the emoji lexicon dealing with Japanese culture to an extent that is not seen for other global cultures and cuisines.

Outside of the Western Anglophone world and Japan, there are very few other cultures represented in the emoji food lexicon. The exceptions to this are a small selection of Central and South American dishes (a taco, burrito, tamale and mate), two Middle Eastern-inspired items (stuffed flatbread and falafel) and the dumpling, which is generically designed so as to represent a broad range of Asian and European dumpling varieties. The limited number of dishes belonging to cultures outside of Japan and the Anglophone world demonstrates the imbalance in not only the quantity of emojis representing different cultures but also the specificity of Japanese and American items compared to the generic nature of items such as 'dumplings' and 'stuffed flatbreads', which are designed to represent as broad a range of foods from different nations and cultures as possible. This is in stark contrast to the specificity of the Japanese dango emoji, for instance, which represents one particular Japanese foodstuff rather than the general concept of 'skewered dumplings'.

The Dumpling Emoji Project, an online project and Kickstarter campaign aimed at the inclusion of the dumpling in the Unicode emoji library, perfectly highlights the issues with the imbalance in which cultural signifiers are included in the emoji lexicon. Prior to the dumpling's eventual inclusion in the emoji canon in 2017, friends Yiying Lu and Jennifer Lee began the Dumpling Emoji Project as a campaign for the representation of dumplings (be they Chinese jiaozi, Japanese gyoza, Korean mandu, Italian ravioli, Tibetan momo, Polish pierogi or any other kind of dumpling) in the Unicode emoji library. From its beginning in 2015 until the dumpling emoji was implemented in 2017, their campaign gained widespread public attention and numerous endorsements from celebrities, highlighting the need for more democracy and cultural variety in the emoji lexicon. The project sought to emphasize the fact that despite being central to the communication habits of internet users all over the world, the emoji lexicon is controlled by only a handful of multinational American tech corporations, with eleven full voting members of the Unicode Consortium each paying thousands of dollars a year for the privilege, eight of those being US multinational tech companies (Oracle, IBM, Microsoft, Adobe, Apple, Google, Facebook and Yahoo). As a result of this imbalance, the Dumpling Project sought to proliferate the idea of emojis by the people, for the people, beginning with the inclusion of widely used cultural cornerstones such as the dumpling. As stated by Eddie Huang, founder of Baohouse and author of American sitcom *Fresh off the Boat*, in support of the project, 'whether it's dumplings or tacos or pizza emojis, the Unicode Consortium is regulating language. People speak with their hands these days and language should be open. I believe that not only should there be a dumpling emoji, there should be a bao emoji too'.

While statements such as the above may appear hyperbolic to some, the Dumpling Emoji Project and similar calls for increased emoji diversity are important. As more and more of our daily communication takes place online, cultural diversity and balance across the emoji library will become an increasingly pressing concern. If issues such as these are not addressed by the White, English-speaking, American-dominated Unicode Consortium, then there is a risk that our global online discourse becomes effectively censored as a result, with only certain cultures permitted to express important aspects of their daily lives through certain modes of communication. As a cornerstone of culture and national identity, food emojis are the perfect place to begin, symbolizing the breadth and diversity of delicious and vibrant foods available across the ever-connected world.

Of course, this does not mean we should limit cultural representation in emojis to food emojis; there are numerous important cultural symbols that have yet to be represented in the emoji lexicon. For instance, although social media use is rapidly rising in the Middle East and North Africa (MENA) region, there has been slow progress in introducing culturally relevant symbols across various social media platforms to serve this demographic. A 2017 social media report estimated that two-thirds of young people in the Arab world used social media at the time, and according to the 2019 Social Media in the Middle East report, this has now climbed to 90 per cent of youths using some form of social media every day.[6] Yet despite this, the cultural needs of the MENA region are underserved in the available emoji options. Progress has been slow in implementing Arab cultural symbols. Apple's 2015 iOS 9.1 update did include the Kaaba of Mecca, a mosque, a palm tree, a desert and misbaha (prayer beads), but it took the efforts of a sixteen-year-old Saudi girl, Rayouf Alhumedhi, to get a woman in a hijab emoji included in the Unicode Consortium selection in 2017. Although there was some backlash at including this emoji, with reasons varying from opposing a symbol seen by some to represent women's oppression to simple Islamophobia, Rayouf sums up the importance of its inclusion well in a CNN interview: 'I wanted to be represented, as simple as that. I just wanted an emoji of me.'[7]

There have been attempts by certain platforms to further emoji representation through non-Unicode emojis. For instance, during Ramadan in 2019, Twitter introduced three emojis to accompany certain hashtags associated with Ramadan: the crescent moon, a glass of yoghurt (associated with breaking of the fast) and a lantern. These were only launched for seven languages (English, Arabic, Bahasa Malaysia, Spanish, Turkish, Hindi and Bengali), and not the entire platform, however. These emojis are also only available for a limited time during Ramadan and can only be accessed through certain hashtags rather than being available for users to add freely to their tweets.

Other emojis relevant to MENA users include the falafel emoji, which was finally introduced by Unicode Consortium in 2019, and the pinched fingers emoji, which was launched on Android platforms on 8 September 2020, and by Apple on 1 October 2020 (Figure 5.2).

The hand gesture was launched in a range of skin tones and is an iconic gesture across the Middle East. It means either 'wait/be patient' or, more threateningly, 'you'll see what happens' when used by a mother to her child. This gesture is not only applicable in the Middle East, however, and has different meanings in other regions. For instance, it can signal frustration in Italy, can represent a dumpling

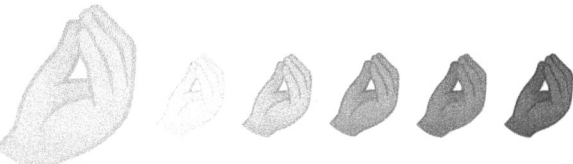

Figure 5.2 Pinched fingers emoji. Source: NotoColorEmoji: © 2021 Google Inc, OFL License.

or a warm sentiment when used by the K-Pop star Yuri, can be used to ask if somebody is hungry in India or can in some cases have sexual implications.[8] In this way, emojis do not have fixed meanings and can mean different things in different regions and (sub)cultures.

Realistic emojis: Representation revision

In 2010, Unicode's vision for emojis was to create a system of symbols that were as neutral and universal as possible.[9] Their official design guidelines recommend that for 'general-purpose emoji for people and body parts [. . .] the general recommendation is to be as neutral as possible regarding race, ethnicity, and gender'[10] (this recommendation does not apply, of course, to emojis intended to have a specific gender or race, such as 'U+1F46F woman with bunny ears' or 'U+1F473 man with turban').

Unicode's guidance is only part of the story, however. Unicode provides a brief description of each emoji and a simple black-and-white guidance image in the Unicode Standard, but a given emoji's final appearance is left up to designers at corporations like Apple and Google, who manage how emojis appear on their platforms. As a result, each platform's emoji designs are subject to copyright, and the appearance of a given emoji will differ, sometimes significantly, between platforms. This means that despite Unicode's design guidelines on gender-neutrality, many designers ended up reproducing gender stereotypes through their emoji designs; for example, in 2016 a group of Google employees pointed out that many of the emojis for professions such as doctor or scientist were depicted exclusively as male while the only female emojis were limited to options like the bunny girls or dancers – a far cry from Unicode's original vision of neutral, universal symbols.[11] In an attempt to fix issues like this, Unicode began introducing gendered pairs for each human emoji in 2016, abandoning the original concept of gender-neutrality in order to ensure platforms did not simply interpret most professions as male. In 2017, Unicode also introduced three new gender-neutral emojis (a child, an adult and an older person) to supplement the gendered pairs of human emojis.[12] In 2019, Unicode expanded these by adding an additional third androgynous/gender-neutral option to nearly all emojis with a male and female variant. These gender-neutral emojis are in line with Unicode's original concept of gender-neutrality, while also being inclusive of non-binary and gender-nonconforming people. An update in 2020 expanded this a little further, adding a gender-neutral Santa Claus, male, female and gender-neutral variants of a parent feeding a baby from a bottle, and a man and gender-neutral person in a wedding veil, among others.

The story of racial representation in emojis is similar to that of gender. According to Unicode's design guidelines, 'emoji characters for people and body parts are meant to be generic', recommending designers use a 'generic (non-human) appearance, such as a yellow/orange colour or a silhouette'. Nevertheless, Unicode's guidelines acknowledge that 'following the precedents set by the original Japanese carrier images, they are often shown with a light skin tone instead'.[13] Indeed, looking at the original set of emojis in Apple's iOS 4.0, it is easy to forget that nearly the entire set of human emojis was originally depicted as light-skinned rather than generic Simpsons-yellow, as is the default now (Figure 5.3).

Figure 5.3 Unicode emojis at the time of iOS 4, featuring mainly light-skinned person emojis. Source: NotoColorEmoji: © 2021 Google Inc, OFL License and Twemoji © 2020 Twitter, Inc and other contributors, CC BY 4.0. See the original image here: 'Apple Ios 4.0'. *Emojipedia*. Accessed 23 April 2021. https://emojipedia.org/apple/ios-4.0/.

Figure 5.4 Person wearing turban (left) and person with skullcap (right). Source: Twemoji © 2020 Twitter, Inc and other contributors, CC BY 4.0. See the original image here: 'Apple Ios 4.0'. *Emojipedia*. Accessed 23 April 2021. https://emojipedia.org/apple/ios-4.0/.

Of the original emojis featured on iOS 4.0, only person wearing turban and person with skullcap look unambiguously non-White. Person wearing turban (Figure 5.4, left) has a brown skin tone, while person with skullcap (Figure 5.4, right) looks like a racist caricature of an Asian person (unsurprisingly, this emoji has been revised since, and has lost its caricatured appearance and is no longer tied to a specific race).

In 2015, however, Unicode made an update to the set of human emojis, allowing each symbol to be combined with a range of five skin tones using a 'zero width joiner' (an invisible character that tells the computer to substitute a single character for a sequence of several), allowing users to choose from five skin tones for each emoji depicting a person, plus a 'generic' yellow variant (see Figure 5.5).

While this was a welcome improvement over the previous system, in which light skin was effectively the 'default', the way multiple skin tones were implemented has also been criticized. For instance, despite the yellow skin tone of Apple's 'generic' emojis, a study by the University of Edinburgh found that both Black and White participants interpreted yellow emojis as being 'more likely to signify White identity'. Upon being shown text messages containing either yellow emojis or darker/lighter skin-toned emojis, 56 per cent of Black participants and 63 per cent of White participants thought that the sender of a message featuring only yellow emojis was more likely to be White. In comparison, both Black and White participants guessed 80 per cent of the time that a message containing a

Figure 5.5 Generic yellow emoji alongside five tones inspired by the Fitzpatrick scale. Twemoji © 2020 Twitter, Inc and other contributors, CC BY 4.0.

darker or lighter skin-toned emojis was written by an author matching the skin tone of the emojis in their message.[14]

Part of the reason for this association could be that White users tend to prefer using the generic yellow emojis over light-skinned emojis. A study by researchers at the University of Edinburgh compared Twitter users' profile pictures to their choice of emoji skin tone and found that 'users with darker-skinned profile photos are more likely to use tone-modified [i.e., not the generic yellow] emoji', while users with lighter-skinned profile photos were more likely to stick to the generic yellow set.'[15] Another study by Andrew McGill examined data from Twitter in bulk, finding that although 'white Twitter users outnumber Black users four to one', 'the lightest skin tone was used the least'. McGill speculated that the reason for this was that going out of one's way to choose a light-skinned emoji 'felt uncomfortably close to displaying "white pride"', leading many users to stick to the generic yellow emojis to 'avoid the decision'.[16]

Despite Apple's attempt to follow Unicode's guidelines of using a non-realistic skin colour for the generic set of emojis, the choice of bright yellow still reads as Caucasian to many; not only do they share the same facial features as the original light-skinned set of emojis, but their bright yellow hair also resembles blonde hair. Additionally, although bright yellow is a non-natural skin tone, it has reminded some commentators of *The Simpsons*, where Black and Brown characters, such as Apu, were given realistic skin tones while White characters were given bright yellow skin.[17]

Paige Tutt wrote an article for *The Washington Post* explaining her mixed feelings on Apple's addition of skin tones to emojis. Tutt writes that she found herself almost forced into identifying herself racially through emojis in situations where she otherwise wouldn't have to: 'Because I'm black, should I now feel compelled to use the 'appropriate' brown-skinned nail-painting emoji? [. . .] Now in simple text messages and tweets, I have to identify myself racially.' Tutt also points out that because only the skin tone of emojis can be changed, not the physical features of the faces themselves, there is 'nothing specifically "black" about an emoji with browner skin', meaning that Black emojis amount to 'white emoji wearing masks'. She acknowledges that Apple most likely wanted to avoid creating caricatures (as they did previously with the person with skull cap emoji), but criticized them for opting out of the design work of doing Black emoji justice, writing that, 'Instead of creating actual emojis of colour, Apple simply allows its users to make white emoji a different color.'[18] Instead, Tutt argues that Apple should have designed their emojis to be raceless and generic from the beginning to avoid the question of representation completely, as Unicode's design guidelines originally recommended.

Indeed, one can argue that the highly rigid, controlled way in which new emojis are introduced serves as a significant obstacle for true representation of different ways of life and experiences through emojis. New emojis must be approved by the Unicode Consortium, which meets four times a year on the west coast of the United States and is primarily made up of representatives from huge tech corporations like Apple, Microsoft and Google, and whose members are predominantly White and male. Additionally, according to Unicode's 'Emoji Encoding Principles', the 'major vendors' (i.e. smartphone producers such as Apple, Microsoft, Google, etc.) have indicated that they want a soft limit of around seventy new emojis and emojis sequences per year, as additional emoji 'can be a burden on memory, UI usability and development cost'.[19] This means that not only are decisions on new emojis limited to a very narrow pool of people (although they do allow the public to submit suggestions) but the Consortium must also make loaded decisions about which emojis are 'important' enough to be included in the roughly seventy new emojis each year.

There is no good way to compare the relative importance of basic human concepts, and the results of these decisions can feel unfair to those looking to be represented through emojis. For instance, the German broadcasting network DW interviewed Tea Uglow, a transgender woman who spent four years lobbying for the inclusion of the transgender flag emoji until it was implemented in 2020. Uglow expressed her frustration at seeing the transgender flag overlooked year after year in favour of adding seemingly trivial emojis like a courgette or a new kind of tractor. She also eloquently explained the importance of representation and diversity in emojis: for her, seeing Unicode reject the trans flag year after year was like them saying, 'You're so small that you don't exist, we cease to matter, we don't need a word to describe us. And that is erasure, in every single definition. To erase a minority from existence. The easiest way to do that is to remove them from your language.'[20]

Unicode itself also seems to acknowledge the problems with the current system. The documentary *Picture Character* interviewed several members of staff at Unicode. One staff member, Lisa Moore, said in interview that, 'we keep talking about getting out of the business of emoji characters because we can't respond to everyone's desires or the true diversity of the world [. . .] Unicode doesn't want to define every emoji character.'[21] The vice chair of the Unicode Technical Committee also stated that 'the future of emoji will not necessarily still involve Unicode. [. . .] We only hope that there would be a better answer for emoji, and one that actually could cater more to the endless imagination of the human mind.'[22]

Determining which symbols are added into the global 'language' of emojis is a huge responsibility, and one that Unicode does not necessarily wish to take on.

One obvious solution to this dilemma of representation is allowing users to directly customize or add their own emojis to the lexicon. After all, every other language on the planet allows speakers to innovate new words to describe new concepts and our changing lives; new words are introduced organically, not decided on by committees. Needless to say, a change like this would require emojis to be reimplemented from the ground up. Creating a more flexible, customizable emoji keyboard that is as user-friendly and convenient as the current system would be a huge undertaking that would likely require the cooperation and coordination of all of the major tech companies to truly succeed, and for that reason is perhaps unlikely to come to fruition.

Some apps have experimented with allowing users to customize emojis or similar symbols, although these are not yet as fully integrated as the standard emoji keyboard. For example, Google's Emoji Kitchen app allows users to combine different emojis to create unique new emojis. Twitter account @Emoji Mashup Bot also automatically generates combinations of different emojis in a similar way and posts the results on Twitter (Figure 5.6).

Figure 5.6 Combine two emojis to create a new one. Source: design by Loli Kim, reproduced with permission.

In 2018, Samsung introduced the AR Emoji feature, which uses AR technology to create an emoji that looks like the user when taking a selfie. Apple also introduced their Animoji feature in 2017 on iOS 11, allowing users to manipulate various 3D emojis characters using their camera so that the emojis mimic the users' movements. In 2018, iOS 12 brought Memoji, which allowed users to customize their own emoji character and to manipulate it using the camera, like Animoji. Users can choose from a variety of hairstyles, facial features and skin tones (including non-realistic colours like purple) to make their Memoji resemble themselves. Users are at no point asked to assign their Memoji a gender; rather, users are free to select features as they see fit without their options being limited to a certain gender. Memoji also offers sliders to allow more skin tone options than the five-tone Fitzpatrick scale used for standard emojis. Because of this additional customization, Memoji manages to be more inclusive of different races as well as non-binary and transgender people.

Customizable emojis like these represent an interesting shift towards allowing users to create their own unique ways of expressing themselves online. In the future, as augmented reality (AR) and virtual reality (VR) technologies become more mainstream, we may find ourselves interacting with each other using avatars like these more often. While this section has focused largely on the standard set of Unicode emoji and the power relations that come into play in their creation, dissemination, recognition and use, in the next section, we will turn to a very different emoji ecosystem.

Demographic diversity: China

Although emojis do not live within languages, different usage emerges within different demographics. Sometimes, these can be small subcultural demographics, and sometimes, entire countries have different emoji usage trends. China is one of those countries that has its own individual emoji styles, though these styles may be employed by the Chinese diaspora and language learners, too. Not all emojis are available to all. Some are limited to certain regions. Due to internet restrictions in China, many popular Western platforms, like Facebook, Instagram, WhatsApp, TikTok, Twitter and Snapchat, are not easily accessible in China, so other platforms are used instead. These platforms come with their own emoji repertoire, meaning that emoji speak among Chinese demographics can look very different because the platform influences our emoji speak so greatly.

WeChat emojis

For users of WeChat, Unicode emojis are of little attraction. WeChat users, largely made up of Chinese nationals, Chinese diaspora and Chinese language learners, tend to use the emoji set created by Tencent (the company that operates WeChat). Tencent's emojis were originally designed for their software QQ, the first Chinese SNS application made available in 1999. Tencent's emojis were then also included in WeChat, when it was introduced in 2011. QQ is differentiated from WeChat in that its focus is more on casual entertainment and making friends, while WeChat has less functionality but is simpler to use. More recently, many users have switched from QQ to WeChat, which now has 1.2 billion active monthly users and is used for work as well as for personal messaging.

In 2020, WeChat updated its emojis twice, adding six new emojis and introducing animated emojis in place of still images. Weibo, a platform filling a similar role in China to Twitter (because Twitter is blocked), also has its own set of emojis. These local sets of emoji are far more popular than the Unicode set used around most of the world, and because of this it is sometimes assumed in China that the rest of the world also uses the Chinese set of emojis. This can be seen in the comments from Chinese netizens in response to an article posted by China Daily on WeChat on the publication of the recent 2021 Adobe Global Emoji Trend Report,[23] in which many commenters assume that WeChat and Weibo emojis are the default collection universally, reflecting their local dominance (Figure 5.7).

China's relationship with emojis, therefore, is somewhat different from our previous examples. The emojis used on Chinese platforms are unique to those platforms and are specifically tailored to the Chinese market. Although Chinese sets of emojis are unique, however, users have a similar relationship to emojis as seen in other countries, and grassroots movements calling for changes to emoji also exist in China. For example, the 'cool' emoji on WeChat used to feature a cigarette. However, following pressure from the Cigarette Control Association of Beijing this emoji 'quit smoking' in the latest version released in 2020.

Figure 5.7 Representation of the types of emojis on the WeChat keyboard. Source: design by Loli Kim, reproduced with permission. See the full keyboard here: https://blog.emojipedia.org/chinese-new-year-theres-an-emoji-for-that/

The Cigarette Control Association argued that associating smoking with being 'cool' is misleading for teenagers using the platform. This change reflects the idea that WeChat emojis function as a beacon for social values, and the campaign to disassociate smoking from 'coolness' shows that in China, too, there is the perception that emojis may have a powerful social impact.

Another example of this occurred during the pandemic. I have discussed how designs of the face with medical mask emoji in Unicode has adapted to the new norm during the pandemic that wearing a mask does not necessarily mean one is sick. This was also the case for WeChat, which also redesigned its equivalent emoji. While the WeChat emoji is still titled 'sick', blushes have been added and the expression is less pained. More noticeably, the updated emoji's mask is a more accurate depiction of a medical mask, while the older design had a plainer white rectangle that could represent a simpler fabric mask. It should be noted that in China, unlike in some other countries, only disposable medical masks are recognized as effective against infection and are required as an anti-coronavirus precaution; the new design reflects this view.

In this way, many of the tencent emojis are specific to the linguistic and cultural background in which they were designed. One informant of Chinese heritage we spoke to expressed difficulty in finding appropriate equivalents for staple Chinese emojis on Western social media. Indeed, many emojis found on tencent platforms have no simple Unicode equivalent.

For instance, the tencent emoji of a smiley face cracking was introduced in 2020 based on the Chinese viral expression '我裂开了', which was made popular by a famous video game player. The expression literally means 'I have cracked', implying 'I have had a mild breakdown'. Although some Western emojis are somewhat similar in general meaning, there is no direct equivalent emoji to this in Unicode at the time of writing.

Another example is this melon-eating emoji, which is also based on a Chinese expression: '吃瓜群众', which literally means 'the melon-eating masses', which refers, in a self-deprecating manner, to onlookers who are uninformed about the facts of a given situation. The phrase was initially used by Chinese netizens to make fun of their own inability to predict the unexpected ways current affairs issues often play out. More recently, however, many people use the emoji to indicate curiosity and the desire to know more about something.

The two emojis our informant described as particularly difficult to find a replacement for on Western social media platforms, however, were not based on specific Chinese phrases.

Figure 5.8 Alternative hugging emoji. Sources (from left to right): NotoColorEmoji: © 2021 Google Inc, OFL License, Twemoji © 2020 Twitter, Inc and other contributors, CC BY 4.0, and OpenMoji, CC BY-SA 4.0.

The shy emoji is used to express humility in response to praise. A typical response to praise in China is to reply with something like 'that isn't true' or 'you are going too far'. It is understood that the person is not really denying the truth of the compliment or feeling bad about themselves, they are simply expressing humility as is socially expected. Young people, however, often find such statements disingenuous and prefer to use this blushing emoji in similar situations online to express reserved appreciation for a compliment. The informant mentioned that this implication of reserve or humility is hard to convey with the blushing emoji on other platforms.

The second emoji mentioned by our informant, the hug, is used primarily to comfort somebody or to offer condolences. This might be used when discussing a serious accident, or simply when someone is complaining about difficulties at work, for instance. Our informant mentioned that this emoji was used in almost all of the responses to the news that a friend's family member had passed away. While hugging emojis certainly exist on other platforms, these tend to feature smiling faces, making it difficult to express the idea of consoling someone who is suffering or grieving (imagine hugging someone with a big grin on your face after they tell you of a recent bereavement) (Figure 5.8).

It seems that Unicode became aware of this gap in the emoji lexicon recently, and added a more neutral hugging emoji, 'people hugging', in Unicode 13.0 in 2020. Although this emoji seems far more appropriate for offering comfort or condolences than previous options, its silhouetted appearance and lack of detail sets it apart from most of the other more vibrant 'people' emojis, making this emoji somewhat less appealing, as well as less readable at small sizes, perhaps making it an imperfect replacement for the WeChat hug emoji.

Chinese characters as emojis

Another interesting facet of emojing in China is the use of Chinese characters as emojis. This is true of the character 囧 (*jiǒng*), which is an archaic character referring to a patterned window or brightness. In 2008, however, it became an internet phenomenon. Netizens began to use 囧 to express embarrassment and gloom, because of the character's resemblance to a facial expression of similar sentiments. In modern Mandarin, 窘, which is also pronounced jiǒng is used to express embarrassment or discontent, so 囧 can replicate its meaning wittily. 囧 has also been used as 囧rz, which is a combination of 囧 and orz. 'orz' is used online in China to visually depict someone kneeling down in defeat. *orz* is often used in gaming situations when one is beaten by another player in a game. Sending the other player *orz* shows the defeated player's respect for the victor. 囧rz is an even more dramatic version of orz, suggesting a greater sense of despair rather than respect.

As we have discussed in this section, China's sets of emojis are separate from the Unicode emojis adopted elsewhere in the world and are tailored to Chinese cultural norms. Despite this, emojis are still recognized as a powerful cultural force, and their designs are updated to reflect changing cultural norms, as with Western emojis. Some of these feature meanings are not found among Unicode emojis, creating linguistic challenges for those switching from Chinese platforms to Western ones.

Catering to different cultures

You might wonder why different platforms have different emojis. If one platform is heavily used by one demographic (as WeChat is in Mainland China), then the platform adapts to cater specifically to that demographic, and their cultural norms. Different countries have different national traits, and different cultures have different gestures and traditions that they might want to be able to present in emoji form. That is why many people in East Asian countries use emojis other than those on the Unicode emoji keyboard. Chinese, Japanese and Korean cultures have specificities that have been made into emojis. It is an interesting occurrence that few other countries have developed.

Douyin is the Chinese version of TikTok. It is also made by ByteDance, but it is only available to Chinese users – likely a choice to stop the platform from being

Figure 5.9 An interpretation of Douyin emojis. Source: design by Loli Kim, reproduced with permission. See the full image here: https://zhuanlan.zhihu.com/p/126498251

banned in China. Douyin also has its own set of emojis. Some resemble WeChat emojis, some resemble Unicode emojis, and some are entirely unique to the platform. There is a feedback loop at work here. The platform's curation of emojis is heavily influenced by the demographic of its users, meanwhile, the users of the platform are influenced by the platform's curation of emojis (Figure 5.9).

In South Korea, KakaoTalk is one of the most popular instant messaging applications. Following the release of the third generation of iPhones in the South Korean market, KakaoTalk was released in March 2010. Around this time, touchscreen smartphones rapidly began overtaking button-based models in South Korea, and instant messaging on KakaoTalk soon began to replace text messaging. Although other mobile messaging services are available, KakaoTalk has consistently been the dominant instant messaging service in South Korea since its release.[24] One of the reasons for this is the popularity of KakaoTalk. KakaoTalk's own 'emoticon' service that was launched in November 2011, soon after the emoji keyboard was implemented on iOS devices. Compared to the emojis on other platforms, KakaoTalk's emoticons are highly varied. There is a range of stickers that are useful in expressing relational and attitudinal dynamics in Korean, such as politeness. Using Kakao Talk's stickers, users can initiate or maintain the proper relationship dynamics that they need to communicate successfully. Whereas Unicode emojis are mostly faces, KakaoTalk stickers tend to show a whole character. South Korean society is highly hierarchical, and Korean speakers have to negotiate respect, politeness and intimacy in every interaction. It is difficult to convey respect with just an emoji face. A character sticker, in comparison, can be much more nuanced.

While emojis are based on the Unicode standard and are compatible across a variety of platforms and devices, KakaoTalk emoticons can only be sent and displayed on KakaoTalk itself. In other words, while emojis can be used on any app, KakaoTalk emoticons can only be used on KakaoTalk. As KakaoTalk is mostly used in Asia and by the Asian diaspora, their sticker packs cater specifically to Asian communities and their preferences for emojis.

Alternative interpretations

In *The Semiotics of Emoji*, Marcel Danesi provided some meanings for a range of emojis.[25] Emojis are not so easy to define, however. For example, they can be misinterpreted cross-culturally, particularly in the case of Unicode emojis in Chinese communication. For example, Danesi defines the winking face as 'suggesting that a word, line, or entire message should not be taken seriously; it has a humorous or flirtatious intent'.[26] However, in Chinese communities, The winking face emoji can be used when the user wants to express sympathy or his understanding about a certain situation. For example, a teacher replying to a message from a student explaining why they have not completed their homework might send a message saying, *Okay, I understand. Don't let it happen again* with a wink emoji at the end. The wink is used to create solidarity in this case, rather than humour of flirtation.

Another example of cross-cultural variation would be the smiling face with open mouth and cold sweat emoji, which Danesi defines as follows: 'Conveys a sense of happiness, but with a nuance of relief. It is often found in texts that portray some negative event that, however, had turned out positively.'[27] In Chinese communities, this emoji may not be regarded as having such positive connotations. It is often interpreted as showing helplessness or being left with no choice. For example, an employee might complain on Facebook about something irreversible or unarguable: 'My boss just told me my salary would be reduced by 30% due to COVID. I've already got many loans. Sigh, what should I do?' They could add the smiling face with open mouth and cold sweat emoji not to show relief, but as a negative expression.

The smirking face emoji is another that shows cultural differentiation. According to Danesi, the emoji is 'used in romantic-sexual messages, providing flirtatious innuendo or entendre to the context'.[28] In Chinese communities, however, the smirking face emoji is commonly used to ask an opinion in a light way. For example, when asking for someone's advice in a friendly way, one might send: 'I bet you have lots of ideas [*smirking face emoji*]. What do you think?' Rather than taking on a flirtatious tone, the smirking face is used in a light-hearted manner. The emoji is an indication of an attempt to build a closer relationship with the recipient so that the recipient will feel comfortable to put forward their ideas.

Towards a more diverse and inclusive nature in emoji: From local to global

Despite the diversity in meanings and visuals represented by emojis, many cultures, minority groups and their associated concepts remain under or unrepresented in emojis. Based on a study on emoji inclusivity by Adobe which surveyed 7,000 respondents, half of them felt that their identity was not represented, 83 per cent agreed that emojis should be more inclusive in their representation and the majority wished that they had more and better options to customize emojis that more accurately reflected their identities.[29] Articles such as '6 Singapore emojis we wish existed' and '12 African emoji we would like to see – including proper sandals and pap', which call for the inclusion of certain country- or culture-specific emojis, highlight a lack of representation of many concepts from less popularly known cultures and further underscore the power of visual representations of cultural concepts which can't be easily explained through words.[30] Despite the wavering attention towards this issue, there are attempts on the ground level to combat this lack of representation and promote a positive image of lesser-known cultures. For example, a graphic design student from the Ivory Coast, created more than 300 different emojis representing things related to his native culture, such as local cuisine, in order to show a more positive side of Africa and combat its negative portrayal in the Western media.[31] Over in Australia, a set of stickers called Indigemoji that showcase the language and culture of the indigenous Arrernte people was launched after a concerted effort by the community.[32] Meanwhile, Finland became the first country to officially publish its own officially sanctioned culturally specific emoji.[33] In other countries like Malaysia and Thailand, special emojis have been released to commemorate important dates in the respective countries.[34] However, despite the numerous ground-up initiatives around the globe, there is still much to be done in order to catalogue all of the world's cultural and linguistic diversity through emojis.

Summary

Most works about emojis tend to define emojis as if their meanings are obvious and ubiquitous. In our emoji speak generation, this doesn't work. Everyone makes and uses emojis in a personalized way. There is so much individual and subcultural variation that it is impossible to generalize. In order to understand the meaning of an emoji, you must know who used the emoji to whom, and the context of the conversation. There is great regional variation, for example, the meanings of emojis on WeChat in China are vastly different to the meanings of emojis on Facebook in the UK. Images speak differently to different people. There is no one way of understanding the signs that we use. More cross-cultural study is needed. In my emoji lab, I am currently building a cross-cultural emoji dictionary, in the hope of eradicating Western bias from current writing on emojis. Our emoji world reflects our world and the Western biases that exist within our world. It is important to recognize these biases in our emoji speak too.

6

Emoji Power

Emoji can have a real impact on us and the world around us, and on how we represent ourselves in the digital world. While emojis may often be considered a juvenile, trivial part of the kind of internet-speak used largely for casual, informal conversations or for teenagers discussing their favourite internet personalities, I argue to the contrary, making the case for emojis as a crucial and impactful part of present-day communication. One simple 'like' button could put you in real trouble. At the same time, you can always excuse yourself – saying that it was a 'technical' mistake. Compared to typing, writing or speaking – which require much more thought and take place over a set time – emoji reactions such as 'liking' something on Facebook can be done at once and honestly. One will also never be entirely sure of the source of this reaction. There is little trace of one's physical presence in emoji interaction – yet it can be considered ever more powerful and impactful than any other human communication.

With online communication becoming an undeniably crucial element of everyday human connections and information sharing, particularly via social media, emojis have quite clearly established themselves as a very real part of our everyday communication. In this chapter, I look beyond an analysis of how emojis are used, considering the impact of emoji use on meaning and how they change sentiment with wide-reaching effects. For example, with emojis constituting a valid element of speech, they can become implicated in legal cases in much the same way as standard speech, particularly with regard to threatening or hate speech online. This raises questions such as: does sending an emoji of a gun represent a threat being made against somebody's life? How can we know and determine someone's intention through the use of their emoji? Can big data be of any help? I also look at the use of emojis in serious real-world contexts, such as social movements or politics on both a local and global scale. Does using an emoji to signify a certain social movement or issue (such as supporting Black Lives Matter or opposing the war in Ukraine) strengthen one's support, and if so, how?

Is an emoji just an emoji?

Sensitive situations often require careful use of language – for example, news articles use words like 'allegedly' to avoid ascribing blame, and politicians often use precise pre-prepared language when referring to contentious foreign policy issues. But are we as careful with our emojis as we are with our words? The consequences of a poorly placed emoji can be just as severe as a verbal blunder, but some of us let our guard down with emojis – perhaps because they are still relatively new to us, or perhaps because their fun, colourful appearance makes us see them as more 'trivial' than 'proper' words. In this section, I will examine some case studies that illustrate how our use of emojis should be just as considered as our use of words.

Our first example took place in April of 2021 and centres on the then-Belgian ambassador to Korea and his wife. The controversy initially started when footage surfaced of the ambassador's wife allegedly assaulting staff at a clothing store after they asked to check that she had paid for the items with which she was leaving the store. The situation became even tenser when the Belgian Embassy issued an apology in Korean that lacked any of the honorific markers which are customarily used in the language, which for some indicated a lack of sincerity. The situation reached a tipping point, however, when the official Facebook page for the embassy used a laughing emoji – using Facebook's 'Haha' reaction feature – in response to a racially charged comment which mocked Koreans for being upset at the incident.

Although there are cases when single-emoji reactions like this one can be quite ambiguous – a 'Haha' reaction might indicate laughing *at* someone rather than *with* them – there is little doubt here that the reaction signals agreement with the sentiment of the comment. As a result of this string of controversies, the Belgian ambassador was removed from his post in May of the same year. This incident illustrates how emojis are not simply a colourful addition to our language but are rather a key part of how we convey meaning online; as such, the way we use emojis can be just as complex as how we use our words, and using the wrong emoji can create serious conflicts in the real world.

Another example of how our use of emojis can backfire in the wrong context happened in one of Cher's tweets. Cher tweeted her prayers for the casualties of an attack on Istanbul's Atatürk international airport that occurred in 2016 and which killed at least 41 and wounded well over 200 more. She wrote: 'WE ALL PRAY FOR INNOCENT PEOPLE IN TURKEY AIRPORT' with the bomb and collision emojis at the end of the tweet. Despite Cher's apparent intention to show her support and empathy for those affected, many criticized her use of bomb and explosion emojis at the end of her message, pointing out a mismatch between the serious subject matter and the fun, somewhat childish appearance of emojis. Cher then tweeted: 'Been thinking about my Poorly Placed,Insensitively Timed"bomb Emoji".No Excuse [broken heart emoji] I'm Used 2 Using Emoji 2Help Say More Than 140 Letters.Sorry [crying face emoji']'. While Cher's subsequent apology clarified her intentions as sincere rather than mocking the victims of the attack, this makes little difference to the discussion around her use of emojis, which arose due to people's differing interpretations of the tone or register of emojis. Cher saw no mismatch in tone at the time of writing her original post because she viewed emojis as a neutral linguistic tool which simply '[helps her] Say More Than 140 Letters'. For those who criticized her post, however, emojis are clearly not tonally neutral; to them, the fun, even 'childish' tone of emojis is inappropriate when discussing a serious tragedy.

Emojis sell

As we are beginning to see, emojis are now a huge component of how we communicate online on messaging apps and social media. Brands have also become aware of the benefits of using emojis in their online marketing and have looked into ways of using emojis to influence our purchasing habits and brand loyalty. There is potentially big money to be made using emojis in marketing, and serious research has been carried out on the effects of emojis in marketing to maximize engagement and profit.

According to Emojipedia, almost a billion emojis are sent on Facebook every day. Additionally, data from HubSpot suggests that 25.4 per cent of tweets featuring emojis receive better engagement, while 57 per cent of Facebook posts receive more likes, with 33 per cent receiving more shares and comments, if they contain emojis.[1] The Emojics blog also reports that 40 per cent of millennials engage with pictures, while the use of emojis in Instagram posts can improve their engagement by 48 per cent, representing a huge increase in the importance of and interest in image and emoji-based content online.

Our brains are hard-wired to connect with others, and we are particularly drawn to looking at human faces. When we look at an emoji, research suggests that our brain reacts as if we had seen an actual person's face, which could explain the higher rates of engagement linked to emojis.[2] Kraus et al. also found that participants who were sent messages containing emojis scored higher when it came to remembering said messages compared to others who received the same messages without emojis, suggesting that emojis can also make messages more memorable.[3] The same study also suggested that using emojis can make customers view your business as friendlier: participants who chatted online with a marketing expert who used emojis in their messaging rated the expert as both friendlier and more competent compared to participants who chatted with a marketing expert who did not use emojis.

Emojis must be used carefully, however. Experts suggest that context is incredibly important when it comes to the use of emojis in marketing. According to popular online social media marketing expert, Neil Patel, 'You need to be careful not to cross the line. Don't use them irrelevantly in your communications in an attempt to increase your user engagement or indicate that you're on top of communication trends'.[4] Which channels to use emojis on is also important. If companies are to make the most of the multiple forums at their disposal, they must research their intended audience and which channels that audience uses the most before deciding which channels are most appropriate to employ emojis on. According to go-to-market intelligence platform ZoomInfo, one of the most popular uses of emojis is within email subject lines, as this can make a message stand out from the other email headings surrounding it.[5] Similarly, experts recommend that emoji marketing is best used when the emojis fit the tone of the social media platform. For example, when using more formal or professional platforms, such as LinkedIn, companies might choose to use emojis that express interest or congratulations, as opposed to images of animal faces or people dancing.

Emojis can also be used to humanize a brand, making it seem more relatable and more like an average social media user. For example, if a brand's Instagram account responds to positive comments on their posts with heart emojis this can help to humanize their online interactions. Furthermore, companies with higher budgets and more sway have in the past created proprietary emojis to help boost their marketing efforts. For example, between 2015 and 2019 Burger King partnered with the Emoji Company to create an anti-bullying campaign.⁶ As part of the campaign, Burger King children's meals featured thirty different collectable Emoji-branded plush toys, which featured both established emojis such as the laughing face with tears of joy, as well as customized proprietary emojis, such as The King, the Whopper sandwich and anti-bullying emojis specifically designed for the campaign in question.

Even in journalism and reporting, which by its nature frequently deals with serious content, emojis have become a way for news sites to engage with readers on a more human level. For instance, it is common in South Korea for news sites to feature different stylized characters with expressions reminiscent of standard emojis; viewers can click on these as a means of reacting to the story in whichever way best represents their feelings on the topic. This, in turn, displays to the company and readers what others thought of the news story, enabling news sites to gather valuable data and determine the types of stories readers are most interested in.

Overall, the use of emojis in online marketing presents an excellent opportunity for brands and companies to draw attention to their brand, foster brand loyalty and engage with their customers in a deeper, more nuanced and more human way. Companies all over the world have been taking heed of studies and expert advice in the area, resulting in a huge increase in the use of images and emojis by corporate social media accounts and websites.

Emoji censorship

Emojis can be a powerful tool of resistance. Although many still view emojis as trivial or pointless, the persistence with which certain political regimes and platform owners crack down on emoji speech that they disagree with shows that emojis are far more powerful than many of us realize. When we think about it, emojis are perhaps perfectly suited for protest movements. Earlier in this book, I explored the idea that emojis act like digital gestures and gestures go hand-in-hand with protest movements. Think of the famous salutes for racial justice on the podium at the 1968 Olympics, or various football teams taking the knee before each game in the recent Euro 2020 football championship (a gesture first adopted to protest against racism by former NFL player, Colin Kaepernick in 2016).

These gestures are effective because they are both instantly recognizable and easily reproducible. Any able-bodied person can show solidarity with the movement by performing the gesture themselves; no equipment nor further explanation is needed. This also makes gestures like these hard to censor. No props or banners are required to make a statement and they are so quick and easy to perform that you could, for instance, perform the gesture on a live TV event before anybody could stop you. The fact gestures like raising a fist or taking the knee are so simple also makes it sound almost absurd to ban them, how can you ban such a basic action?

Emojis have a great deal in common with gestures like these. They are highly graphic, can be posted on nearly any platform by anybody with a compatible smartphone or computer, and are usually multipurpose or ambiguous in meaning (making it harder to censor a particular emoji as it may also be used innocuously). Given that some real-life gestures also have the corresponding emojis, there is great potential for a crossover between real world and digital forms of protest; for instance, when showing support for the Black Lives Matter (BLM) movement, one could either raise one's fist in real life or simply post the raised fist with black skin tone emoji. Most people would likely understand that both are essentially forms of the same gesture in either online or offline spaces.

However, just as even the most peaceful real-life protests can be forcibly shut down (often violently) by police, emoji protests can also be subject to censorship, albeit using different methods. The Chinese Communist Party (CCP) is well known for its surveillance and censorship of the internet, and, perhaps unsurprisingly, emojis have also been subject to bans. For instance, since 2012, the CCP has been silently banning the candle and cake emoji from Weibo (a Chinese social media platform similar to Twitter) every Fourth of June, the anniversary of the 1989 Tiananmen Square massacre.[7] Each year, the candle, birthday cake and Olympic torch emojis (which are used as signs of mourning – the birthday cake and Olympic torch taking on this meaning because they include or resemble a candle) disappear from the Weibo emoji keyboard on the third and fourth of June, and searches for those emojis are also blocked. This indicates that censorship of textual and photographic content online alone is insufficient for the CCP and that the Chinese government is sufficiently concerned about emojis attracting attention to certain issues that it takes steps to restrict their use and prevent people from seeing them. The candle was also removed upon the death of Nobel Peace laureate Liu Xiaobo in 2017 to prevent users from mourning the death of somebody who had been publicly critical of the ruling CCP.⁸ While censoring emojis of candles may be less violent than, say, for example, the UK police violently disbanding a candlelit vigil paying tribute to the murdered Sarah Everard in early 2021, both online and offline censorship deny people important opportunities to mourn and to protest injustice.

Emoji censorship can take place with the cooperation of global tech companies, too. Take, for example, the case of the Taiwanese flag. The Taiwanese flag emoji was banned from the emoji keyboard on iOS devices where the region is set to mainland China, the Hong Kong Special Administrative Region, or the Macau Special Administrative Region following the release of iOS 13.1.1 in late September 2019. Chinese-model iPhones or iOS devices set to the Chinese region will not display this emoji on the emoji keyboard and will instead show the missing character (☒) in place of the flag when reading messages sent from elsewhere which include the emoji. It also cannot be used or displayed in any apps, even by copying and pasting.

It is interesting to note that the removal of this emoji was enacted in September 2019 amid the anti-government protests in Hong Kong, where activists protesting the Chinese government promoted independence for Hong Kong. This period prompted the Chinese government to crack down on the movement in order to emphasize its sovereignty over Hong Kong. By the same token, because of Taiwan's political status, the People's Republic of China considers any mention of or allusion to its independence as an offence against its sovereignty.

The Chinese government has also intensified its efforts to pressure global companies on how they refer to Taiwan in recent years. PayPal displays a generic globe instead of the Taiwanese flag in its region picker, something which it does not do for any other region.

The South Korean company Samsung has also removed emojis referencing Japan in the past, likely due to the tense relationship between South Korea and Japan concerning the Japanese government's continued refusal to apologize for atrocities committed against Korea during the first half of the twentieth century. For instance, Samsung changed the crossed flags emoji (which usually features two crossed Japanese flags) to feature the South Korean flag in 2015, before removing it completely alongside other emojis explicitly referencing Japan, such as 'map of Japan' and 'chart increasing with

Yen' in 2016.⁹ These emojis appear to have been reintroduced, however, in an update since.

Depending on the cultural context, even relatively innocuous emojis can become controversial. Anti-feminist backlash has resulted in the censorship of cute cartoon stickers on South Korea's popular messaging app KakaoTalk earlier in 2021. The controversy stemmed from the word *heobaheoba* (허바허바), a viral word that supposedly originated from a woman making fun of the sound of her boyfriend messily eating.¹⁰ Because of this, anti-feminists began reporting stickers featuring the word, claiming it was a misandrist slur.¹¹ Although these complaints seemed to have been made in bad faith, KakaoTalk still banned stickers featuring the term as a way to avoid the controversy altogether. Incidentally, anti-feminists also launched an offensive against South Korean Olympic archer, An San, during the Tokyo 2020 Olympic Games for using these slang terms in the past, even attempting to get the Korea Archery Association to take back her medals because she was a feminist.¹²

Another case of tech companies banning seemingly innocuous emojis occurred when Facebook and Instagram restricted the use of the 'aubergine', 'peach' and 'sweat' emojis to cover parts of an otherwise naked body or for descriptions of sex. On their Community Standards page, Facebook prohibits writing messages that offer or ask for sex and feature 'suggestive elements', including 'Contextually specific and commonly sexual emojis or emoji strings': (such as those listed earlier).¹³ This rule was intended to crack down on advertising sex work on these platforms but is another example of how emojis are often subject to censorship.

Emojis as social movements

In recent years, the creation and use of emojis have come to take an important role at the core of social movements. Emojis can be used to promote diversity and make our linguistic landscape more innovative and inclusive. There is plenty of evidence for the use of emojis as part of a social movement in the Hong Kong context. For example, the simultaneous use of the 'five' and the 'one' emojis is common in the social media bio of teenagers from Hong Kong. These emojis are used together to show one's support of the 2019 Hong Kong protests – 'Five Demands, not One Less'. Similarly, the yellow ribbon emoji, which was originally used as a symbol of sorrow or empathy (e.g. the yellow Ribbon Campaign and Sewol Ferry Protest Movement in South Korea), is also used as a representation of the user's political stance, with the yellow ribbon standing for the support of the protest demonstrators, in contrast to the blue ribbon standing for the support of the Hong Kong police force. In order to avoid being too political on their social media page, some people or some shops who support the protestors would instead use a yellow heart emoji to represent their political views.

Businesses and shops of this nature form a 'Yellow Economy Circle', where customers who support the demonstrators would only visit and spend their money on the shops that label their stand as 'yellow' by putting a yellow heart emoji or a yellow ribbon emoji on social media (e.g. Instagram). Despite there being no blue-ribbon emoji, shops that support the police force could also display a blue heart emoji to indicate their political stance. However, they normally avoid doing so as it runs the risk of their being boycotted by those with opposing views. Some shops that neither put a yellow heart emoji nor a yellow ribbon emoji may also be considered by consumers to be supporting the police, again leading to a boycott of their services. It can be seen here that emojis, far from just fun pictures, can become incredibly politically sensitive and affect individuals, businesses and society at various levels.

Certain emojis have also gained a politically significant meaning in mainland China, frequently leading to their censorship despite their, on the surface at least, seeming rather innocuous to an outside observer, such as social media platforms Sina Weibo and WeChat's annual censorship of candle-related emojis in response to attempts to commemorate the 1989 Tiananmen Square Massacre.

Emojis are also used in a Chinese social media context as a way of circumventing censorship around politically sensitive or non-government-sanctioned topics by means of homophones. Chinese feminists have also come to use emojis to avoid censorship, following the suspension of many feminist accounts on WeChat and Weibo, including the account 'Feminist Voices'. For example, a combination of the rice and rabbit emojis, pronounced in Chinese as *mi* (meaning rice) *tu* (meaning rabbit), is used as a subtle reference to the #MeToo movement without drawing unwanted attention from regulators. This use of emojis further demonstrates their ability to be used creatively, outside of their stated purposes, to further social causes online.

Emojis and the law

Although emojis entered our awareness as an informal, light-hearted form of communication, their increasing use across a broad spectrum of society means that they have taken on important real-world implications. Emojis are no longer just peripheral images confined to the digital realm; they now form an important part of how we understand and communicate with one another in almost every setting. Using the wrong emoji can cause confusion, put off customers, end a budding romance or even land you in court.

In recent years, there have been several high-profile court cases around the world in which emojis played an important role, either as evidence or as part of the alleged crime. But, as I have discussed, the meanings of emojis are hugely subjective, and although Unicode provides names and labels for individual emojis, there are no set rules for the various ways that they are used and interpreted in practice. So how are emojis dealt with in court? And should emojis ever be used to determine someone's guilt or innocence when it comes to allegations of criminality?

So far, courts have shown varied understandings of how emojis function in communication. In some cases, they have demonstrated a nuanced understanding of emoji use. For example, courts have found that an emoji can be used to render the preceding text sarcastic.[14] In other cases, however, their approach to emoji use has been controversial. For example, a series of apparently threatening emojis have been interpreted to be legally equivalent to a death threat, and the use of smiley faces has undermined plaintiffs' claims of sexual harassment.[15]

One of the key problems that emojis present to courts is the interpretation of their meaning and what that says about the attitude of the sender. Emojis are designed to be universally recognizable, but that does not mean that they have a universal meaning; rather, their meaning is highly contextual. In one US sexual harassment case, the plaintiff's experience of harassment was called into question because they continued to communicate with the defendant, at one point using a smiling emoji:

> During the time when Ms. Murdoch claims to have been sexually harassed by Mr. Berger, she regularly sent him unsolicited emails asking him how he was doing or how his travels were going. AF No. 14.2. For example, on February 11, 2015, Ms. Murdoch sent an email to Mr. Berger while he was out of town stating: 'Just checking in. Is all as enjoyable there as you had hoped?' AF No. 14.3. *Ms. Murdoch ended the message with a smiley face emoji.* AF No. 14.4.[16] (emphasis added)

The court's line of reasoning here demonstrates a misunderstanding of not only the dynamics that often appear in cases of workplace harassment and abuse but also the ways emojis are used. A smiley face does not always indicate that the sender is happy, but is often used to set the tone of interaction, punctuate the text or soften a message. Two people who greatly dislike one another may well use smiley faces in their digital communications as a mutually understood symbol indicating that they 'come in peace'. In a similar case, the defence also concluded that the use of emojis undermined the plaintiff's allegations: 'Needless to say these responses *do not indicate distress*'[17] (emphasis added). Again, the interpretation of how emojis are used in communication lacks nuance here; our emotions do not necessarily map directly onto the emojis we use.

There have also been legal questions about the extent to which the use of emojis can be said to represent the intention to act. In a case in Israel, a potential tenant for a property sent an emoji-laden message to the landlord saying, 'Good morning. Interested in the house. Just need to discuss the details . . . When's a good time for you?' with the emojis in Figure 6.1.[18]

The landlord interpreted this message as confirmation that they would rent the property and proceeded to take down the relevant ads. Ultimately, the prospective tenants did not rent the property and the landlord filed charges for financial compensation on the basis that the prospective tenants had negotiated in bad faith.[19] The court concluded that the defendants had indeed acted in bad faith because they did not go through with the arrangement despite the landlord interpreting their communications as a very positive indication of their intention to rent the property. The court statement stated:

> The [emoji laden] text message sent by Defendant 2 on June 5, 2016, was accompanied by quite a few symbols, as mentioned. These included a 'smiley', a bottle of champagne, dancing figures and more. These icons convey great optimism. Although this message did not constitute a binding contract between the parties, this message naturally led to the Plaintiff's great reliance on the defendants' desire to rent his apartment. As a result, the Plaintiff removed his online ad about renting his apartment. Even towards the end of the negotiations, in the same text messages sent at the end of July, Defendant 2 used 'smiley' symbols. These symbols, which convey to the other side that everything is in order, were misleading, since at that time the defendants already had great doubts as to their desire to rent the apartment.[20]

Figure 6.1 Emojis used in a text to a landlord. Source: NotoColorEmoji: © 2021 Google Inc, OFL License.

However, as Goldman notes, a smiley face does not necessarily indicate optimism or agreement and is often simply a way of managing or punctuating a conversation.[21] Someone may very well write, 'Good morning [smiley face] I'm really sorry, but I won't be able to make it this afternoon [smiley face]' without contradicting themselves. Their initial smiley face was not necessarily misleading, deceptive or sarcastic, but simply used to set a friendly tone before moving on to some possibly disappointing news. Taken in context with the rest of the message, the prospective tenants' message is certainly positive and indicates interest, but it is questionable whether it was enough to confirm acceptance of a contract or negotiation in bad faith; exuberance does not equal commitment.

Emojis have played a crucial role in more serious criminal cases, too. There have been cases in which teenagers' emoji use has been interpreted as demonstrating the intent to commit acts of violence. For example, a twelve-year-old child in the United States went through questioning by the police for using a gun, a sword, and a bomb emoji on her Instagram post with a caption reading, 'Let's meet up at the library on Tuesday.' This was interpreted by police as a potentially serious threat of a school shooting or similar violence, and she was charged with 'threatening the school' and 'computer harassment'.[22] In a similar case, a seventeen-year-old child was arrested in New York for posting several gun emojis pointing towards an emoji of a police officer, following his frustrations with police violence towards Black people.[23] Once again, this was interpreted by the police as a threat of violence. Yet, as the child's attorney Fred Pratt has argued, 'I think something is definitely lost in translation [. . .] These kids are not threatening cops, they are just trying to say, "I'm tough." It's posturing'.[24] The fact that both these cases involved children's use of emojis also calls into question whether there is an element of intergenerational difference at play.

Young people have grown up with social media and emojis. As discussed elsewhere in this work, emojis are a central part of the way young people communicate. This is not always the case for their elders, who have had to adapt to the use of emojis in speech at a much later stage of life. Young people often now speak publicly on social media and use emojis about topics that would previously have been spoken about verbally and in private. Furthermore, emojis are not always a literal form of communication (after all, as we know, an eggplant emoji does not always mean an eggplant). Is it the public nature of these messages that have led them to be perceived as a threat? Or are the visual symbols used to convey frustration being taken too literally?

The law already has provisions to respond to verbal threats, which can also be metaphorical rather than literal, but are at least usually intentionally and specifically directed towards an individual. Can or should a series of potentially metaphorical symbols be interpreted in the same way? Given that we know how the meaning of an emoji can differ hugely based on cultural or individual preferences, it seems dangerous to ascribe a legal precedent determining a specific meaning and intention to the use of certain emojis, especially if such interpretations lead to the criminalization of children.

Furthermore, Goldman also flags the potential misunderstandings that come about as a result of 'platform dialects', referring to the different appearances of certain emojis depending on the platform and version of the technology one is using. Due to a desire to protect intellectual property, emojis on different platforms that share the same Unicode code point may appear very differently. Notably, in connection to the examples used, on the Apple platform, the gun emoji appears as a water gun rather than as a real firearm. If a teenager were to post an emoji of a water gun pointing at a person and tags their friend, but this appears to the friend as a gun pointing at their head, should this be perceived as a threat under the law?[25] Goldman argues urgently for a comprehensive dictionary of emoji meanings and for platforms to relinquish their IP in order to standardize cross-platform emoji use. But would this limit the expressive possibilities of emojis? Speaking of the legal context, he writes, 'Platforms' emoji substitution implicitly constitutes a form of misrepresentation. In effect, the recipient's platform puts "words" into the sender's mouth that the sender did not utter. If confusion results, arguably it is the platform's fault'.[26] Indeed, this can sometimes be an issue when communicating between platforms. For instance, while most providers have changed their depiction of the gun emoji to a water pistol, some platforms have yet to do so or have taken longer than others to do so (see Figure 6.2). If one sends what appears to be a water pistol emoji from one's own device and it shows up as a gun for the receiver, one may have inadvertently sent a death threat through no fault of one's own. As Goldman argues, this seems to be a serious issue, and one that must be dealt with if emojis are to be properly interpreted in legal contexts.

Figure 6.2 Different versions of the gun emoji. Sources (from left to right): Twemoji © 2020 Twitter, Inc and other contributors, CC BY 4.0; OpenMoji, CC BY-SA 4.0; and NotoColorEmoji: © 2021 Google Inc, OFL License.

Summary

I have explored the different ways emojis can have an impact on the real world and our lives, proving that emojis are far from a trivial or pointless addition to our communication. They are an important means of communicating in the digital age that warrants further study. Their significance is widely institutionally recognized, as demonstrated by the fact emojis are now censored as potentially dangerous speech by oppressive regimes. The wrong sequence of emojis could potentially land us in court or have us taken in for questioning. Emojis can also mean millions of dollars in extra returns for a large company's marketing campaign, provided they are used sensitively and appropriately. Emojis are also used every day as a representation of one's beliefs and sense of self-identity, and an appropriate range of emojis is important in enabling us to represent minority identities in our online speech.

7

Emoji Emotions

Human feelings and emotions are complex and unique to humans. When Detective Spooner in the film *I, Robot* (2004) asked Sonny the robot why he murdered Dr Lanning, Sonny answered, 'I was frightened', to which Spooner famously replied: 'Robots don't feel fear. They don't feel anything. They don't eat. They don't sleep'. We see numerous works of science fiction which aim to explore this, and in our recent technological development, a new field known as *affective computing* has been developed. One day we may be able to prove Detective Spooner was altogether wrong.

Indeed, the robots in Web 3.0 may be able to understand human emotions and even be sympathetic to us. The Kismet project by a team of scientists at the Massachusetts Institute of Technology (MIT) proved that it is possible to build a robot which can understand human sympathy. Cynthia Breazeal and colleagues at MIT have constructed a robot called 'Kismet' with moveable eyelids, eyes and lips. The range of emotional expressions available to Kismet is limited, but they are convincing enough to generate sympathy among the humans who interact with him.

With the advent of social media and its development as a prime channel for daily communication, emojis and emoticons have become a cornerstone of the way people communicate with their friends, family, colleagues and strangers every day. Even young children now learn how to use emojis early on. However, in this increasingly digital world, it is important to query whether condensing our thoughts and feelings into simple, abstracted symbols is good for us as human beings. Multi-modal communication is becoming increasingly innovative and expressive, through emojis and memes. However, what could the long-term impact of such imagery be? Could the use of simplified reproductions of human emotional expression have long-lasting effects on our interpersonal communication and emotional understanding in years to come? How do the user interfaces offered by social media sites, as well as functions like predictive text, shape our language? Is there a chance that we, as humans, will become conditioned by the algorithms of companies who possess our emoji data, in a way similar to that of Kismet's programming concerning the expression of emotions?

During the last two years of an almost experimental, unprecedented scope of virtual interactions, we all have realized what technology can and cannot do. Sure, it's great to be able to meet up and discuss matters online – yet most people feel that this is not enough and that doing a Zoom social isn't so much fun. I think we all discovered the gap which technology cannot fill; we now value more than ever the physicality of human communication which carries our feelings as they are. Having said that, the emoji world is constantly evolving to cater for our everyday expressions. Would this world soon find ways to fill the gap we have experienced?

Another big question I have is, how are young people, who grow as natives to the world of emojis, influenced by their emoji behaviours? Will they gradually lose the ability and capacity to project complex feelings? Could emojis oversimplify our expressions? Further to this, given the way in which big tech companies manufacture and monitor our emoji behaviour constantly, would our feelings perhaps – unconsciously – become conditioned by them? This is a chilling idea, yet in one sense it could be quite close to our reality. One of the great conveniences of emoji speak is the predictive emoji; we don't need to think twice but simply choose what is given. Nevertheless, it is also true that our feelings could be trained like a machine in a sense to react in a particular way.

This chapter will delve into issues considering the representation of human emotions by emojis, and whether it is truly possible for them to do a good job. Emojis often function similarly to facial expressions and other physical gestures in face-to-face communication, helping to bridge the gap between online and offline interactions. However, a crying emoji is not identical in meaning to actually crying; in fact, when describing a real tragedy, one might avoid using emojis as a way of respecting the gravity of the situation. This raises the questions: where are the limits of emojis for conveying emotion, and how do they compare to real facial expressions and gestures? I will look at the pros and cons of using emojis and their impact on the emotional development of both adults and children, discussing whether the use of emojis could, contrary to their intended use, end up restricting our emotional expression.

Emojis as reactions

Of course, there are many ways we express our feelings. Often, expressing feelings can be difficult, leading us to delay our talks and seek different forms of negotiation. Using emojis to convey emotions could be life-saving, in that it can create an atmosphere in which one can talk without worrying about the other's reaction. The emoji world can be a safe space, in which happiness and *kawaii* have prominent roles, and parties are able to relax more, without a need to be so serious. Emojis also enable quick responses and a fast turnaround for the conversation. We can no longer imagine emoji-less social media or smartphone communication. Even if one sends a message expressing positive feeling or agreement through words – for example *fantastic, great, brilliant* – if all that appears on the screen are just these letter words, the recipient will generally sense that something is still missing. This shows how, in the span of less than a decade, we have all become emoji trained!

The use of emojis as quick ways to respond to posts and comments online has been encouraged by the companies that run the social media platforms we use. Instagram, for example, prominently displays a range of one's preferred emojis above the text box for commenting on other users' posts, allowing one to respond instantly with an emoji. Other messaging services, such as Facebook Messenger and WhatsApp, have introduced a similar feature in their direct messaging services which enables users to react to each other's messages by choosing from a selection of emojis, such as the following: a thumbs up, a heart, a laughing face, a shocked face, a sad face, or an angry face.

In one way, reacting through an emoji helps us to be more efficient, but many may still feel uncomfortable – is it enough? Is an emoji really enough?

Emojis as tone indicators

As previously mentioned, one vital function of emojis is to convey emotion. Emojis are rich in emotional meaning, allowing users to communicate how they feel in a manner that is not possible using letter-driven text alone. Emoji speak – which by definition includes multi-modal resources in communication – enriches our communication with feelings and attitudes of all sorts. This means that emojis provide an important clue in detecting the tones of a conversation. Furthermore, emoji behaviour shows a great resemblance to bodily expressions – though there is a significant difference between the two. Oftentimes, people say that emojis soften the tone of exchange and make the conversation smoother. Bodily expressions have such functions, but these are not their main functions. Serious emotions are difficult to capture with emojis. In fact, people tend to use emojis to convey somewhat safe feelings. Feelings that are too personal or too serious are better expressed in another medium. Emoji speak, after all, doesn't seem to fit in well with sincere or serious talks.

Have some heart

With the depth of human emotions in mind, I pose the question of whether emojis can cope with their complexity. Can we truly replicate the depth and intricacy of human feelings through simple images? Of course, we can make more emojis, but will we ever have enough? Generally, the emotions that emojis represent are rather limited; people are hesitant to use an emoji that could harm a relationship. In the emoji world, everything could appear rather rosy. According to a Unicode report, the most frequently used emojis in the world are heart emojis or their related emojis:[1]

Does this suggest that the world is full of love? Or are people full of love for each other? Can this be interpreted as foreshadowing the bright future of humanity? People try to understand the meanings of emojis all the time. Yet, it is never straightforward. People tend to use heart or smiley emojis not to express the genuine sentiment of their heart, but as a social mask to avoid any possible conflicts. In Asian contexts, such 'benevolent' emojis are often sent multiple times. In Korean contexts, the '^^' symbol, which depicts your eyebrows in a smiling face, is repeated almost every time one wraps up their turn in the conversation. It appears that the overuse of emojis reflects social insecurity and a desire for approval.

In the emoji world, we find it difficult to express our discontent or disagreement. Just today, I was asked about four or five times to provide feedback about services that I received – twice in the supermarket, once in the gym and lastly in a taxi – by picking out an emoji. Hardly anyone would dare to pick the angry emoji. Choosing an angry emoji fails to properly express your view and, more often than not, makes you look bad. Feedback via emojis is indeed observed in every sector of our life, but it is tiring and demanding. They prompt us to avoid thinking deeply about how we feel; instead, we arbitrarily click or press a button. Yet, at the same time, we have become hyper-sensitive to the views of others: how many likes do we have? How many reactions have we received? We are so accustomed to pressing a heart emoji for all things. It may be true that, overall, we are indeed being trained by big data machines and conditioned to think and react as predicted. In order for one to express deep and complex feelings, one must be aware that they need to step out of the screen.

Do emojis actually help us?

In this era of machine learning and big data, we should consider to what extent we are truly aware of the emojis we are using. Nowadays, social media platforms and our smartphones collect vast amounts of data about how we communicate with each other, thereby enabling said platforms to nudge us towards the patterns of communication they have learnt that we use. For instance, the autocorrect function on smartphones learns which words we tend to use in certain situations and recommends them when it thinks we are likely to need them. Autocorrect also suggests appropriate emojis when it detects that we are talking about subjects with a corresponding emoji. Social media platforms, too, encourage us to react to posts by choosing from a predefined set of emojis that provides their platform with even more detailed data about our thoughts on that post. In my case, when I want to respond to a person's message or post, my most frequently used emojis appear first – and all seem to express a happy emotion. On the one hand, this can be interpreted as a positive feature for it helps users to express particular emotions more efficiently. However, the way these systems nudge us towards words and emojis that we have used in the past runs the risk of creating a closed loop, in which we find ourselves being guided into narrower speech patterns. This leads us to wonder: would we communicate with each other differently without these AI-driven suggestions? And can we still consider our words to be our own when they are informed by the tailored suggestions of a computer?

Six emotions

The 2015 Pixar animated film *Inside Out* follows the five personified emotions of Joy, Sadness, Fear, Disgust and Anger in the mind of a young girl, Riley, as her parents move her from her home in Minnesota, United States, across the country to San Francisco, uprooting her life in the process. The film's plot culminates with the protagonist realizing that Riley's memories cannot be ascribed to a single emotion, but rather her emotions become entangled and intertwined with each experience she gains. According to digital anthropologist Pamela Pavliscak, limiting reactions to a select set of emotions stems from theories that are well established in evolutionary psychology. One prominent theory in evolutionary psychology developed in the 1960s by psychologist Paul Ekman also suggested that humans experience six core emotions across the board (joy, surprise, anger, disgust, sadness and fear) and that their corresponding facial expressions are universal, regardless of culture or upbringing.[2]

Although academic debate concerning the complexity and universality of human emotions is far from settled (Ekman himself later added more emotions to his model), it is inarguable that these basic six emotions are easy to recognize and group together, particularly by machines. This makes emoji-based reactions and comments very valuable to social media platforms looking to monetize their user base. For example, advertisers can collect data on how many users have reacted to their posts or ads in certain ways, allowing them to create more targeted and effective campaigns in future. In fact, emojis have become an important part of marketing for companies the world over, providing them with more granular data about how people are reacting to their advertisements.

Therefore, while these quick emoji reactions are undeniably convenient, what effect does our liberal use of simplified representations of emotions have on human communication? Pavliscak warns that compressing the range of emotional reactions that we regularly employ flattens the way in which we talk to each other, causing us to forget the full range of emotions that we could, or should, be using in certain situations. These more complex, compound emotions are an important part of how we communicate and help establish both our relationships and identities. When it comes to emotional intelligence, the more concepts one has, the more distinctions one can make, and the more coping strategies one can develop. The use of a select set of emojis could theoretically limit our emotional expression and risk changing how we understand our feelings in the future. With fewer distinctions and nuances, our basic emotions could become more intense and less regulated.

A further risk of using this basic range of emotions in our daily communication is that of cross-cultural confusion. With the Internet and online social media being so international in nature, users from different cultural and linguistic backgrounds communicate with one another and often come into contact with the same content online. However, the intended meanings of certain images and emojis, and the emotional responses they provoke, might not be uniform across users from different cultural backgrounds. While some emotions, such as Ekman's original six, may be considered universal (or at least very widely recognized) across cultures, symbolic gestures, such as nodding or shaking one's head to indicate yes or no, or the ok gesture with one's hands, are indeed culture-specific.[3] For this reason, it is important to be wary of cultural differences in our use of emojis, ensuring that we respect and maintain cultural nuances.

We now look at how the same emoji is represented differently depending on the platform. In 2016, GroupLens, a social computing research lab at the University of Minnesota in the United States, published a study investigating how the differing appearances of emojis on different platforms can lead to different interpretations of their meaning. This, in turn, potentially results in miscommunication when users of different platforms send each other emojis. The study pointed out significant differences in how the grinning face with smiling eyes emoji was interpreted to represent different emotions depending on which platform it was displayed on.

GroupLens asked participants about their impression of the emotion displayed by the above emoji on a scale of 5 (positive impression) to −5 (negative impression) through a questionnaire survey. Results revealed that while Google's grinning face with smiling eyes emoji emoji design made a positive impression, with a score over four, Apple's design was interpreted as slightly negative overall. This means that, theoretically, somebody sending this emoji from a Google device (on which the emoji looks positive) to an Apple device (on which the emoji looks more negative) could have created confusion by adding a negative connotation to the message unintentionally (Figure 7.1).

Indeed, Apple seems to have become aware of this inconsistency with other platforms soon after GroupLens' study was released, as they redesigned the emoji in 2016 to be in line with other platforms, giving the emoji a more positive expression.

Part of the problem with the old design may have been that it shared the same mouth section as the grimacing face emoji, leading users to interpret it as having a similar meaning. In this way, we can see how although each platform must create their own designs for each Unicode emoji due to copyright,

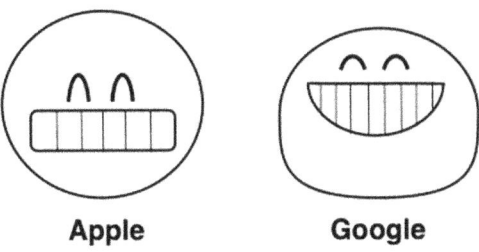

Figure 7.1 Interpretation of the grinning face with smiling eyes emoji across platforms. Source: Emoji design by Loli Kim, reproduced with permission.

there is significant pressure to ensure that their designs do not stray too far from those used by other platforms. Differences like these demonstrate that misunderstandings outside of one's control can quite easily arise when using emojis across platforms.

Emojis and children: Tools or trouble?

Children are coming into contact with technology and the internet at an increasingly young age. One study of 350 US children found that around three-quarters of children had their own mobile device by the age of four, while the majority of children in the study began using mobile media devices before the age of one.[4] Children may encounter emojis at a young age through either their personal devices or while using a parent's or guardian's device.

According to the 2017 Common Sense census the most common use of these devices at younger ages (0–8) is to watch videos on platforms like YouTube Kids,[5] while according to a study published by Ofcom in February of 2020, around 70 per cent of children aged —twelve to fifteen have a social media profile. Of these, 27 per cent said Snapchat was their main social media platform, with Instagram at 24 per cent, Facebook at 23 per cent, and WhatsApp at 14 per cent. Ofcom also found that a quarter of ten-year-olds who go online claim to have a profile, with this rising to 43 per cent of eleven-year-olds – despite the minimum age for most social media platforms being thirteen.[6] Over the course of the following years, during the global pandemic, these statistics all increased.

In her book, *Reclaiming Conversation: The Power of Talk in a Digital Age* (2015), American psychologist and sociologist Sherry Turkle observed that the extensive use of phones diminished children's empathy and their ability to engage in deep conversation. This presents the irony that, while a new means of communication such as emojis may allow more efficient delivery of the user's emotions, this is to the detriment of the depth and richness of empathy in life offline. For young children who are in the process of developing their emotional intelligence, the use of simplified emojis might be much more problematic than it is for adults. Getting accustomed to the simple tapping of an image to convey one's feelings could potentially undermine a more profound exploration of what one is feeling at that moment, and perhaps even stunt emotional maturity and development.

However, we should not be so quick to blame phones for everything. We need to understand both the pros and cons of emojis and the use of digital devices for our young people, as well as examine their educational and psychological impacts more rigorously. Emojis are an important aspect of online communication for young people. Very young children often enjoy scrolling through the list of emojis and selecting ones they like even before they can read, while children and teens use emojis in more sophisticated ways to communicate with each other effectively online. However, concerns are frequently raised about the increasing use of social media by young children and the potential socio-emotional problems such trends can bring.

That said, there is also evidence of some benefits associated with using emojis. For instance, emojis have been introduced in Austrian classrooms as a part of a language education research programme (SELFIE project: Strengthening Effective Language of Feelings in Education), among primary school students across three schools in socio-economically challenged areas. The idea behind the programme is that learning to express oneself through various visual media (including emojis, animations, memes and GIFs) can help a child to better process and describe their own emotions and perspectives. In short, this is an attempt to enrich the emotional development of children by using emojis as a new learning tool. Indeed, Professor Mills, the leading researcher behind the programme, describes how students' use of emotional language transformed from basic descriptions to a more sophisticated level of expression after participating in the programme.

Other studies have also confirmed the benefits of using emojis for socio-emotional development in children as an effective communication tool,[7] and as an intervention tool to enhance empathy in children with autism spectrum disorder (ASD).[8] There have also been attempts to facilitate emotional health through emoji expression. An app called 'Emoodji' was developed to help youths monitor their mental health. The app allows users to take selfies and add emojis that fit the user's feelings that day, creating opportunities to express negative emotions without stigma. These studies and initiatives show that this new mode of communication has the potential to both simplify and enrich children's emotional experiences.

The grey area: Irritation or boredom?

Emojis live in context. Even the very obvious-looking smiling happy face emoji can be very often used to convey a sarcastic mood by Chinese users. The one I always find difficult to understand is the face with tears of joy emoji; it is so popular but I'm not quite sure whether the laugh is a so-called 'good and innocent laugh' or a sort of 'mocking laugh'. To be on the safe side, I don't use this emoji much, and I found that this is the case for many of my Asian colleagues and friends. The same emoji doesn't always have the same interpretation and reaction in all situations by all people.

The interpretation of the so-called unamused face emoji or face with rolling eyes emoji is much more hotly debated. In what context can we use it? It shows some sort of irritation and displeasure but we cannot be sure what level of irritation this emoji represents. Yet, surprisingly, the same emoji can mean boredom. There are indeed many kinds of emotions conveyed through emojis which we are unable to accurately describe. Cultural interpretation is also very different. Here are some emojis, whose meanings in a Chinese context are not what I believe most of the readers might have imagined (Figure 7.2).

Short Code	Image	Meaning
[smug]		Dislike, unsatisfied, disagree
[duh]		So boring
[speechless]		Embarrassed, do not know what to say
[angry]		Angry, embarrassed, worried

Figure 7.2 Emojis and their typical interpretations in a Chinese context. Source: emoji design by Loli Kim, reproduced with permission.

For the final set of emojis on the bottom row, one may initially label the expression as 'angry', but in reality, it could also mean 'embarrassed' or 'worried'. When we don't see the colour, for instance, you could think it signifies 'worried' more than 'upset'. However, the red colour makes the face look angry. It is interesting that colour matters; you will see that these emojis are red in the e-book format of this book, thereby leading you to associate the face with anger, but in the paperback format you are unable to see the colour and will be less likely to link the face to anger.

Kawaii emojis

It has also become common for social media companies to develop their own in-house characters to use in their unique emojis for their apps or platforms, particularly in Asian regions. These unique characters are designed to encourage customer engagement and attachment through their cute designs.[9] Eventually, these characters can become familiar to large numbers of people, allowing companies to expand said IPs into merchandise lines and cartoons.

There are currently three main players in the emoji business in Asia: KakaoTalk, Line and WeChat. KakaoTalk was one of the first companies to design emojis featuring unique characters intended to capture the daily emotions that people experience. KakaoTalk incorporated catchphrases and gestures from popular TV dramas, movies, webtoons and cartoons to enhance their familiarity and accessibility to users. At the end of 2016, KakaoTalk expanded its range of character emojis by launching its *Little Friends* range of emoji characters aimed at younger users. This was a great success, particularly among female users who were drawn to the characters' cute, delicate designs, enhanced by the younger appearances of this line of characters. The awkward personalities of the characters also helped to endear them to users.

In comparison, although WeChat has not had the same success in creating one single iconic collection of characters, it does have an extensive range of sticker packs available for free and through purchase. WeChat's sticker packs range from cartoon figures of every animal imaginable to images of food and stickers of regional dialects that may become popular to use due to their use on TV shows and in other media. Often, people also take pictures of their pets and make them into emojis, sometimes adding captions to the pictures, trying to illustrate what their pet was 'thinking' at the time. A unique feature of WeChat is that each sticker has its own title, and if a user types the title in their message,

Figure 7.3 A likeness of a real image sticker pack.

then those emojis with that title will pop up. This happens especially with common conversational phrases, such as 谢谢 (*xiexie* thank you), 拜拜 (*bai bai* bye), 好的 (*haode* okay), 对 (*dui* that's right) and 你好 (*nihao* hello) (Figure 7.3).

Line has also created its own range of emoji/sticker characters, with a focus on characters that are more dynamic and have more striking facial expressions. Just as Line's early emoticons were derived from Ekman's six basic emotions,[10] their emoji/sticker characters have evolved to cover a wide range of visual expressions mimicking common facial expressions, gestures and relatable situations. These images are so exaggerated and expressive that they are able to convey a strong sense of the emotion they are depicting without the need to rely on text to explain their meaning.

Indeed, the instant recognizability of the facial expressions of these Asian emoticons reminds us of Ekman's six basic emotions (joy, surprise, anger, disgust, sadness and fear). In fact, on the messaging app Line, stickers are presented to the user arranged into a table labelled according to these six emotions, perhaps backing up Ekman's hypothesis that these emotions are universal.

Then again, given the popularity of the Line app in Japan, some culture-specific features can also easily be discerned. For example, these emoticons also draw heavily from the visual language of anime and manga. Elements of the style of classic *shōjo* manga that appear to influence emoji design include the presentation of characters with long eyelashes, decorative elements like sparkles and rose petals, and 'speed lines' often seen in manga to add a feeling of movement or intensity to an image.

Although platforms like Line and KakaoTalk offer paid sticker packs for purchase on their stores, the free character emojis/stickers they offer are extremely well known and popular among users. These emoji characters are designed to be broadly appealing and suitable for adapting to branded goods and commercialization, and goods featuring Line and KakaoTalk characters are highly profitable for these companies. In fact, in 2017, Line Friends opened twenty-two offline stores across nine countries, including China, Japan and Thailand. Similarly, Line even created an animation to expand its characters to wider audiences to grow the influence of their brand and characters.

These non-verbal visual signs are so prevalent in instant messaging (especially in Asia) that reading through these messages almost feels like reading a Japanese manga due to the large number of expressive images used to convey meaning. The manga-like image in Figure 7.4 is called a *jjalbang* in Korean. This term refers to photos, images or videos, which are mostly comical and used as an alternative to typed text in the course of written online communication, generally to express the sentiment of a user's reaction to something. This is similar to the use of gifs

Figure 7.4 Jjalbang. Image source: Naver jjalbang

made easily available on platforms such as WhatsApp, although the form more closely resembles that of a meme. The name *jjalbang* is an abbreviation composed of the word stems *jjal*, which means to cut, and *bang*, which means prevention. The meaning of *jjalbang* is therefore literally 'prune prevention', referring to the images posted alongside forum posts on imageboards which required an image to be posted alongside every comment. In the past, when users wanted to make a comment but had no relevant image to post, they would attach random images simply to prevent their post from being deleted by moderators – hence these images came to be called 'prune prevention', a name that stuck even after this context became irrelevant.

The characters used for emojis/stickers are usually either humans or animals due to their expressiveness and ability to convey relatable emotions. To strengthen the visual impact of these emojis, each brand establishes personalities for each character, matching their expression in each image to fit their personality. Users often gravitate towards characters with a similar personality to themselves, or whose emotions they can relate to. The range of these emojis/stickers is becoming increasingly diversified, allowing users to choose from a wider range. For instance, illustrators are free to submit their own sticker packs for purchase on platforms like KakaoTalk and Line after passing an evaluation system, therefore allowing for a huge variety of expressive options for those who are willing to pay.

People are drawn to characters able to express their exact thoughts and feelings, or which express their own identity. These personified character emojis therefore allow users to express their thoughts and feelings more intuitively and more expressively. Emojis and emoticons developed in Asia also draw from the visual lexicon established by manga to represent various emotions. Users can find characters they identify with and express their emotions through different stickers featuring those characters depending on the situation. Sometimes, the highly exaggerated expressions of these characters can enable us to express ourselves more effectively than realistic descriptions of how we are feeling.

Summary

Despite concerns from some that by flattening our emotions into simplified emoji forms we may flatten the range and complexity of our own emotions, we have seen that emojis are used to encode a far greater range of information than our basic emotions. Emojis have a nature that is more constructive, than destructive. How an emoji is interpreted also depends on the cultural context and social dynamics, meaning emojis are less simplified than some may think. Emojis are equally as important as the tone and style of written language in the online space, and emojis provide a new, unique insight into pragmatic language use. All social media users consider the relative status of their addressee when deciding which emojis to use or whether to use them at all. Meanwhile, there is also a noticeable difference between the types of emojis used by different cultures.

The result of the increasing adoption and evolution of emojis is a new form of linguistic expression, whereby social media language use has become a visual performance. Each social media user is culturally informed about the performative use of emojis by their own observations of emoji use by other social media and messaging users. Users learn the nuances of trending emojis from their online communities, going on to use those emojis themselves on that basis. However, users are not passive recipients of the nuances and accepted meanings of emojis, but are also participants in constructing and adding to their meanings. In the social media community, each user becomes a creator and propagator of each emoji's significance, creating a continuous cycle in which the meaning and pattern of use of emojis are constantly created and updated. The use of emojis and the development of their nuanced meanings is an emerging topic of study that merits further examination. In the study of linguistics, there is a lot more to be learnt about pragmatic language use, and how cultural features of the language are transferred to and altered by an online environment.

8

Emoji Sensitivity

Emojis are a perfect fit for our busy life; they help us to be efficient by streamlining conversation. In our ever diversified, multilingual and multicultural life emoji speak is the most pragmatic and emphatic way of communication. As a reminder, in this book, emojis are understood as any image or symbol which is found digitally and online, often on a (smartphone's) screen, such as a smiley face. One heart emoji can bind people of all linguistic and cultural backgrounds and help to build solidarity. For example, since the Russia–Ukraine conflict has begun, we have seen blue and yellow emojis being used across the world to show solidarity with Ukraine. The simplicity of emojis is invaluable as we can show sympathy and unity without necessarily knowing another's language. However, as we all know, this doesn't mean that emojis are straightforward. A red rose, for example, can be used to show respect in Chinese culture, whereas in many other parts of the world it can carry a romantic connotation. The multifarious use of emojis is complex and their meanings are sometimes culturally bounded.

General emoji etiquette

Indeed, emojis require sensitivity. A smiley face can be easy and casual if you know the person to whom you are 'emojing' well enough. However, it may not be so easy when you use one with a person to whom you are not close or with a work colleague. You have to think twice about whether the smiley face could in fact cause a problem at the other end. You don't want to sign off a message too seriously, yet at the same time, you don't want to make yourself look too casual. For relationships in which you know the other person is sensitive, one needs to be careful in using emojis. Sometimes even a mere exclamation mark (!) or a (repeated) question marker can make a person feel nervous and rattled. These are just a few things to consider in emoji etiquette. Emojis don't, after all, exist in a vacuum.

One's culture matters greatly in the use of emojis and their interpretation. For instance, in Asia, age and gender greatly matter when choosing emojis. Politeness from in-person communication needs to be expressed through emojis too, somehow. Context and register also play important roles. Whether you are talking to one person or to a group, or with a close friend or group of colleagues, context is key. In our ever-diversified world, cultural sensitivity matters more than ever before. The symbolic meanings of an emoji will be hugely different from one culture to another. A winking face, for instance, could be considered as a light-hearted gesture in one culture, but in another where people do not casually wink, it could be perceived in a negative light. It is crucial to grasp the situation, understand the dynamics of the people involved and judge the suitability based on the context.

Sensitive emojis

Emoji mistakes are very plausible, partly because we message so quickly, so mistakes are unavoidable. In our ever-evolving emoji world, it is possible to misunderstand an emoji, since nobody is sure about the exact meaning of each one: even somewhat obvious-looking emojis may have entirely different meanings depending on the context. Consider the poo emoji.

The sender may have used it in a fun way, but humour always comes with a risk of being ill-received; the recipient might take offence. In a Chinese context, the poo emoji is used as a reaction of strong disagreement. One Chinese participant said that he would use this emoji as a response to rubbish talk or offensive words.

Another example from our corpus of messages is the combination of the red rose with the beckoning finger, used in the Chinese context. Elsewhere, the red rose is often used to convey a romantic sentiment, yet here this rose means 'tired'. Hand gestures also vary in meaning. The beckoning with a crooked finger gesture. means 'come and join' in a Chinese context. However, for me, this emoji feels a bit uncomfortable. In Korean culture, this would be considered rude and insensitive.

Most of the emojis studied in the linguistics field are ones that are less sensitive to different cultures, what I call 'safe emojis'. Studying emojis in linguistics is relatively new. To this day, the field has focused mainly on emojis used in English and Western European contexts. It is important to reconsider the lens through which we study emojis. We must improve our approach to the topic in future research, in order to bring fuller justice to our emoji use in an ever-growing multicultural world.

Emojis at work

Different cultures may have differing views on when it is appropriate to use emojis. For example, in a Western context, it is generally uncommon to text and use emojis regularly in a professional setting. However, in China, where a lot of communication takes place through the multi-functional messaging app WeChat, emojis are common in work-related messages. This shows how some cultures have integrated emojis into their registers of formality. For example, emojis such as the red rose in the Chinese context can also be used to indicate 'gratitude', therefore they appear frequently in Chinese work-related chats (Figure 8.1).

The rose, sun and coffee emojis can be used to show care at the workplace in China. They can be used between colleagues regardless of seniority, unlike some other hierarchy-sensitive emojis. Similarly, in Korea, work colleagues regularly use KakaoTalk emojis with each other. After all, being connected through phones can increase response rates and yield faster results for work-related matters. Nonetheless, there is an issue concerning privacy and the implicit demand to work out-of-work time. In the West, Portugal has just banned employers from contacting employees by phone, message or email outside of their work hours as part of new laws brought in to promote a healthier work–life balance amid a rise in remote working.

There is also a great personal difference and one Korean participant attests:

The emojis I use depend on what kind of work I do with the person. *If it's someone I work with for a short period of time, I don't use emojis at all. Using emojis in formal work-related conversations could seem impolite.* But with people

Figure 8.1 Rose, sun and coffee. Source: Design by Loli Kim, reproduced with permission.

you work with on a regular basis or on long-term projects, *it can feel too blunt without emojis, especially as you spend more time together. Without any emojis in texts, it can feel too business-like and formal.* In such cases, I use emojis but only simple ones like a smiley face. It's my way of telling the person that even though we are in a business relationship, we are not all formal and that we are quite close. It's my way of showing friendliness to the person. (Emphasis added)

Hong highlights that varying patterns of emojis are used in the workplace. Hong analysed conversation data between recently employed workers (in their twenties to thirties) and senior position employees (in their fifties to sixties) in Korea.[1] The younger employees were more cautious and passive when it came to emoji usage in conversations with their professional seniors. In contrast, senior employees were more proactive with their emojis and generally did not exhibit as much caution as their junior counterparts. Most of the preferred emojis for use with socially distant targets in formal conversations had static and geometric properties rather than personified or realistic visual characteristics. Interestingly, static and geometric emojis were viewed as a safe 'public language' to be used in formal contexts. In addition to the nature of the conversations (whether informal or formal), people adjust their emoji behaviour according to the receivers' personalities, often 'emojing' in a similar style to the person with whom they are talking, thus shortening the social distance between them.

Emoji politeness

Unlike Western languages, in which the hierarchical relation between the speaker and addressee does not directly influence the grammar of the language, social hierarchy matters at every level of social interaction in many Asian languages. For example, there are emojis that you can use to your seniors and teachers and emojis that you cannot use. Language use, including the use of emojis, pictures, stickers and other features of computer-mediated communication, is influenced by complex interpersonal dynamics and the relative sociocultural position between two or more interlocutors. Multiple factors within the field of interpersonal dynamics influence the use of emojis in online communication, with the most dominant being: age, intimacy, gender and relative positions within a shared organization or family, etc.

Although the use of emojis is typically considered to be a highly peripheral feature of computer-mediated communication that softens various expressions,[2] such a view tends to underestimate the role of emojis as a feature of online communication that is more often than not obligatory. Emojis can make or break a linguistic exchange; when used correctly, they can lead to a heightened sense of solidarity, closeness and enjoyment, but when used incorrectly, there is a danger of offence, a perceived lack of sincerity and even conflict.

We now turn to a discussion of how relations influence the use of emojis and other non-linguistic features in texting and computer-mediated communication. Although we will introduce each relational characteristic later separately, it is important to keep in mind that these do not exist in isolation. Each feature is intertwined with the others, and it is their particular configuration in a given situation that determines the (in)appropriateness of emoji use in online communication. For instance, you may be able to send some emojis to your boss – but not *all* emojis (Figure 8.2).

In my Jamboard workshop, I asked participants what they thought of the exchange between a professor and a student as seen earlier. Some thought it was okay and friendly, whereas some said it looked disrespectful. People's opinions vary greatly when it comes to emoji appropriateness. My Jamboard

Figure 8.2 Emoji Interpretations. Source: Design by Loli Kim, reproduced with permission.

workshop on emojis was hosted by the Korean Education Centre attached to the Korean Embassy to the UK. It was an interactive online workshop. Most of the participants were those who are interested in Korean culture and reside in the UK. However, I didn't know their linguistic and cultural background. Not all of them were, in fact, from the UK. One participant was from Bulgaria, and another was from Nigeria. We spoke in English, but participants came from a wide range of backgrounds. I did not know their age, gender, linguistic and cultural backgrounds in detail. This is an apt illustration of the emoji world that we live in – it is multicultural and incredibly diverse. In fact, emoji speak by nature happens across languages and cultures. Nevertheless, the freedom with which one can use emojis inevitably means a variation of meanings and interpretations. With such diverse and unique interactions, misunderstandings are unavoidable. With this in mind, it is all the more important that we use emojis sensitively.

Age and hierarchy

In order to emoji sensitively, one needs to consider their relation to the interlocutors – in this case – age and hierarchy matter. This is especially true in Asian cultures, and even more acutely so in East Asian cultures, where persisting Confucian values require younger people to honour their elders. People will typically show their respect to an older individual through their gestures, speech style and general conduct. This level of respect should be maintained to curtail any awkwardness or conflict, as a perceived lack of respect may result in unwanted friction. Respect for one's elders must also be preserved in computer-mediated written communication, where it manifests in several ways. In this, conventional grammatical forms and punctuation are typically maintained. When one forgoes features such as full stops, commas, capitalization and so on, one could be perceived as having a lack of respect.

The liberal use of emojis can be seen as rude. Emojis are often perceived as superfluous and demonstrate a lack of sincerity when sent by a younger person to an older recipient. This can cause a serious problem as one may end up being scolded for being cold and disrespectful to the elders. Therefore, younger generations are particularly careful when using emojis when talking to their seniors.

> The emojis I use when talking to seniors are almost fixed. *I avoid funny emojis with seniors. These are fine between friends but with older people, they are not.*

Emojis that look too dynamic and active, such as bears dancing or bears eating, are rarely used in my formal conversations. (Emma, 25, female) (Emphasis added)

I think I use emojis and texts together when I send messages to seniors. I may sound rude if I use emojis only, so I send an emoji indicating gratitude and write 'thank you' additionally. (Chris, 23, male)

Yes, if I am using banmal (casual form), it would mean that I am close with the person so I would be able to use any types of emojis including funny ones, whereas with people using honorifics I wouldn't feel comfortable to use those funny emojis – it wouldn't be polite. (Alice, 26, female)

Generally speaking, for elders or people whom I am not that familiar with, I usually use the cute stickers, such as cats and dogs, and then some simple ones, such as a blushing or happy face, and more of the built-in emojis in WeChat. [...] *I must pick one that is polite enough, and understandable to the other person*, because there are still some emojis that have puns, etc. I use very *straightforward* emojis and stickers with elders. (LY, 22, female) (Emphasis added)

My Chinese interviewees said that they tended to use standard friendly emojis to those older than them. One of our Chinese respondents noted that he mostly used 'straightforward' emojis, that is to say, emojis without any hidden connotations to those older than him. Straightforward emojis include emojis and stickers that have a simple greeting function – 'Hi', 'Bye', 'Nice to meet you' – as well as expressions of gratitude or agreement. Almost all our Korean and Chinese interviewees reported that one of their biggest concerns was that an elder recipient may not appreciate the same emojing style as the one they use with their friends. They were keenly aware that emoji styles popular among young people may seem confusing, or that they mean something different to an older recipient.

One of the most 'straightforward' emojis is the smiley face. While the [Smile] in WeChat, represents a sign of friendliness and kindness, and is perfectly acceptable to use for people in their forties or older, it actually implies a certain degree of sarcasm in younger people's eyes. Young people would rarely send the [Smile] to their friends if they wanted to create a friendly tone. Instead, they would use the [Joyful] emoji or other smiley faces which have additional stylistic elements. To younger users, the [Smile] appears demure and rather inexpressive; it may even be interpreted as an uncomfortable smile. This is in contrast to older users, for whom the [Smile] is simply a happy smile. It should be noted that this is not only the case in China but all over the world. Users of WhatsApp similarly stated that Apple's equivalent smiley face emoji can be perceived as mocking.

In relation to age, it is also important to recognize that the social media platform matters in regard to the use of emojis and how they are understood by interlocutors. Snapchat is particularly popular among teenagers, and this is also the case for TikTok, as the majority of TikTok users are aged nineteen to twenty-nine (35%), with a large proportion below eighteen years old (28%).[3] These age ranges correspond approximately to the age range of the Gen Z born between 1995 and 2010, whose top three preferred social media platforms include TikTok and Snapchat.[4] TikTok is projected to gain more twelve to seventeen-year-old users than Snapchat by 2024, with Snapchat being predicted to remain as the most preferred social media platform among Gen Z due to a forecasted higher usage rate among the 18- to 24-year-olds.[5] Due to the large user base of Gen Z-ers on TikTok and Snapchat, it is also observed that patterns of emoji usage in TikTok and Snapchat are age-sensitive, often being influenced and led by this very generation. Similar to how language changes, the meanings of emojis on these platforms are constantly being redefined by each successive generation – Gen Z inherited the common usages of emojis from the preceding generations and elevated it through a mixture of uses that 'enriches communication'.[6] Compared to preceding generations, the use of emojis by Gen Z is more 'nuanced', and similar to how slang and new linguistic forms are often formed by this generation. New uses of emojis can also be spread via this generation, such as how the usage of soft emojis like hearts to express sarcasm in sentences was popularized by this very generation on TikTok.[7] There also seems to be an age-based division in the use of some emojis. For example, use of certain older emojis like the Face with Tears of Joy is no longer considered 'cool', with some of the Gen Z agreeing that these emojis should be used only by the older generations.[8] Therefore, age indeed plays an influential role in the use of emojis and, when coupled with how they are used on various social media platforms, intergenerational misunderstandings and tension may arise when the meaning of the emoji is not understood by both parties.

Many of the interviewees also mentioned that there is a 'safe' category of emojis, which are used to exchange greetings without any additional implications. These emojis are often cute and simple. Figure 8.3 shows a collection of 'safe' emojis that can be sent to older people. The sticker pack, entitled 'Chubby Sheep', shows a cute sheep making mostly friendly gestures. The expressions are all very earnest and could be sent to an elder without fear of misunderstanding or causing offence.

Most internet users would agree that the tone in a serious conversation should be composed and 'business-like'. In such situations, the Chinese

Figure 8.3 Cute sheep sticker pack. Source: Design by Loli Kim, reproduced with permission. See the real 'Chubby Sheep' sticker pack here: https://tinyurl.com/chubby-sheep

students that we interviewed stated that they adjust their emoji behaviour according to the behaviour of the person to whom they are speaking. In a standard serious conversation, they would usually refrain from using many emojis and stickers, if any at all. However, if the superior(s) in the conversation were to use emojis, then the interviewees felt it natural to follow their lead and use emojis of a similar style. The individual differences and preferences of the addressees play a significant role in the interlocutor's use of emojis. Our respondents highlighted that the personality of the addressee(s) was crucial in deciding whether to send emojis to someone of senior status. Participants stated that they would take into consideration whether the addressee(s) are open-minded or not, and whether they comprehended or participated in the same texting culture as young people. Accordingly, intimacy and closeness between juniors and seniors can also affect the use of emojis and the style of emojis used. For instance, juniors who are close to their seniors may be able to express themselves more casually, and thus will be able to use emojis more freely.

Intimacy

Intimacy also matters greatly in emojing. By 'intimacy', I refer to the closeness of the relationship between interlocutors and consider the professional or cultural circumstances that would influence this closeness. A close relationship tends to allow for more freedom of expression through creative emoji use in online chatting environments, while a less close or more professional, the relationship would demand more restraint. Intimacy also encourages or allows a certain level of originality and innovation. For example, in a chat with a close group of friends or individuals belonging to the same fandom, innovative uses of emojis can arise that would be incomprehensible to an individual that is not part of that friend group or fandom. Thus, we see how intimacy leads to a great capacity for creativity and fun when emojing online.

Degrees of intimacy are also important. However, oftentimes hierarchy and intimacy need to be considered together in order to find an appropriate level of emoji usage. For instance, Jenny, a British woman whom we interviewed, married a Korean man. She mentioned that when she interacts with her in-laws – who are all close – she needs to consider the hierarchy. In practice, this means that she needs to use fewer emojis less frequently or more carefully with her in-laws. In contrast, she uses emojis much more freely with her sister-in-law who is younger than herself. Emoji politeness is certainly becoming much more hard work as we interact and engage with the ever-diversified, multilingual, multicultural world.

Gender

The third relational dynamic is gender. Although gender is less obviously significant in terms of sociocultural hierarchy, it still has an impact on texting behaviours. Past studies have found that women tend to use emojis to create humour, while men tend to use emojis to express teasing/sarcasm.[9] In Korea, women use more emojis on the KakaoTalk platform than men. Wolf suggests that this is due to women having a greater ability to infer other people's emotions and consider the perspectives of others.[10] She finds that female students are more likely to use emoticons to express emotions or intimacy and manage message meaning than male students. The most frequently used emoji in Korea is the face with tears of joy. The second most frequently used emoji for women in Korea is the loudly crying face, and the second most frequently used emoji for Korean men is the folded hands. I seek to add to this understanding of emoji use from a different perspective: how do people change their emoji use when speaking to the opposite gender?

Marília et al. examined whether gender differences are consistent regardless of age. It was found that women reported using emoji more frequently and a more positive attitude towards their use, and that these 'gender differences for emoji frequency of use and attitudes were particularly evident for younger women'. It was also found that younger (versus older) participants used more emojis and identified more strongly with motivations for their use.

Marília et al.'s findings add to the emerging body of literature on emojis and emoticons by showing the relevance of considering age and gender, and their interplay, when examining patterns in the use of these features. For example, the study builds upon research suggesting differences between the frequency of emoji and emoticon use, observing gender and age differences that converge with past findings – that women use more emojis and have more positive attitudes towards their use than men.[11] Findings that showed younger participants use emojis more often and have more positive attitudes towards their use likewise confirm previous studies.[12] However, the interaction of age and gender was also found to be significant. This important evidence indicates that typical gender differences, as reported by previous studies may be more salient among younger samples (e.g. university students).[13]

The existing literature gives a good overview of the different states of research in Western and Eastern contexts. On the one hand, Western studies of emoji use a framework based on gesture research and underestimate the importance of interpersonal relationships in their approaches. On the other hand, Eastern language studies tend to look more deeply into the modulators of emoji use and consider the influence of complex interpersonal dynamics. There is notably less scholarship about emoji use in Asian languages, so this chapter will focus on how Asian cultures affect emojing habits.

I do not aim to establish what exactly are the different emojing habits of men and women; there are previous studies dedicated to that cause. We, instead, look at how emojing habits change when one is talking to the opposite gender. Whether in a conservative or liberal culture, no one wants their messages to be misconstrued as having romantic connotations. This is especially true of the case studies that I will look at in Jordan and South Korea. However, age, intimacy and status all affect emoji use across genders, so various styles are employed. Of course, personal taste will always have an influence, too. When talking with professors, bosses or other people of a higher social status, concerns about misconstrued romantic interests seem to give way to other social norms: one's behaviour should change to conform to the identity one possesses, as well as to the relative social distance and the power dynamics of the relationship. Our interviewees emphasized that they would not send any emojis to any of their professors, regardless of gender, otherwise they feared that they would come across as not being serious.

Emojis between genders

The use of emojis between genders can require sensitivity and careful thought. In the set of emojis in Figure 8.4 – which are collected from participants from China, Korea and Jordan – some can be used freely across genders and some cannot. This is all decided by culture and context. For instance, smiley faces and laugh-cry emojis are commonly used as they are straightforward in expressing positive emotions and do not denote any underlying meanings. Even the doggy head emoji, which comes from a famous meme that is widely known in China, will not be perceived negatively and can be used as a tool for building a closer relationship between the speakers. On the other hand, emojis with hearts, lips or kisses are not often used across genders. This is because they may convey hidden romantic meanings which might not be appropriate if the speakers are not in an exclusive relationship (Figure 8.4).

Indeed, culture matters in the use of emojis across genders. Some cultures are particularly sensitive to cross-gender emojing, whereas others are less so. In the following section I will show how my interviewees (which are comprised of South Korean, Jordanian and French participants) react differently to certain emojis.

Korean cases

First, some context on South Korean society. Despite having undergone many changes, South Korean society is built on the foundations of the Joseon Dynasty,

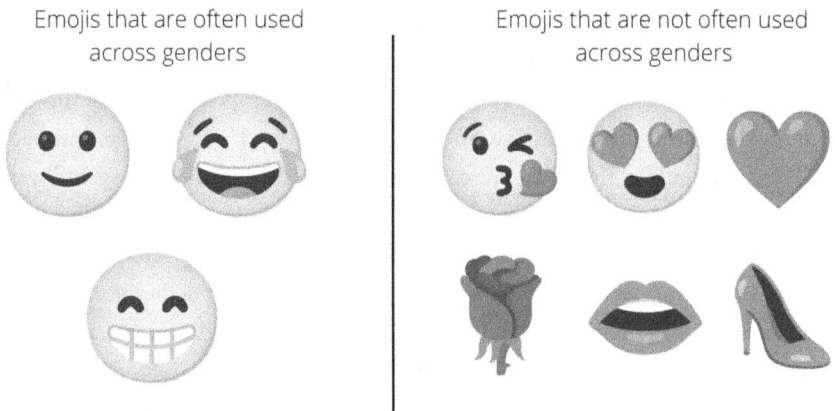

Figure 8.4 Emoji diversity across genders. NotoColorEmoji: © 2021 Google Inc, OFL License.

a time when Neo-Confucian doctrine was the orthodoxy. From the sixteenth century onwards, there was strict segregation between men and women. Though this has gradually changed since the turn of the twentieth century, it was still taboo for men and women to be friends as late as the 1950s and 1960s. Echoes of this societal standard remain in online communication. Korean people would rarely send affectionate emojis to those of the opposite gender. The most frequently stated reason for this was the risk of the recipient misinterpreting the intention of the emoji. Even when the sender did not have to worry about such misinterpretations with close friends, the speaker still felt no need to use an affectionate emoji with opposite-gender friends:

- I would never send a heart-shaped emoji to a male senior (opposite gender). I feel that it's in our tradition to show caution when expressing affection to the opposite gender. We have to be very careful about sending heart-related emojis to the opposite gender. For example, I would only send heart emojis to my boyfriend. Whereas I feel that in Western cultures, people are more liberal in saying 'I love you' and sending heart-shaped emojis. It seems to be a natural part of their culture so I would feel more comfortable sending those types of emojis to my American friends. (Female Korean speaker, 20s)
- Yeah, I can send heart emojis more easily with people of the same gender especially if I am closer to them. If I am talking to my male friends, I would not use heart emojis at all. Just in case they misinterpret my intentions. (Female Korean speaker, 20s)
- I wouldn't worry about my close female friends misinterpreting my intentions for using heart emojis, but I still wouldn't send affectionate emojis to my female friends just because I wouldn't feel the need to. I would send funny emojis though. (Male Korean speaker, 20s)

In Figure 8.5 we present a screenshot of conversations between a Korean woman named Eunji in which she is chatting with a female friend.

In Figure 8.5, we see two women talking together. Noticeably, there is a high frequency of emoji use, with affectionate emojis, like heart eyes and cute stickers. Comparatively, in Eunji's instant messaging conversations which have a cross-gender dynamic in our data, there are no emojis used from the emoji keyboard. Instead, she and her interlocutor tend to stick to graphemes, such as ~, ㅋㅋㅋ and ㅠㅠ, to add character, but not intimacy, to the conversation.

This differs greatly from the typical patterns of emoji use we observed for male message senders. In male–male conversation, notably, there are no emojis used at all. This is interesting in itself and may be related to concepts of masculinity,

Figure 8.5 Conversation between two female participants. Reproduced with permission.

which may be idealized overall as a less affectionate gender. In cross-gender conversation, although no affectionate emojis used, stickers are occasionally added in a friendly, personable manner. Once again, any hints of intimacy are avoided.

Our data also included an example of a multilingual (English and Korean) cross-gender conversation. Once again, there is no use of affectionate emojis. The participants stick to basic emojis, ':((', " :)', and '~'. These types of emojis are visibly more distant than their Unicode counterparts. They add a tone of friendliness to the conversation, but also draw a clear line, showing that the participants are not too close. The conversation can take on a pleasant air but will never reach the point of intimacy with such emojis.

We see again that particular emojis, especially hearts and cute stickers, are gender sensitive. Women tend to use affectionate stickers more often when talking with their female friends. In comparison, men may not feel the necessity to use any emojis with their male friends and may use friendly, yet polite, emojis with their female friends. Women also are careful not to use overly affectionate emojis with men. Both genders fear that their friendly intentions may be misconstrued as romantic ones, and therefore, tend to use more neutral emojis with the opposite gender.

A Jordanian case

The strictest form of emoji uses in cross-gender conversations that we came across was from my participant from Jordan. When asked about her emojing habits, Amira responded that she would never send affectionate emojis to those of the opposite gender. Amira stated that she felt comfortable sending affectionate emojis to female friends: 'When it comes to our female friends, that's okay, we send these [affectionate] emojis on a daily basis.' However, when it came to male friends, she expressed the same fear of misinterpretation: 'If I send a heart emoji to my male friend, he could misinterpret it as a love message and our families – his parents or my parents – could also misinterpret this as me trying to express my love towards him.' In Amira's case, it is not only the risk of creating awkwardness in her relationship with a man that she took into consideration, how parents may perceive affectionate emojis was also important to her.

Amira's motivations to avoid using affectionate emojis goes beyond simple disapproval; to be seen flirting with a man could have serious consequences if seen as an honour crime:

> Girls can be killed for dating or even texting a man and the people that kill the girl would be her brother or father. They would say, 'She stained our family's honour', and the action of killing the daughter would prove to people that the family's honour was protected. So yes, we are very cautious when interacting with men and hence, there would be a lot of restrictions with using love-related emojis.

Amira is happy to use emojis to male friends in general, but she is careful to make a distinction between those that would be interpreted as affectionate and those that would not: 'We can use a pink flower emoji but not a red rose emoji. Red has a feeling of love so I can't use it with any men. But when it's white or pink or any other colour, it's okay as long as it's not red.'

Though this is the case in Amira's family who view marriage in a traditional manner, it is not true of all Arab families or countries.

> 'When talking about the Arab world, we have so many countries and different cultures. The Palestinian culture tends to be conservative. Jordanians are also conservative. Lebanese are liberal and open-minded, so I know some of my Lebanese friends that shake hands with men and text each other using heart emojis. This would all be fine but, in my culture, I cannot shake hands with men or kiss them, hence no heart emojis.'

It is also not the case for all generations:

> I was in a Facebook group with students of mine from different refugee camps and one day, I noticed that one of my female students used a white heart emoji at the end of a thank you message to another male student. When I first saw this behaviour, I was very shocked. Then, I noticed some of my other female students used a white heart emoji as well. I found this odd because I would not do that with any men. Perhaps, the emojing culture is changing with the younger generations. I feel that they have more flexibility than I do with these emojis.

As such, Amira's case is one of the more extreme cases, but it once again shows that the gender of the person to whom we are speaking may affect our use of semiotic resources.

French cases

Despite what we have seen earlier, there are some people who do not view emojis as being so indicative of their true intentions or feelings. Some users will happily send messages with emojis of possible romantic connotations to any of their friends, regardless of their gender. Let us look at the case of Maylis here, a French university student. When asked about sending heart emojis to her friends, Maylis replied that she would be happy to send them to both male and female friends. She states that if she were to send a heart emoji to a male friend, then he would know that 'It's not that deep' because 'we both understand each other really well in knowing that the expression is not on a deep level'. When asked about how often she expresses love or affection, Maylis replies, 'Yes, in France, we don't have a problem expressing love. Most of the time, it's not that deep when we send "I love you" or heart emojis to friends. But you know we really mean it when we're texting someone we're dating'. Maylis' response demonstrates that context is everything. She seems to have a lot of comfortable cross-gender friendships, and she does not need to worry about them misconstruing her meaning. It is only when a relationship has been established as romantic explicitly that there is a possibility for emojis to take on a deeper romantic significance.

Nonetheless, when asked whether she would send affectionate emojis to a male professor, Maylis responds with a decisive 'No'. Notably, Maylis does not say that this is because of the possibility of misconstrued romantic interests but instead emphasizes that she would not send any emojis to any of her professors, regardless of gender: 'If they are professors, we won't use emojis. It's not seen as appropriate, so nobody uses emojis.' For Maylis, the key lies in the nature of the interpersonal relationship: if the person with whom she is messaging is friends with her in an informal comfortable way (regardless of age), then she will use whichever emojis that she wishes. However, if they have a formal relationship, like teacher–student, then she sees emojis as inappropriate, as they do not suit a formal communication style.

Another French student, Pierre, who is male, demonstrates similar emojing habits. Pierre often uses emojis with friends, family and peers. For cross-gender conversations, his emoji behaviour depends on the nature of each relationship. With male friends, he uses fewer emojis, often to create humour. With female friends, he 'texts bisous' (kisses) sometimes, but in a restrained way. Interestingly, Pierre mentioned the blue heart emoji. There are twenty styles of heart emojis on the Apple emoji keyboard. Among them, Pierre believed that the blue heart would be interpreted by recipients as having a sense of coldness. Conventionally, the red heart emoji is for love in most cultures, as with French people. However, for Pierre, the blue heart emoji is a sign of kindness or friendliness, the unofficial 'friendzone' emoji. It conveys the intimacy between close friends, teammates, school classmates and work colleagues in a platonic manner. The blue heart is therefore mainly used to show feelings of affection to someone else, but only in a friendly manner. Women use the blue heart emoji with men whom they see as friends, and they avoid the red heart emoji which has the connotation of romance. If a man sends a red heart emoji to a woman, she will respond with a blue heart if she doesn't want to reciprocate his affection. Nonetheless, Pierre would never use affectionate emojis with his female friends. Overall, Pierre demonstrates similar sentiments to Maylis, as he is fairly free with his emoji use – particularly if we compare his responses to the case studies from Korea and Jordan. Nonetheless, we also see that he is slightly more cautious than Maylis in expressing affection to the opposite gender.

That said, like Maylis, when asked whether he would send emojis to a male professor, Pierre's response was a decisive no. He explained that he would not send any emojis to any of his professors, regardless of gender. In a formal relationship like teacher–student, emojis are inappropriate, as they do not suit a formal communication style thus it is very strange to use them. In some cases, if the professor uses emojis first, he will also use them. However, generally speaking, he won't.

In all the cultures explored, we have seen some level of sensitivity towards age, seniority and the opposite gender. Naturally, no one wants to come across as rude, and no one wants their intentions to be misunderstood. Consequently, our participants all changed their use of emojis to varying degrees, according

Interpersonal Dynamic	MM or FF	MM or FF	MF	MF	Junior-Senior	Junior-Senior	Older-Younger	Older-Younger
Intimacy Level	Close	Not close	Close	Not close	Close	Not close	Close	Not close
Affectionate Emoji Use Frequency	Frequent, but degree of use based on personal preference	Frequent, but degree of use based on personal preference	Personal preference*	Infrequent	No use or some use of "safe" emojis	No use	No use or some use of "safe" emojis	No use or some use of "safe" emojis

Figure 8.6 Table summarizing findings.

to the interpersonal dynamics of the conversation. In regard to gender, we have not collected evidence to say that men and women's emojis are different. Instead, we have focused on how people all over the world use emojis differently when speaking to someone of the opposite gender. Thus, our findings are summed up generally in Figure 8.6.

Even though one's emojing habits are the result of social norms and also an exemplification of them, young people today are encountering social media content from all over the world. Moreover, their interactions with people from other cultures, educational, recreational and so forth, are unimaginable for earlier generations. It is thus inevitable that their perception of emojis and social media interactions are influenced by, and at the same time influence, the overall social environment. For many Asian countries, the influence of Western culture is in terms of social media, films and TV series. Therefore, traditional Confucian or religious concepts of gender differences might no longer maintain as much significance as before. As a result, people may use affectionate or cute emojis and stickers in cross-gender conversations when the relationship between them is close enough in order to avoid any misinterpretations.

'Safe' emojis

In every culture, there exist what we may term 'safe' emojis. For instance, for Amira, the olive tree and smiley face emojis are safe emojis. In general, emojis expressing a smiley face are safe across cultures. Figure 8.7 shows some examples of Chinese 'safe' and 'sensitive' emojis. Without doubt, there will be individual differences, however, my Chinese participants widely agreed that the emojis on the left-hand side are safe to use to people in general, but those on the right-hand side are not.

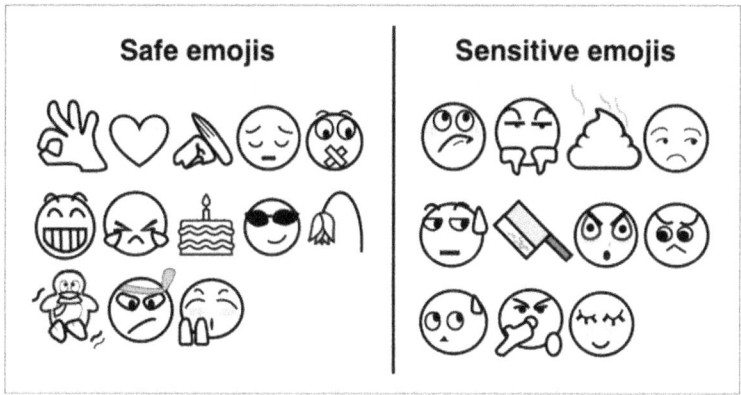

Figure 8.7 Safe and sensitive emojis. Source: Design by Loli Kim, reproduced with permission.

Figure 8.8 Emojis that are okay to send to your seniors (Chinese). Source: Design by Loli Kim, reproduced with permission.

The set of emojis in Figure 8.8 shows emojis that are acceptable to use with your seniors in a Chinese context. The ability to determine the appropriate use of emojis, avoiding offence, can be quite difficult and not very natural. Indeed, it is important to demonstrate competence with emojis, and in order to do so, you need to know the culture!

Individual matters

It is impossible to generalize emoji behaviours. Some people, for example, use emoji extensively and very often, whereas others do not. For some, limited use of emojis is fine, whereas for others it can lead them to feel insecure or hurt. Indeed, understanding and using emojis can be deeply personal. One's style matters greatly. What I found by interviewing different people over the last nine years for my study on emojis is that you cannot simply dismiss emojis as an activity of young people. Broadly speaking, the old and young distinction alone when it comes to smartphone communication will be less significant in comparison to an individual's style of multimodal communication. Perhaps, affordability and digital acceptability may mean more. If you own a decent smartphone and are keen to navigate the emoji world, no matter how old you are, you are very much able to do so.

Someone in their fifties once told me how a new emoji brightens his day, whereas my 76-year-old mother complained to me one day about my sister-in-law who sent a very big emoji to her. My mother was upset because my sister-in-law sent her an emoji rather than phoning her. For her, emojing itself is too casual and disrespectful, considering matters such as age and hierarchy. Indeed, this can be the case for a number of people: emojing is too casual. While emoji behaviour is sensitive to cultures, more often than not it also concerns personal choice and habits. One interviewee told me:

> I feel that emojis for me are something that I would more commonly use with my female friends. So, for example, *specific emojis like heart emojis. The ones blushing and the ones that show more affection*, I think I would use more with my female friends. Whereas with my male friends, I would use the thumbs up and hand emojis or the 100 with the line under, like those types of things, ones that aren't maybe as emotive in certain ways. Because usually they'll send a funny text, and I'll send a laughing emoji back, *where there's nothing sort of affectionate* (Ellie, 22)

From this, we can see that there is nothing which shows the informant's nation-state or cultural traits, nor her heritage or background, though her ability to emoji sensitively may give a hint as to her age group. The emoji world is one in which notions of culture and nation-state do not set the boundaries; no two people across the world will use emojis in an entirely identical manner.

Group chat matters

Belonging and group identity also matter greatly in emoji speak. In languages like English, language stylistics may be less sensitive in terms of individual or collective dynamics; whether you are talking to one person or a group will not change your actual language significantly. This is not the case in most Asian languages, for your language stylistics change dramatically whether you are talking to someone in a private space one-to-one, or whether you are talking to a group of people. Furthermore, when in a group chat, not only does it matter whether you know the group or not, but the relationship dynamics, such as a senior–junior relationship or peer relationship, are also important. All of my Asian informants told me how their emojing habits will change altogether if their teachers are included in the group chat – even if they are not talking to them directly. This is what we also observe in face-to-face communication. The presence of spectators matters greatly in Asian languages. Though you may be talking very casually to your friends or your family, you may change your ways of talking immediately and instantly slip into a more formal tone when an outsider comes to the scene.

Cross-cultural sensitivity

The internet has radically transformed our relationship with the rest of the world. While globalization chips away at the importance of national borders in the physical world, in the online world, there is not a whole lot to chip away at. Outside of state surveillance and censorship of the internet in some parts of the world, the internet is not structured along national borders, and users from all over the world often share the same online spaces, interacting freely with each other.

The typical online comments section is a melting pot populated with messages from languages all over the world, written in scripts that are familiar or unfamiliar. Even English comments, which usually comprise the majority due to the status of English as a global lingua franca, are incredibly diverse: British and American Englishes exist alongside World Englishes, such as Singaporean English, as well as alongside the plethora of English comments written by second-language speakers. In the online world, where free translation tools like Google Translate can instantly give you the general gist of a foreign-language message (or else spit out a stream of gibberish – but hey, we're not all perfect!), language is not an impenetrable barrier to participation in discussions. As such, we are exposed to a greater variety of languages and cultures online than ever before.

With such a blend of different languages and cultures, however, one can hardly expect communication to always go smoothly. Language is only part of the equation; culture also plays a big role in influencing what we say and how we say it, as well as how we interpret what others say. We don't always literally mean what we say, and in such cases some interpretation is necessary. This is especially the case with emojis. For example, sending a smiling emoji could potentially transmit a wide range of conflicting, and often unintended, meanings – smiles connote joy in American culture, while it has an added nuanced meaning of hiding 'embarrassment', 'displeasure' and 'anger' in Japanese culture.[14] A look at lists of emojis most commonly used in each country also gives us an idea of what is more culturally accepted or emblematic of the culture in that particular country. For example, here are excerpts of some findings from a study on instant messaging data in sixteen languages and regions regarding differences in emoji usage across countries: Arabic speakers tended to use emojis like male-centric icons, while French speakers used the heart emoji more than 50 per cent of the time.[15] It is also important to be sensitive to how certain emojis might be interpreted differently from your own culture or another culture that you are familiar with. For example, while sending the thumbs-up emoji might be seen as a positive sign of approval in many cultures, this same emoji could be interpreted as an offensive gesture in Greece and in the Middle East.[16] Therefore, it is useful to have some cultural knowledge in hand when using emojis so as to prevent any instances of committing offence.

One step further is the more coded and cipher-like use of emojis in the digital world which, when used in particular cultural contexts, may incur severe consequences. One area in which cultural (in)sensitivity in the use of emojis can result in significant political and/or social ramifications, is emoji censorship. As an example, recall how the Chinese government clamps down on any form of commemoration of the 1989 Tiananmen Square massacre by removing the candle, cake and breeze emojis from social platforms Weibo and WeChat every year prior to the anniversary of the tragedy.[17] There have also been instances in other countries whereby certain emojis are banned for various reasons, or can incur legal actions if used. In the United Arab Emirates, sending a middle finger emoji online makes one liable for legal prosecution, which can result in a jail term or hefty fine.[18] Similarly, in Saudi Arabia, sending a red heart emoji via WhatsApp amounts to harassment as it is a 'gesture with sexual connotations' even if it was only sent digitally.[19] Meanwhile in Indonesia, intolerance from religious conservatives in the country has led to gay-themed emojis being removed from the Line messaging application, with additional governmental pressure on other social media platforms to follow suit as well.[20]

Therefore, when using emojis in certain situations and environments, it is vital to consider the numerous factors (such as social, cultural, political and religious) that may be involved in defining what the emoji means within a certain culture and react appropriately according to the constraints of the culture. If Weibo emojis were used outside of a Chinese context, they lose all relation to the Tiananmen Square massacre, and take on new meanings in the new context. As such, emojing is a constant process of negotiating across different contexts, gaining the appropriate cultural competence and adjusting one's emoji usage according to what is acceptable.

While emojis have been censored due to their offensive connotations in specific cultural contexts, they can also be used as a tool to rebel against censorship and authoritarianism. An image consisting of a number seven emojis and multiple persons walking emojis spread throughout social media. It was used as a kind of coded phrase to indicate one's intention to join the protest against Russia's invasion of Ukraine.[21] This was meant to be a way to avoid strict censorship in Russia. Likewise, an emoji can become a regional symbol of protest. Recall again when Twitter launched a special emoji for the Milk Tea Alliance, a movement which united Taiwan, Thailand and Myanmar in their common fight against authoritarianism in their respective territories.[22] These emojis of protest gained meaning within their specific contexts of use because they were created for people who were directly involved. However, their meaning is opaque to those who do not have at least some pragmatic knowledge about the cultural context being implicated in the emojis. Therefore, having a clear understanding of how others interpret these emojis as well as cultural competence is essential if one wishes to emoji successfully within certain contexts.

Emojis do not have fixed definitions. There is no official dictionary that one can go to when one is unsure about an emoji's meaning. Instead, the meaning of an emoji is gradually built up based on how it is used. It is certainly a bottom-up process in which meaning is constantly in flux due to the constant negotiation by users. This is a culturally specific process, however, and the meaning that is settled upon in one community may be totally different from the meaning in another community. This can lead to miscommunications when different communities interact online, each bringing their own interpretation of an emoji's meaning.

Interpreting a smile

Many people think of emojis as having a universal meaning. After all, people all over the world smile when they're happy, right? Therefore, it isn't a big leap to assume that a smiling emoji would simply mean that you are happy, no matter where you are from. Yet strangely enough, even the most basic emojis are interpreted differently in different cultures – this includes the simplest of smiles!

How an emoji is interpreted depends on the cultural background of the sender and recipient, the context of the conversation, and subtle variations between similar emojis that impart their meaning based on their differences. For instance, there are several different smiling emojis, each with slightly differently shaped smiles and different expressions in the eyes. A smiling emoji with inexpressive eyes might therefore be interpreted as less sincere than a smiling emoji with happy-looking eyes, for example, thereby imparting the emoji lexicon with a diverse range of meanings.

This can also apply to smiling in the offline world. In Vietnam, for instance, a smile can be used to express one's happiness, contentment, agreement, acceptance, desire and tolerance. The same smile, however, can be used to show disagreement, discomfort, embarrassment, confusion, anger and even contempt. A smile can further serve as a response in the place of verbal expressions in a range of situations. For example, when someone says 'hello', Vietnamese people often simply smile at that person rather than respond with the same word. This is particularly prolific in the workplace, where senior Vietnamese employees rarely reply to the greetings of subordinates with verbal expressions and typically only smile in response. Within Vietnamese culture, the interpretation of which meaning is being expressed by a smile often comes down to the understanding of the situational context and its combination with the expressions of other facial features. Paying particular attention to the eyes can be crucial to arriving at the correct interpretation of a smile's intended meaning. For example, when smiling for the purpose of the agreement, the eyes are often closed partly so that the eyes move with the smile.

The Vietnamese interpretation of a smile clearly differs from other interpretations across the world. For example, in Korea, non-verbal expressions play a vital role in the completion of verbal expressions. Using a non-verbal expression in place of a verbal expression tends to be interpreted negatively. Therefore, a smile in replacement of a verbal utterance would potentially carry attitudinal meanings that the smile would not convey in the same situation in a Vietnamese context. These differences inevitably extend to emojing, not only in how different emojis are used but the types of visual resources used (whether emojis, emoticons, stickers, etc.) and their recognition between Korean people and Vietnamese people. For example, in an interview with a 23-year-old Vietnamese woman, she discusses her first encounters with the Korean smiley and sad face emoticons, and how initially she did not understand what they meant:

The first emoticon I came across was the double caret ^^ which resembles the eyes of someone smiling. One day I entered a chat site on my PC and someone typed hi to me with this emoticon. Back then I did not know what this symbol meant, and I remember asking for clarification. Koreans also express sad faces with the Korean vowel combinations, such as ㅠㅠ, ㅜㅜ, and ㅜㅡ, indicating tear drops.

Emoticons such as the smiling eyes/eyebrows ('^^'), crying eyes ('ㅠㅠ' and 'ㅜㅜ'), squiggle ('~~'), and various forms of e-laughter such as 'kkk' ('ㅋㅋㅋ') and 'hhh' ('ㅎㅎㅎ') are popular among Korean speakers and are generally not recognizable outside of East Asia except by Korean language learners and those involved in Korean popular culture fandoms (K-fandoms). As such, emojis and emoticons are often regional – be that in their existence in the first place, or in their interpretation once used.

Prayer or greeting?

The folded hands emoji is another example of a widely recognized emoji with an array of meaning potential depending upon the cultural context. In Western countries and religious contexts, this emoji is often used to reference prayer. In Japan, pressing both palms together in this manner is an expression of supplication or gratitude, seen often at Shinto temples as part of a ceremonial greeting. The Japanese platform Docomo even provides a fuller version of this emoji. In comparison, this emoji is often known as the 'namaste' emoji in India and is often used in introductory messages, placed after an addressee's name or after the initial greeting. Many have also adopted this emoji as a means of high-fiving someone online. In China, however, it is used to refer to sex – attempting to high-five a Chinese person using this emoji could result in a serious misunderstanding! Similarly, angel emojis are believed to be a sign of death in China, and sending one could be seen as a threat. In contrast, in the West, this emoji may have no deeper meaning other than perhaps expressing innocence.

Happy, tragic or ridiculous?

Another example is the tears of joy emoji, which is also often used by Westerners to express the idea of crying with laughter. In Korea, however, this emoji is to express a tragicomic nuance and emotional duality, in situations that are both funny and sad. Meanwhile in China, this emoji is used when a person is lost for words in circumstances that are felt to be ridiculous.

Figure 8.9 Love hotel or hospital? Source: NotoColorEmoji: © 2021 Google Inc, OFL License.

Love hotel or hospital?

Then there are the less obvious emojis, that are specific to a particular culture and do not hold the same meaning elsewhere, or which are represented in different ways in different cultures leading to misinterpretation in other cultures (Figure 8.9). Japanese emojis provide a good example of this because emojis were first introduced in Japan and many of these early emojis were created with specific reference to Japanese cultural items. For instance, the U+1F3E9 emoji is commonly interpreted as representing a hospital outside of East Asia. This misinterpretation is based on the emoji's depiction of a large building with an 'H' and a heart symbol, which can easily be interpreted as standing for 'Hospital', with the heart representing the care provided there. However, originally, this emoji was created to represent a 'love hotel' – a form of hotel catering to guests looking for a discrete place to stay, often by the hour, which is well known for being used to conduct extra-marital affairs and by young couples who are unable to bring their girlfriends/boyfriends to their parents' home overnight because of the cultural unacceptability of this in Japan (and other East Asian regions). If users do not live in a country where love hotels exist, then they are unlikely to intuit this meaning from the emoji, which could lead to misunderstanding and embarrassment when messaging people from those regions. Emojipedia now has confirmed that the emoji indeed means 'love hotel', but this does not stop people from misunderstanding.

Summary

Emojis do not exist in a vacuum. In the Western context, grammar is typically not modulated by relational hierarchies. The opposite is true for Asian languages, such as Korean and Japanese, where grammar is sensitive to hierarchical dynamics. Emojis are shaped by the same interpersonal dynamics as offline speech, namely: age, intimacy and gender. These are the three dominant factors that determine whether emoji use is appropriate or inappropriate. Appropriate emoji use can lead to a greater sense of community, closeness, kinship and solidarity. Inappropriate emoji use can have the opposite effect, causing tension, friction and conflict. Unlike in Western contexts, images associated with humour are typically avoided in online texting spaces, because people from Asian societies tend to avoid potentially rude or silly expressions, even among family. Emoji use is the product of complex interpersonal dynamics that have often been overlooked in contemporary linguistics. In mirroring face-to-face communication, juggling interpersonal relations adds a complex dimension to the world. This often creates problems for learners of Korean or Japanese, as they need to be careful with their use of emojis so as not to offend recipients. There are many potential instances where the wrong use of an emoji can cause a negative response and damage one's relationship with a friend or colleague. Emojis are sometimes used to rescue awkward situations due to the ambiguity of their meanings, but this function does not always follow through; sometimes when emojis are used to fill awkward silence it has an adverse effect of seeming insincere.

Emojis play a significant part in our current digital age in which social media platforms have a prominent role and enable increasingly diverse interactions between people from a range of backgrounds. With this in mind, it is therefore important to possess a level of competency regarding the use of emojis. Taking into account the context of a conversation in which one may use emoticons, for instance, is vital to enable smooth and expressive communication. There are a number of emojis that have thrived, survived and even died (in metaphorical terms) throughout the years, and what is notable is that we cannot really predict which ones will make it. The world of emojis is certainly a bottom-up approach, a grassroots initiative. Despite what Emojipedia may state, the exact meanings of emojis are in constant negotiation by different groups of people and individuals. There is no central authority that is able to dictate how an emoji should be used and received. Indeed, emojis exemplify the fluid, dynamic, and creative nature of human communication, in which pragmatic elements (a.k.a context) must be taken into consideration.

9

Emoji Stylistics

When my father-in-law first met my mother and a few of my friends, he winked at them. We knew it was just a funny joke made by an old man, but it is not so common, in Korean culture at least, for older men to be humorous and wink. To a less understanding crowd, the gesture could have been perceived as inappropriate, as there is a high expectation for how older men should behave in Korean society. I, too, would rarely wink at someone, if ever. This permeates into my emoji use too. Even though I have lived in England for many years, I still can't use a wink emoji freely because of the flirtatious connotations it could have. Even though my husband often suggests I add a wink to the end of a message to soften a request and make my messages light-hearted, I still can't. A wink's other connotations always linger in my mind, so I am hesitant to use one.

How we emoji matters a lot. It says a lot about us to other people and can even indicate where we belong. In other words, emojis signify both our personal and group identities. Emojis don't exist in a vacuum. We need to know which culture or subculture they have been used in to understand their nature. Thus, a top-down prescriptive approach is no longer valid as emoji speak adapts fluidly to the needs of subcultural groups and everyone as individuals.

Emoji stylistics

In this chapter, we will be looking at something that I have termed *emoji stylistics*.[1] This is how one adapts the use of emojis, memes, stickers and other digital communication features to suit the intricate interpersonal dynamics between two or more people in dialogue and their respective sociocultural standpoints. In fact, numerous factors shape emoji use, with some of the most dominant factors being age and gender. The notion of emojis being a marginal function of digital communication for the purpose of delivering a message in a gentler tone dismisses their effectiveness. It makes it seem like an obligatory norm, rather than a function that is useful and sought after for its efficacy.[2] Emojis can serve a more fulfilling function, as they can aid users in establishing an amicable bond with the recipient when used appropriately. If misused, emojis can upset communication and create tension. Emoji stylistics are used by everyone, regardless of their language, but in the following, we will consider how they are used in Korean. Korean society is a good example because it is heavily hierarchical, so Korean speakers have to pay careful attention to their emoji stylistics.

Asian languages are notorious for their socio-pragmatic complexity, and Korean is no exception. The honorific system of Korean is the most systematic among all known languages,[3]. Still, other Asian languages such as Japanese, Chinese and Javanese also exhibit rich systems of honorification that encode the relative social hierarchies between the speaker, addressee and referent.[4] In my book *More than Polite*, I propose that how Korean people express their feelings and attitudes is almost like a performance, even before they open their mouths to speak. Most respectful and deferential meanings that are so important in Korea's hierarchical society are expressed through non-verbal expressions, including bowing, nodding, hand gestures and eye contact. Saying one thing but not visually indicating your position with your body can make you seem insincere. Before emojis, written and typed Korean had no way of showing such body language. Now that we live in an emoji era, body language can be transferred into online communication. Hence, emojis matter all the more.

For Korean speakers, it is crucial to choose the right emojis for each conversation. The right emoji can be chosen only after considering the person with whom they are speaking and what level of respect, deference or intimacy is appropriate. This process can be thought of as similar to the process we go through when selecting an outfit for a particular occasion. Depending on where we are going, we choose an outfit in an appropriate style. We wear pyjamas to bed, not to go to work, and we wear a suit to work, but not to go to bed. We wear a thick coat and scarf in the winter, but not in summer. Other aspects of the environment are also taken into consideration. We might dress more formally when meeting someone for the first time, such as on a first date, and then dress more informally as the relationship develops. We might even be influenced by further factors, like meeting a friend who always tries to dress well, and so we do too. In Korean communication, speech and gesture styles also need to be selected for the occasion, and similar factors to those considered when choosing what to wear are considered when deciding how to communicate.

Let's look at Korean honorifics. Korean has different levels of speech styles that show different levels of politeness. These speech styles can be broadly divided into casual, polite and formal styles, but their distinction becomes almost inapplicable as we embrace our emoji speak. Conventional speech styles become totally outdated. There is even a speech style used mostly in online messaging alone that uses non-standard grammar to find a halfway point between the honorific and casual styles.[5] So, the question arises, does having different speech levels make emoji speak harder in Asian languages than in Western European languages? Well, yes and no. Yes, because using the wrong emoji and being disrespectful can have serious consequences. No, because the proper use of emojis can help to further demonstrate one's respect or deference towards the recipient. The misuse of honorifics leads to conflict and is considered ungrammatical in most instances. This linguistic phenomenon naturally transfers to the online space, where the relational standing between speakers is to be considered when choosing punctuation and emoji.

Younger users tend to end sentences with emojis rather than morphological endings on social media, especially Twitter.[6] This raises the question: could emojis replace standard grammatical endings? Sometimes final consonants (ㅇ *ng*, ㅁ *m*, ㅂ *b*), which do not have any grammatical status or function in traditional Korean grammar, are used in instant messaging.[7] It is not apparent what meaning difference each of these final consonants is making. Despite the absence of any apparent grammatical function, they add some emotional meanings that somewhat reflect the speaker's willingness to communicate with the other party and their friendly attitude.

In the following example, the propositional meaning of each sentence is the same. Yet, each model exhibits different emotional and attitudinal meanings. The last four examples have somewhat happy emotions, whereas the first is liable to be interpreted as more formal and serious because of the use of a full stop.[8] Emojis mean that one sentence can significantly vary in attitudinal meaning. There is far more variation and complexity in our communication now that we have emojis. All of the following options are all acceptable; you would simply pick one according to your style and desired emotional tone. Note that there is no neutral sentence: (a) has a more serious and/or clipped tone, whereas (b) to (e) have friendly tones. Emojis require us to 'show our hand' regarding our emotions or attitudes. There is no such thing as a neutral tone now that we have emoji speak.

a. 알겠습니다.
   algesssumnda 'ok, I understand'.

b. 알겠슴니당
      algesssumnidang 'ok, I understand'.
   c. 알겠슴니당 ㅋㅋㅋ ~~~~
      algesssumnidang kkk 'ok, I understand'.
   d. 알겠슴니당 ^^;
      alkgesssumnidang 'ok, I understand'.
   e. 알겠슴니당 ^^
      algesssumnidang 'ok, I understand'.

I have analysed a database of youth messaging from Korean speakers in Seoul.[9] Within this database, I found very few messages that used punctuation marks. This was also the case with question marks. When other morphological or contextual cues were provided, those punctuation markers were less likely to appear. In instant messaging, one unit typically appears within one speech bubble. Hence, the grammatical function to 'finish' a sentence through punctuation markers seems to be unnecessary.[10] In addition, I found that Korean spacing conventions were frequently violated.

When asked about their usage of the full stop, participants responded in the following ways:

   a. 'I use a full stop when I want to show that I am serious.'
   b. 'I don't use a full stop because I can't see it in my keyboard immediately and just because I can't be bothered.'
   c. 'I can't be bothered. This is my habit.'
   d. 'I've hardly ever seen my friends use a full stop. Really no one around me uses it.'=

Responses along the lines of (c), that using a full stop is too much effort, were the most common.

When asked about their usage of emoticons, or specifically the use of non-verbal signs instead of punctuation markers, participants responded as follows:

   a. 'Well, if something is really funny, I use ㅋㅋ (laughter) signs for about five lines. If it's not too funny, I use ㅋ signs once or twice.'
   b. 'ㅋ (laughter) signs can be used to show that you can't be bothered to respond. Using ㅋ more than three times can mean that it's really funny.'

The participants showed that the number of the laughter signs ㅋ used varies based on how humorous the message they are responding to is. It can also be used as a substitution for a word-based response when the responder cannot be bothered to type out a response.

My participants mentioned that they often use the enter key, which sends the message, in place of a space or full stop ending the sentence. The participants prioritize speed and efficiency and would prefer to break messages up into smaller chunks rather than obey grammatical conventions of full stops and other sentence breaks. Efficiency often played a crucial role in that if grammatical patterns were redundant, participants did not bother to use them. A critical characteristic of instant messaging is the speed of responses. One can often see whether the other party has seen one's message or not, and if a reply is delayed after the message has been read, it can create a misunderstanding. In a situation such as this, where a quick response is required, the time restriction and the accompanying rule of efficiency play a crucial role.

Emojis for transparency: Tone indicators and tone tags

The tone of written messages can be difficult to interpret even when interacting with somebody you know well, but this is made even harder in public online spaces like social media, where one can interact with thousands of strangers in a short span of time. The rapidity and scale of these interactions often make it difficult to interpret them in a nuanced way, and there is plenty of room to misinterpret or misunderstand others' comments in these public online spaces. A sincere compliment might be read as sarcastic, causing hurt feelings or a sarcastic joke might be interpreted as the commenter's genuine opinion. In rare cases, users may even intentionally misinterpret the tone of another user's comment or take them out of context to harm their reputation. As such, communicating one's intentions and tone clearly in these public spaces is especially important. This is one area in which emojis can help us: attaching a winking emoji to one's message can often indicate a joke, for example. However, emojis are also usually open to interpretation and may be used ironically or sarcastically, complicating matters. The matter of interpretation can also be especially hard for neurodivergent users (for instance, those on the autistic spectrum) who may have particular difficulty accurately reading tone online.

In order to solve the issue of accurately interpreting tone online, some users have introduced a system of 'tone tags' or 'tone indicators', where users label the tone of their messages in specific terms, leaving no room for error. These take the form of forward slashes followed by combinations of letters, such as */j* ('joking'), */li* ('literal'/'literally'), */s* or */sarc* ('sarcastic'/'sarcasm'), */srs* ('serious') and */gen* ('genuine'). Although such a systematic implementation of tone indicators is a relatively new phenomenon, these tags formally resemble those previously used online, which mimicked those of HTML. Much earlier uses of tags among earlier internet users came from those familiar with coding languages, such as enclosing sarcastic comments with <sarcasm> </sarcasm> or ending a ranting message with /rant.[11] Indeed, while most of these tone indicators may be incomprehensible to non-Gen Z users, /s may be the exception, as the use of this particular tag for sarcasm far predates the systematized Gen Z tone indicators and is likely a holdover from the earlier HTML-style tags. The fact that a tag for sarcasm was introduced before the rest of these tone indicators may be because sarcasm and irony have been perennial problems in text-based communication even before the internet; an inverted exclamation mark (¡) was proposed to indicate irony as early as 1968.[12] Once again, online communication demands that we make our intentions completely transparent. Labelling is one thing, but is this constant transparency actually healthy?

Tone indicators are still far from mainstream or accepted part of internet language, however. According to a New York Times article by Ezra Marcus, these are popular 'within some Twitter and Tumblr communities of young people with overlapping interests in identity representation, anime and K-pop fandom, twee aesthetics, and sensitivity towards mental health and gender issues'.[13] As mentioned before, they are especially useful for neurodivergent users. For his New York Times article, Marcus interviewed Twitter user Michael Guazzelli, who identifies as neurodivergent. According to Guazzelli, although tone indicators are 'mostly used by neurodivergent people', they have increasingly been 'spreading to all people who find them useful or just want to be clear and help nd [neurodivergent] people understand things (which is most appreciated by us!)'.[14]

Tone tags are also generational, most strongly associated with Gen Z users. Because each tag is highly abbreviated, usually consisting of one to three characters, most terms are not immediately comprehensible to those unfamiliar with the tag system. As such, proponents of the system have created reference resources providing lists of common tags.[15] Despite the goal of these tags being to eliminate ambiguity in one's tone, however, it seems that there is no one central authority determining what the established meaning of each tag is. Members make numerous unofficial resources of the communities using the tags, but because anyone can make their own list of tags it seems possible that a clash of meanings could arise. As for the future of these tags, it seems likely that they will remain in use within the communities for which they are most helpful, such as among neurodivergent users. It also seems likely that some of the more valuable and intuitive tags, such as /gen and /srs, could enter more mainstream use online.

Emojis as collectors' items: Creating stickers on WeChat

China's most extensive instant messaging service, WeChat, offers a unique feature called 'custom stickers' in its emoji and sticker section. Under custom stickers, users can create their stickers for free, using images or videos from their camera roll. To these images, users can add text and other stickers to make the image's meaning clear and/or add humour to the image. After sending one of these custom stickers, other users can save the stickers to their custom sticker collection. As such, emojis on WeChat are like collectors' items. Users creatively make stickers, using their wit and humour, creating images that may be sardonic, sarcastic, cute or endearing. One person sends their custom sticker out, and users gradually save and send on the sticker, resulting in a snowball effect. A custom sticker can gain popularity exponentially (Figure 9.1).

Users often create custom stickers using images of celebrities. For example, it is ubiquitous to see custom stickers of children starring in a primetime Korean reality show, *The Return of Superman*. Similarly, images of online celebrities and child models are selected for custom stickers, too, as their pictures are highly cute. There are also stickers featuring scenes from dramas, in which iconic lines are featured on the sticker, and/or iconic expressions are captioned with novel phrases. New stickers emerge from subcultural groups, further reaffirming language development's move from central authorities to the grassroots.

Figure 9.1 WeChat offers a 'custom sticker' feature, to which one can save stickers. By clicking the '+' on the left, the user can create their own stickers using images from their camera roll.

These images are creative commons, so users have a right to use them, but questions of copyright and rights to circulation may arise as this culture grows.

Users have no legal rights to use these images, yet this has become a widespread emojing culture in China. The original pictures are captioned with words or contain small icons, to enhance the facial expressions and actions depicted in the images. The captions may not have the same meaning as was present in the original situations; instead, the emoji-maker manipulates the image creatively to represent their own interpretation. These self-made emojis are employed in conversations with close friends or family, where there is space to be cute or sarcastic without the risk of misunderstanding. These emojis would not be sent to those with whom one is not familiar. Despite this, these stickers gain such popularity that a featured character, who may have started with one or two custom stickers, becomes so widely used that they are added to WeChat's official sticker gallery.

In China, and for the broader population of WeChat users, using emojis is an opportunity to create and innovate. Upon seeing something funny, cute or entertaining, users can easily share the image with their friends, saving the image to their personal library for later use. On the other hand, users view emojis also as collectors' items. If they see an emoji that they believe is particularly humorous or impactful, they can easily save it to their stickers collection. Then, when they wish to send a sticker, they can look through their own personal collection of stickers to find the sticker with the perfect nuanced meaning. WeChat users uniquely endeavour to create and collect the funniest, cutest, most popular sticker collection in an individual yet crowd-sourced manner.

Emojis as generational emblems: The case of TikTok

TikTok is the platform of Gen Z. Over 60 per cent of the platform's users were born after 1996.[16] As of 2021, the app has recorded more than 1 billion users (with Douyin alone recording around 600 million users in China) and is the fifth most-used mobile application.[17] TikTok is most used in Southeast Asia (198 million) with significant user numbers in North America as well (105 million). In particular, TikTok's most considerable user numbers can be found in the United States, Brazil, Indonesia, and India (before the banning of TikTok there).

TikTok has its own graphically unique emojis. There are forty-six secret emojis that can be 'unlocked' by typing certain codewords in square brackets, which can only be used in the TikTok application.[18] For example, if you were to remember ✎ to ✎ take ✎ out ✎ the ✎ trash

Figure 9.2 A style of comment used on TikTok, whereby each word is punctuated by an emoji. Source: Emojis from NotoColorEmoji: © 2021 Google Inc, OFL License.

type [smile] in TikTok, a pink variant of a smile emoji will appear. There are also a series of flattop emojis. There are two advantages of such emojis specific to TikTok. First, they can signal one's insider expertise about the 'secret language' of TikTok.[19] Second, these secret emojis are graphically rendered in the same way across all mobile operating systems, which removes any ambiguity of meaning.[20] These features establish the aforementioned secret emojis as uniquely belonging to TikTok, which accords a special status of being part of a subculture.

TikTok also breathes new life into existing and well-established emojis by imbuing them with some new meanings. This can largely be attributed to Generation Z or Gen Z (loosely referring to those born from 1996 to 2010), who have popularized the use of alternative meanings of Unicode emojis, making them specific to TikTok.[21] An example is the replacement of the laughter emoji with the chair emoji, which initially emerged as an insider joke among a group of TikTok users that later went viral. On other platforms, the chair emoji generally does not have any other special meanings other than an actual wooden chair. Additionally, the *writing hand emoji*, which usually refers to the general act of writing on other social media platforms, refers specifically to the act of taking mental notes on TikTok. In this platform-specific usage, *writing hand emoji* normally accompanies every word in the sentence, to punctuate that the sentence is being noted in Figure 9.2.

A trend of combining emojis has also arisen on TikTok. A combination of the pleading emoji (which represents begging, adoration or feeling moved) and the left and right-pointing emojis together to present ideas of bashfulness, awkwardness and/or apprehension. This unique style of emoji created by TikTok's Gen Z users showcases more specific details of the body language related to awkwardness.

Emojis as created by subcultural groups

What does () mean to you? Nothing? In Korean Buddhist communities, a pair of parentheses () signifies a greeting. In the screenshot in Figure 9.3, we see one sender end their message with several pairs of parentheses () () (), and then the other members of the group chat respond with three () too.

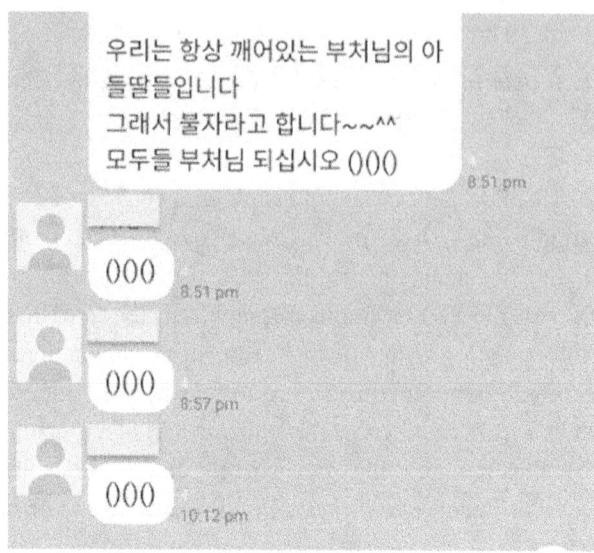

Figure 9.3 Conversation in a Buddhist group chat.

This is a form of greeting only known in Buddhist communities. Outside of these spaces, a () would be totally unintelligible, appearing like nothing more than a typo. This is a totally innovative use of parenthesis that has emerged in one particular group of society. The emoji is used to create solidarity between members of the community and to indicate belonging to the group via specialist emoji knowledge. Rather than coming from a central linguistic authority, the subcultural group themselves created this emoji.

Emojis as badges: Emojing communities in K-pop fandoms

The internet has been revolutionary for fan communities. Geographical barriers are no longer an obstacle to the formation of communities centred on particular interests. The internet allows fans to 'form communities that could not otherwise exist', while also providing 'mountains of information for the devout follower'.[22] Additionally, the internet has 'lower[ed] the barrier for the creation and distribution of content', disrupting the previously established divisions between audiences and producers. Fans no longer need to wait for official producers to drip-feed them new information or content. Fans are free to create and distribute their own theories, clips, memes, fanworks and the like, with few barriers stopping other fans from enjoying their creations. This is not to underplay the creative efforts made by fandoms pre-internet. The internet has simply made these fanworks far more accessible to more fans than ever before. As with any community, communication between fans is hugely important in these online fandoms, and emoji help make this communication friendly, fluid and fun. Emojing can help members communicate with each other more clearly and signal their membership in the community. Fans can also express their emotions more intensely, form inside jokes within their community, and support their favourite creators. We can see how this manifests when we analyse their emoji use.

Online fan communities are very real social spaces; some users spend most of their time online within fan communities to which they belong, and deep and lasting relationships are often formed within these spaces. As such, users often come to strongly identify with their fandoms and may wish to signal the membership of their fandoms to other users, both as a badge of pride and as a way of finding other members of their community – especially on sites like Twitter, where dedicated message boards for particular subjects do not exist and all users post on the same universal platform.

For example, K-pop fans on platforms like Twitter or internet forums often use hashtags and emojis to signal fandom membership and support their favourite artists and band members. Using hashtags of the name of one's favourite group or group member can help other fans (or even the group itself) find one's post, potentially sparking conversations about a shared interest. For example, supporters of the girl group TWICE may use hashtags like #TWICE, #sana or #jihyo. Emoji are a more visual representation of one's support and love for a group, and by using emoji associated with one's preferred group, one's account becomes immediately recognizable to other users within the fandom. The meaning of these emoji or emoji combinations is also more opaque than hashtags; users unfamiliar with one's fandom are unable to interpret which fandom or group members they are associated with, creating a sense of shared knowledge among fans.

One example of these fandom emojis can be seen with fans of the group GFRIEND. The GFRIEND fandom incorporates the official colours of the group into their fandom emoji. K-pop groups often have official colours to represent the group's aesthetic and concept, and these colours are often used in the group logo, merchandise like light sticks and supportive banners made by fans. These colours are a way for fans to associate with the group, both online and offline.

Because GFRIEND's official colours are identified as Pantone's Cloud Dancer, Scuba Blue and Ultraviolet, the white, blue and purple heart emojis have been adopted as the fandom emojis for the group. The group members have endorsed this idea by using these emojis to express love and gratitude for their fans, as depicted in the image earlier. These emojis have also become a tool for fans to express their support for GFRIEND online.

GFRIEND is not the only group to incorporate their official colours in their fandom emoji: BTOB's official colour is sky blue, so their fandom has adopted the blue heart emoji, while ChungHa's fandom uses green, blue and purple heart emoji and a crescent moon emoji, because ChungHa's official logo is a crescent moon filled with the three colours blended together. You may have noticed some overlap, as the blue heart emoji is associated with all three groups just discussed. This is because although the specific shades of the official colours differ from each other (as identified on the Pantone colour scale), the emoji repertoire is too limited to represent the precise shades of the official colours, and so multiple different fandoms represent different shades using the same emoji.

Custom K-pop emojis: BTS and EXO

In exceptional cases, however, a K-pop group may be provided with a custom emoji for themselves and their fandom on social media platforms like Twitter. BTS is an example of this: while they are usually associated with the purple heart emoji, Twitter added a specific BTS emoji (a bulletproof vest with 'BTS' written on it) in 2016, which would automatically be added to posts containing specific hashtags (e.g. #BTS). This emoji reflects the group character, as the group name 방탄소년단 (*Bangtansonyeondan*), literally translates into 'Bulletproof Boy Scouts', which explains the bulletproof vest. The BTS-specific emoji creates a heightened intimacy and connectivity, as no other fandom can use this emoji. As mentioned earlier, there are frequent cases of different fandoms having overlapping emoji, but creating a unique emoji tailored to the image and identity of the group creates a special means of recognition in online spaces. They would never be confused for another fandom and can stand out among the millions of K-pop fans online.

BTS also played a role in popularizing the 'finger-heart' gesture. The gesture is a heart shape made by crossing your index finger over your thumb (Figure 9.4). The gesture gained popularity among K-idols and is commonly used when K-idols pose for photographs. It became so widely used that even former South Korean president Moon Jae-in and North Korean leader Kim Jong-un have been photographed using the gesture.[23] This gesture started offline and then moved into online spaces when Unicode added it to the emoji keyboard. Then later,

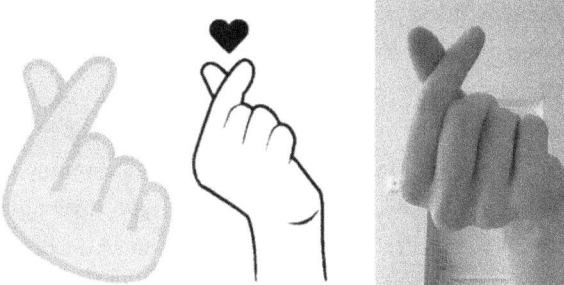

Figure 9.4 A finger heart emoji (left and middle) and the real-life gesture (right). Left emoji by NotoColorEmoji: © 2021 Google Inc, OFL License, and middle image designed by Loli Kim and reproduced with permission.

the term 'finger heart' was coined. This means that the finger heart first existed as a gesture, then an emoji and finally a letter word. The finger heart originates from a subculture, and now it is used all over the world, and this is due to the power of the K-fandom. Now that the finger heart lives on the emoji keyboard too, it is used across the globe by users who interpret it in their own way. The finger heart gesture is thus important because it shows how emoji words exist across online and offline spaces, and how letter words are becoming of lesser significance. Most people outside Korea cannot understand the Korean alphabet and yet they can understand this emoji. There is a parallel between our online and offline gestures, as the finger heart demonstrates.

Emojis provide a deeper and more personal connection than simply using a hashtag. While using a hashtag is a mere reference to or mention of the group, emojis have an underlying expression of endearment. The use of emojis when discussing the group not only shows solidarity within the fandom but also connects the K-pop artist to the fandom, as seen by the common use of the same emojis by GFRIEND members and their fans. Using a designated emoji is not the only way of expressing a fan's support and love, fans can also deliberately mimic the way their favourite singers use other emojis too.

In one thread on the website Quora user grace xin yu has observed which emojis are most frequently used by individual BTS band members. For instance, they note that BTS member Jungkook has not been using many emojis in his feed except for one that 'has a drop of sweat coming down the forehead and is smiling'. Here, emojis are a part of wider online behaviour along with the use of hashtags and captions. Possessing knowledge of such behaviour and preferences can be a marker of a fan's dedication to the group, as it is evidence of how they have devoted their time to follow the group on social media.

Another example is using particular emojis in association with the image of each artist in a given group. Some K-pop forum users have assigned each member an emoji according to their looks, likes, tendencies or personalities. One Reddit user posted a list of emojis they thought represented the K-pop group EXO. They allocated the bear face emoji to EXO member Kai and a bunny face emoji to Suho, as they apparently physically resemble their respective animals. Physical appearance is not the only criterion used for selecting an emoji, however. Xiumin is identified with the blue butterfly emoji as he calls EXO-L (the official fandom name of EXO) his butterflies. These emojis may be used to identify and visually represent the artists on social media and forums, but it is also a sign of a fan's love for the group, like a pet name. According to the Reddit thread 'Are idols aware of the emojis we use to represent them?'[24] some emojis associated with individual members become so widely known within the fandom that the artists also use them on their social media captions or Vlive titles (Vlive is a Korean live video streaming service) to embrace the image given to them by their fans. The emoji become the artist's alternate face on social media, as a symbol or an icon of their identity. Such emojis are common knowledge among fans, and being aware of each member's emoji is essential in proving one's support towards the group itself.

The use of emoji ultimately creates a sense of unity for the K-pop fandoms, both among the fans and between the fans and artists. Within K-pop fandoms, emojis are a tool that ties the fans together and expresses their love towards the artists. This goes both ways, and the artists reciprocate this support by using these emojis in their social media as well. Being aware of the different types and combinations of emojis and using them appropriately is an expression of one's presence and identity. Fans can use these emojis to connect with fellow fans or show support for the artist, and the artist may use them to express gratitude and love for their fandom. Although the fans may not always speak English, most K-pop groups have fan bases stretching beyond mainland Korea, and emojis break language barriers and connect the fandom and the artist, as a non-verbal expression of endearment.

Emojis for expression: Reaction images in K-pop fandoms

Reaction images and gifs are highly prevalent within online fandoms, particularly those concerning fans' attachment to particular characters or celebrities, such as K-pop. These reaction images and gifs function as non-verbal expressions that simply depict one's own emotions by matching them to the emotions felt by the subject in the image or gif. As we will see, this type of non-verbal expression is

Figure 9.5 A sample reaction image used by a fan. Public Domain Image from FreeSVG.org and tear drops from NotoColorEmoji: © 2021 Google Inc, OFL License.

popular in these communities that are built upon fans' extreme attachment and affection for their favourite character, celebrity or group member. These reaction images are often highly exaggerated, allowing users to express the full depth of their attachment. For instance, Figure 9.5 shows a sample of the kind of reaction image that a fan might send.

This image expresses the intense affection the fan feels for Yoongi upon seeing the picture using a hamster that resembles *Ebichu*, from the anime series *Oruchuban Ebichu*, tearing up with emotion. This example is quite representative of reaction images, which often use cartoon characters or pictures of animals to depict the emotion felt by the speaker; they are not limited to photos of humans.

Users are not restricted to the use of just a single image, though, and it is possible to use a sequence of several images to tell a simple story using Twitter's ability to attach multiple images to a post. The sequence of images follows the same grammar as the panels of a comic book and can be read as a short narrative. This is a highly creative way of taking advantage of a social media platform's features to create new avenues of non-verbal expression online and shows the creativity and agency users have in shaping the forms of online communication.

Although we have only shown one example of a BTS fan expressing their intense emotions using reaction images, some K-pop fans do attempt to use text to represent these emotions by using 'keysmash' text. 'Keysmash' text is generated by pressing your hands on your keyboard to generate a random sequence of letters. This works to convey a sense of extreme excitement or emotion as if one has totally lost control and cannot put one's feelings into proper words. Another aspect of K-pop fandom language worth noting is their absorption of Korean terms into their communication in English online. For instance, the use of the Korean word *selca*, above, a shortening of the English words 'self camera' that is equivalent to the English term 'selfie'. This illustrates how online fandoms often serve as good entry points for introducing foreign terms into English.

While the meaning behind the reaction images and gifs like the one we discussed earlier can usually be straightforwardly grasped without additional context, some memes are far more obscure and can only be understood by a relatively limited niche of users. When used in this way, memes can function as a way of signalling one's membership to an in-group, while displaying one's wit and sense of humour; in other words, memes are one way of purchasing social capital online.

Emojis as inside jokes: Memes in Manga and Anime fandoms

Within online subcultures, such as anime communities, memes are also used in a similar way to create solidarity with other fans by referencing shared knowledge within the community. For instance, anime is a medium with a huge number of genre tropes ranging from common character archetypes such as the *tsundere*[25] to stock scenarios such as the 'beach episode'. These tropes are often so ubiquitous that more self-aware anime series will frequently subvert them or break the fourth wall to comment on them. Fans also notice and discuss these tropes within anime communities, and they often become inside jokes within said communities.

One common trope, for instance, is showing characters who are late to school running with a piece of toast in their mouth, as they had no time to eat breakfast. This trope became so common that it is now more often parodied than invoked seriously. For example, in the series *Daily Lives of High School Boys* one character is shown running to school while eating a plate of curry.

Another more recent trope comes from the *isekai* subgenre of anime. *Isekai* means 'alternate world', and series within this subgenre typically begin with the dissatisfied, boring protagonist dying suddenly in the real world, only to be reincarnated in a fantasy world inspired by fantasy role-playing games. The way in which the protagonist dies is of minimal importance to these stories, however, and many shows opted for the lazy method of having them be hit by a truck. Like the toast trope, this became so ubiquitous that many anime protagonists in this subgenre now acknowledge the trope by having the protagonist be particularly aware of the danger of being run over by a truck, for instance. English-language anime communities also picked up on this trope and began personifying this deadly truck as 'Truck-kun' (with the Japanese *-kun* suffix implying a sense of affection for the truck) because of the way these trucks effectively improve the protagonists' lives by taking them away from the dissatisfying real world to a fantasy world filled with magic.

So well known is this trope that it has even spawned an English-language meme that references several ways trucks are used as plot devices in modern anime. Screenshots from multiple animes, each of which features being hit by a truck as a significant plot device, are combined into a static montage.

Sometimes these memes become more than non-verbal methods of communication and have a lasting impact on the verbal language used within these communities. For instance, poor translations and eccentric 'fansubs' (episodes unofficially translated and subtitled by fans) have provided online anime communities with a large number of amusing phrases and expressions that are often invoked to build solidarity with other fans.

For instance, one common phrase is 'just according to keikaku', meaning 'just according to plan' but substituting the English word 'plan' with the Japanese equivalent *keikaku*. This came from an absurd fan translation of Episode 24 of *Death Note*, which used the word *keikaku* within the English script while adding a translator's note explaining that the word simply means 'plan'.

This phrase is often invoked in response to a plan that is needlessly overcomplicated and convoluted to achieve a simple goal.

Another image widely shared (and mocked) by online anime communities, which has subsequently achieved the mimetic status, is taken from the series *Fate/stay Night*. The subtitle text is a fairly literal translation of the original Japanese, 人は殺せれば死ぬ (*hito-wa korosareba shinu*). The English, however, sounds somewhat absurd and overly obvious, whereas the original Japanese has more of a simple yet impassioned tone. The Japanese language occasionally allows these kinds of tautological sentences that fail to translate well into English, presenting translators with a difficult challenge.

As we have explored in our previous discussions of memes, remixing and combining memes is a huge part of meme culture, and this is just as true in anime communities. Memes in the anime community often combine several common inside jokes to create an amusing new meme; for instance, the 'Truck-kun' meme has been combined with the *Fate/stay night* meme to amusing effect. The joke, in this case, is that the protagonists of *isekai* do not really die when they are hit by a truck but are reincarnated in another world. The creative recombination of memes is an important part of how online communities build solidarity and bond with each other as a community and even affects the verbal language used by these communities.

Emoji use in Japanese Vtuber fandoms

Vtubers, or virtual YouTubers, are YouTubers who use avatars instead of their real faces. Vtubers' usual content is streaming videos in which they either play games or respond to fan submissions. That said, most channels will have shorter videos in which they might sing songs, demonstrate cooking, teach Japanese, etc. The Vtuber phenomenon has most famously taken off under the Japanese company Hololive Production. This company employs multiple Vtubers, who then collaborate on live streams and do other combined projects such as merchandise releases. Because of the concentration of Vtubers within this company, most fans of Vtubers are fans of, or at least very aware of, multiple Vtubers. This leads to a strong fan community both in Japan and abroad. This is supported by heightened interactivity between creators and fans. Creators are constantly reacting to submissions, money and messages from the fans during their streams.

The interaction from fans comes in the form of typed comments that unfold alongside the video, which the streamers will read and respond to in the video itself. Emoji use is extremely common in fan comments, where comments will often appear in extremely rapid succession, and longer conventional written messages would be lost in the churn. It is also notable that emojis are often repeated several times in a single message, which makes them more noticeable.

The evolution of emoji speak can be clearly seen in one instance drawn from these kinds of live comments that appear in our data. Here, the use of the kanji 草 (kusa, meaning 'grass'), which appears twice (although one emoji, which has the script 'くさァw' an appears in the fifth line, is closely related and will be explained as well). This is a good example of the kind of in-group online communication that requires experience of the space for understanding. *Prima facie*, the Japanese word for 'grass' appearing in isolation in the comments section is fairly opaque in meaning, and the video's content was completely unrelated to grass. This kanji is used to express laughter, and its origin is far from self-evident. The Japanese *wara* (written in the phonetic hiragana script as わら,

or in kanji as 笑) which refers to laughing or smiling was (and still is) used in this function. For the sake of efficiency, this evolved into simply 'w' as users only hit the first key for this word. Returning to the superficially baffling 'くさアw', we find an explanation in the practice of Japanese netizens using longer strings such as 'wwwwwwwwww' to express their laughter. It was ultimately decided that these strings of the letter 'w' looked like grass, and this explains the eventual adoption of 草 in the same role. The 'くさアw' emoji contains the hiragana for 草, followed by the katakana (an alternative phonetic script used for emphasis of sound effects, foreign words, etc.) ア (a) which extends the sound of kusa to express excitement and the roman character 'w' (the meaning of which has already been described).

The Hololive community also involves relatively complex interlingual in-jokes and puns, with an understanding of Japanese and basic English seemingly expected of fans.

On screen, Hololive avatars appear to the left and the Japanese words and puns that fans are expected to be able to decipher appear to the right. To give an example from our data, the Japanese word 同じ, which is pronounced *onaji*, appeared next to an avatar who always wears a shark costume. Fans are expected to know that the English translation for this word is 'same', and then work out that 'same' is also how the Japanese word for shark would be transliterated (even though the pronunciation of the Japanese word is quite different to that English word), which explains the appearance of 同じ in this context.

In these Vtuber communities, we often see emoji styles that are inaccessible to outsiders without the appropriate knowledge required to understand them. This heightens the exclusivity of these communities, and in turn, strengthens its identity. It is a dynamic space where new communication styles emerge and flourish. This enhances the experience for all who engage with it. They are privy to a virtual world that makes innovative and exciting uses of emoji in a multilingual context.

Summary

We have explored how emojis are used within subcultural groups to help us bond with each other and bring warmth to our online interactions. Emojis and memes can help us construct our identities. The iterative, collaborative process of creating memes can help fandoms bond over a shared understanding of inside jokes and references. Often, these emojis require a high-level understanding of the fandom's source material; as we saw with some of the Vtuber fandom memes, some even required competence in multiple languages to 'decode'. We also saw how K-pop fandoms use emojis almost as 'badges', signalling their fandom of certain groups using particular emojis with established meanings in that fandom, allowing members of that fandom to identify each other and show their support for their favourite group or member.

On the other hand, emojing can also have the opposite goal; the recent innovation of 'tone tags' does not aim to produce a feeling of exclusive in-group knowledge, but rather aims to ensure complete transparency and understanding even with those who might be outside of one's in-group. Similarly, expressive stickers and emojis can be used in one's in-group to more accurately depict how one is feeling. Emojis are highly effective tools for creating solidarity, in both public and private settings, while creating a sense of fun and warmth in our online conversations.

10

Vision for the Future

In *1984*, George Orwell devised the concept of 'Newspeak', the official language of Oceania designed to suit the ideological preferences of Ingsoc, an abbreviation of English socialism. Newspeak was designed to simplify and reduce language, and thus the concepts that people were able to talk about, so that language in Oceania, by its very essence, only allowed for positive discussion, and hence thought, of Ingsoc's ideology. Newspeak was intended to replace 'Oldspeak' by 2050. As of 2022, we have not seen the emergence of anything quite like Newspeak, however, we have seen the rise of what I call, 'emoji speak'. Far from having the sinister undertones of Newspeak, emoji speak refers to an innovative, new genre of speech that started off as the addition of typed emoticons, like :), in computer-mediated communication and has developed into widely used emoji keyboards, sticker packs, gifs and more.

Though the comparison between a fictional dystopian language and light, humorous emoji speak may at first glance seem rather absurd, when we look at the purpose and grammatical rules of Newspeak and compare them to emoji speak in the present day, the two turn out to be less different than one might think. Newspeak was aimed at cutting down all the words referring to an 'organization, or body of people, or doctrine, or country, or institution, or public building' into 'familiar shapes'. It was meant to create a new, smaller and simpler vocabulary, with broader meanings. Is this not very similar to emojis? They take our foods, sports, transports, animals and even complex human emotions and turn them into simplified images. For each emoji that you read, you do not say any words in your head. For example, you would not read a message as 'Can't wait to see you! Face with party horn and party hat, glasses clinking'. No instead, you just read the text and take a vague sense of meaning from the emojis as you see them. Like Newspeak in which the vocabulary was limited, simplified and broad in meaning, emoji speak too provides a general sense of simple meaning.

The similarities do not stop there. In Newspeak, new forms of extra-efficient grammar were introduced. One way in which this took form was by the universal use of affixes for all word forms. These affixes included plus- and doubleplus-affixes, which could be placed in front of any adjective – Orwell gives the examples of *plus*cold and *doubleplus*cold, meaning 'very cold' and 'superlatively cold' respectively. Is this not similar to using one emoji, two emojis or three emojis for different levels of emphasis? For example, one party emoji at the end of an excited message will seem less excited than two party popper emojis, which will both seem less excited than three party popper emojis.

Of course, we know what the purpose of Ingsoc's Newspeak was intended to be in Orwell's fictional world, but do we really know the purpose and significance of emoji speak in our own world? This is one of the questions that I hope to have begun answering in this book. I have considered how emoji use differs between different countries and cultures, which factors affect the way that we emoji, and how the meanings of emojis are created and changed.

A league of its own

As it stands, emoji speak has not only entered the communication playing field over the last few decades but also created a league of its own. No longer a sub-genre of communication, emoji speak, as I have termed it, is constantly growing, spreading throughout internet users and developing at an astonishingly fast rate. In the linguistics field, there has been a lot of discussion around 'grammatical' and 'ungrammatical' communication, but emojing is a form of digital communication which fits neither of these moulds. It is playful, spontaneous and lawless. Neither spoken nor written, emojing bridges the gap between the two, allowing for the user's intentions to be observed more clearly. They facilitate a style of texting that is more multi-modal, enriching our conversations on a regular basis.

Far from a frivolous social media trend, emojing has significance for every individual who uses smartphone to communicate. In fact, I would go as far as to say that one's emoji style is a unique identifier of each individual, even comparable to a fingerprint. After reading this book, I am sure that you may be able to hazard a good guess of the age, gender or home country of a user based purely on their emoji habits. Similarly, we all have friends or family that regularly use certain unusual emojis, and as such, we don't even need to see the name of the sender to work out who the sender was. Just like handwriting, emojing style is unique to every user.

We can almost profile users according to their emojing habits. We form an idea of a person's personality purely according to their emoji use, in a manner that is far more enriched than what we can tell from writing alone. On the flipside, this means that every user consciously chooses emojis according to how they think they will be perceived, revealing little titbits about themselves in the process.

The ability to transfer one's personality through the internet is something that relies on what could be called a 'hivemind' of shared knowledge, common references and mutual understanding. When an emoji gains a certain significance or popularity that it did not originally have, a wave of semi-conscious awareness sweeps over the hivemind, who adopts and appropriates the emoji's meaning, thus propagating yet also creating its new significance. Of course, this hivemind is segregated according to many factors: country, continent, age, language, fandom, etc. We saw this in particular in Chapter 9, where different fandoms gave different significance to certain emojis. However, it also happens on a larger scale, meaning that there is an element of crowdsourcing in emojing: a constant feedback loop, where one action affects all of the others.

Like it or not, emojis are here to stay. They are not just for the young, but are largely being adopted by everybody, be that your grandma using a typed :) or your dad using the thumbs-up emoji to reply to your every message. The more time passes, the more we all grow accustomed to emojing. Emoji speak, as I call it, is a mode of communication completely autonomous to any pre-existing communication style. It has its own unique features and connotations that mean that it is a law unto itself. This new genre of speech has allowed for a new dimension to be added to multi-modal communication. Significant meaning can be gleamed from emoji use and, as such, they are a revolutionary creation that has changed the very meaning of communicating online.

The future is hazy

We have established that emoji speak is here to stay, but do we really know the implications of this rapidly evolving speech genre? Though we can say for sure that emoji speak has completely revolutionized computer-mediated or smartphone-mediated communication, how do we evaluate the effect that it is having on our world? We can easily sing the praises of emoji speak, as we can easily see just how emojis enrich our communication, but what about the negative implications? We haven't quite figured it all out yet.

Further study about emoji use and its effects on users must be carried out with respect to a variety of demographics – in particular, young children, teenagers and the elderly. We must consider the amount of time spent engaged in emoji speak, and what this might mean for people dependent on age, socio-economic status, their country of residence, culture and so on. We need to answer questions like does emoji speak alienate the elderly from our daily communication? Could emojis be made more accessible for the elderly demographic? What effects does emoji speak have on our mental health? Does heavy use of emojis in children inhibit their progress in reading and writing? Without the answers to questions like these, we are unable to fully assess the impact of emojis.

Another key area that must be examined is the effect of emojis on our perception of the world: of different countries and cultures. As discussed, the selection of emojis on the emoji keyboard that we have access to is controlled by the Unicode Technical Committee, which is far from representative of the entire population of the world. Although creators can put out sticker packs on apps like Facebook and WeChat, the fact remains that a small group of people, made up mainly of Americans, control the emoji keyboard, which forms the main basis of how users emoji. At this point, we cannot know whether this is worrying or not. Further study into how emojis influence our perception of the world is crucial in this case so that we can understand whether emojis are enforcing racial or nationalistic biases.

Nothing is black and white, however. From a different perspective, we can see that emojis lower language barriers by allowing a form of pictorial communication to take place. Though nuanced meaning will not be conveyed, people from all across the world can achieve basic communication purely by using emojis. On this note, however, more study is also needed into digital inequality and emojis. What is the difference, if any, between the communication styles of those who are exposed to emoji talk regularly and those who never use it? This is another question that needs to be answered for us to truly understand the influence of emoji speak.

As we saw in Chapter 6, emojis are being cited as evidence in court cases, suggesting that they are of great significance – but do we really know this for sure? Just how clearly do emojis demonstrate our true feelings and intentions? This is another area which certainly needs more study. Some would argue that emojis are frivolous additions to CMC, which demonstrate our feelings on a surface level but should not be read into. However, with emojis being used as evidence in court cases, we really need to compare the use of emojis with our true intentions in a quantitative manner so that emoji speak is not manipulated to mean more or less than it actually does.

In summary, without clear evidence of the effect of emojis on the way we think and behave, and without clear evidence of how emojis link to our true thoughts and feelings, we are powerless to evaluate the true nature of emoji speak and which aspects of it are positive or negative. We know emoji speak is here to stay, and we know that it will continue to evolve at rapid rates. However, without further study, we cannot know what efforts need to be made to ensure that emoji speak develops in a positive, inclusive manner. We also do not know how best to protect children and teenagers from their influence. Moreover, we do not know how to bridge gaps in emoji fluency, related to digital inequality or age discrepancies. Thus, although we do know that emoji speak has enriched and revolutionized CMC, far more study is needed to be able to truly understand the nature of emoji speak.

Emojis in a post-pandemic world

Since the outbreak of Covid-19 in early 2020, we have all taken to online communication more than ever. With work and social life being forcibly moved to online spaces during lockdowns, we have adapted to the extent that our habits have been permanently changed. We no longer feel that it is necessary to travel to meet with work colleagues, or even friends and family if they live far away. We have all adapted to new platforms that we were hardly aware of pre-pandemic, namely Zoom and Microsoft Teams. During an endless number of video meetings for work, people of all ages have learnt how to clap, heart and laugh react to happenings on Zoom, and to thumbs up and heart react to messages in the chat on Microsoft Teams. Similarly, families communicating on video chat platforms have exposed children to heightened emoji use. As such emojis have gained even more significance and relevance in our lives than ever before.

With online working looking like it is here to stay, and international travel remaining difficult, emojis may hold the key to keeping our communication exciting. They help us to be personable and loveable. They allow us to create humour, making it easier than ever to employ joking or even sarcastic tones. They let us express affection, joy and warmth. Even though there are questions still left to be answered about emoji speak, it is undoubtable that emojis are a permeant addition to our digital lives. We need them. As long as we can mediate their use, emojis will continue to facilitate enriched communication for many years to come.

Towards emoji linguistics

Emoji linguistics is still an emerging field. Despite the continuing cultural and linguistic impact that emoji have had since their rise to massive mainstream popularity in the early-to-mid 2010s, traditional linguists have been reluctant to treat emoji as much more than a short-lived fad with little communicative value. Perhaps part of the issue was that there wasn't necessarily a clear home for emoji within academia. Where did they belong? Linguistics? Communication studies? Graphic design? All of the fields that intersect with emoji could tell us something interesting about them, but I believe that the linguistic value of emoji is their most important and interesting feature. Whether they become widely accepted as part of linguistics or not, they are drastically shaping how we communicate, and it is essential that we understand the ethical issues involved with emojis and the impact they are having on language acquisition, our legal system and laws, censorship, our relationship with technology and far more besides.

As we study emoji and improve our understanding of emojis, we may also discover unexpected benefits to their use, and in doing so, unlock the full potential of emoji as a valuable addition to how we communicate. Emojis create a new entry point to online communication that isn't based on the written word, meaning that they essentially remove some of the barriers to entry into online spaces. For anybody who struggles with traditional written communication for any reason – be that dyslexia, learning disabilities or other forms of neurodivergence – emojis could be a valuable tool for broadening their communication horizons. Emojis have the potential to make online spaces more inclusive, diverse and accessible, and further research into how this potential could be unlocked could be incredibly helpful for many people.

On the other hand, the fact that so much of our lives is now mediated through technology does present some cause for concern. For instance, while autocorrect software may be helpful when it corrects our clumsy errors, the fact that it learns our communication habits and nudges us into reproducing them again and again could make our communication less creative as we end up reinforcing our established habits. Autocorrect is essentially a feedback loop: it learns from what we type, yet it also suggests what we should type. Emoji could also be implicated in surveillance capitalism online: if Facebook were to notice, for example, that posts with a lot of 'angry' reactions generate the most engagement, and therefore the most advertising revenue, then Facebook would be incentivized to show users more divisive and controversial posts, resulting in an increase in divisive rhetoric and an increasingly emotionally negative experience for users on the platform. It is essential that we also consider the ethical issues behind emojis to ensure that they do not have negative effects on society and our communication styles.

One thing is for certain: the way we communicate will never stop evolving. And as big tech companies gear up for a new stage of the internet that they predict will be characterized by metaverses, avatars and Web 3.0 technologies, it seems likely that embodiment and visual forms of communication will play an increasingly large role in our online communication. Of course, as of the time of writing, it is still unclear as to what exactly this future will look like – even the companies pouring billions of dollars into developing the tech required to realize their vision of the metaverse seems to be hazy on the details. As such, it is hard to make informed predictions about how emojing will evolve going into this new iteration of the internet. If we find ourselves navigating metaverses through VR headsets with sensors that bring our real-life gestures into the virtual world, perhaps we will see more traditional gesturing make its way into online spaces. The gestures we use today may have to undergo some changes in their transition to the virtual world, however: if these VR devices require hand-held controllers like current devices, our hands may not be as free to gesture exactly how we do in the real world.

I have written this book in the hope that it would spark readers' curiosity about this under-researched field, and perhaps even inspire a few of you to investigate emojing for yourself and contribute something new to the field! As emojis are a relatively new development in communication, there is still plenty left to explore and discover, making it a fertile ground for creative and interesting studies. So where do emoji linguistics go from here? A couple of relatively unexplored areas include how emoji are processed in the brain; how young people acquire emoji competence; how users innovate and build upon emoji meanings; and more. In my next project on emoji, a book series on emoji linguistics, I aim to tackle some of these questions in further detail in collaboration with other linguists in the field.

Emoji are constantly changing and evolving. When emojis went worldwide in 2011 when Apple first implemented the emoji keyboard, they were looked upon as cute curiosities, more of a novelty than a serious addition to communication. Yet now, over ten years later, emoji have evolved into a set of symbols densely layered with interlocking meanings – so much so that even the most seemingly unambiguous emoji could have multiple alternate meanings depending on context and who you are talking to. Emoji are not dumbing down our language – on the contrary, they are making communication far more complex. The meanings emoji obtain in different cultures are intertwined with our language, history and culture and only enrich our relationship with language. They are also not trivial decorations to our texts: if you were to break down how much the average person communicates via text versus emoji, emojis would make up a much larger chunk than most would expect. After all, we have never communicated with just words alone, our body language, facial expressions and tone of voice are just as important as the words we say. Emojing doesn't threaten language; it simply gives us back something that we had previously lost in the transition to text-based online communication with a little extra too.

Notes

Preface

1 Both 'emoji' and 'emojis' are commonly seen as the plural of 'emoji'. In this book, I generally use 'emojis' where fidelity of a quotation has not led me to do otherwise.
2 Caleb Spencer, 'Coronavirus: Digital Poverty "A Threat to Children in Care"', *BBC News*, 2020. https://www.bbc.co.uk/news/uk-wales-52654426.

Chapter 2

1 *Statista*, 'Smartphone Users 2026', 2022. https://www.statista.com/statistics/330695/number-of-smartphone-users-worldwide/ (Accessed 26 January 2022).
2 Simon Kemp, 'Digital 2022: Global Overview Report', *Datareportal*, 2022. https://datareportal.com/reports/digital-2022-global-overview-report.
3 As of the first quarter of 2021, the microblogging platform had over 199 'monetizable million daily active users'. https://s22.q4cdn.com/826641620/files/doc_financials/2021/q1/Q1'21-Shareholder-Letter.pdf, Facebook had approximately 2.85 billion monthly active users and 1.88 billion daily active users (https://s21.q4cdn.com/399680738/files/doc_financials/2021/FB-Earnings-Presentation-Q1-2021.pdf) on its eponymous service and approximately 3.45 billion monthly active users across its full social media family (Facebook, WhatsApp Instagram, and Messenger) (https://s21.q4cdn.com/399680738/files/doc_financials/2021/FB-03.31.2021-Exhibit-99.1_Final.pdf).
4 Vyvyan Evans, *The Emoji Code: How Smiley Faces, Love Hearts and Thumbs Up are Changing the Way We Communicate* (London: Michael O'Mara Books, 2017).
5 Marc Prensky, 'Digital Natives, Digital Immigrants Part 2: Do They Really Think Differently?' *On the Horizon* 9, no. 6 (2001): 1–6.
6 World Data Lab, 2021.
7 GSMA, 'Sub-Saharan Africa', *The Mobile Economy*, 2021. https://www.gsma.com/mobileeconomy/wp-content/uploads/2021/09/GSMA_ME_SSA_2021_English_Web_Singles.pdf.
8 Pew Research Centre, 2021.

9. Herbert P. Grice, 'Logic and Conversation', in *Speech Acts* (Boston: Brill, 1975), 41–58.
10. Christopher Potts, *The Logic of Conventional Implicatures* (Oxford: Oxford University Press, 2005).
11. 'emoticon, n', *OED Online*, March 2022. Oxford University Press. https://www.oed.com/view/Entry/249618?redirectedFrom=emoticon (Accessed 26 April 2022).
12. Rachel Wilkinson, 'The Father of the Emoticon Chases His Great White Whale', *Narratively*, 2022. https://narratively.com/the-father-of-the-emoticon-chases-his-great-white-whale/ (Accessed 26 April 2022).
13. For example Evans, *The Emoji Code*, 155.
14. Arielle Pardes, 'The Wired Guide to Emoji', *Wired*, 2018. https://www.wired.com/story/guide-emoji (Accessed 20 February 2022).
15. Mark Davis and Ned Holbrook, 'Unicode® Technical Standard #51', *Unicode.org*, 2022. http://www.unicode.org/reports/tr51/#Introduction (Accessed 16 January 2022).
16. https://emojipedia.org/stats/
17. Gretchen McCulloch, *Because Internet* (2019), 241.
18. Richard Dawkins and Lalla Ward, *The God Delusion* (Boston: Houghton Mifflin Company, 2006).

Chapter 3

1. Michelle Ruiz, '2019 Was the Year of the Celebrity Notes App Statement', *Vogue*, 2019. https://www.vogue.com/article/best-celebrity-notes-app-statements-2019.
2. Laura Silver, 'Smartphone Ownership Is Growing Rapidly around the World, but Not Always Equally', *Pew Research Center*, 2022. https://www.pewresearch.org/global/2019/02/05/smartphone-ownership-is-growing-rapidly-around-the-world-but-not-always-equally/ (Accessed 15 February 2022).
3. David Crystal, *Language and the Internet* (Spain: Cambridge University Press, 2006).
4. M. Iqbal, 'Snapchat Revenue and Usage Statistics (2022)', [online] *Business of Apps*, 2022. https://www.businessofapps.com/data/snapchat-statistics/ (Accessed 8 June 2022).
5. Ibid.
6. Barton and Lee, *Languaging Online*, 2013, 7.
7. Zappavigna, *Discourse of Twitter and Social Media...*, 2012.
8. Liyang Yu, *Introduction to the Semantic Web and Semantic Web Services* (Boca Raton, FL; London: Chapman & Hall/CRC, 2007).
9. Javad Zarrin, Wen Phang Hao, Saheer, Lakshmi Babu, and Bahram Zarrin, 'Blockchain for Decentralization of Internet: Prospects, Trends, and Challenges', *Cluster Computing* 24, no. 4 (2021): 2841–66.

10   'Sexual Solicitation | Transparency Centre', *Facebook.Com*. https://www.facebook.com/communitystandards/sexual_solicitation (Accessed 22 April 2022).
11   Mary Bellis, 'Arpanet: The World's First Internet', *Thoughtco*, 2018. https://www.thoughtco.com/arpanet-the-worlds-first-internet-4072558.
12   Kristine L. Nowak, and Christian Rauh, 'The Influence of the Avatar on Online Perceptions of Anthropomorphism, Androgyny, Credibility, Homophily, and Attraction', *Journal of Computer-Mediated Communication* 11, no. 1 (2005): 153–78.
13   Merriam-Webster.com Dictionary, s.v., 'Avatar'. https://www.merriam-webster.com/dictionary/avatar (Accessed 27 April 2022).
14   'Rethinking Our Default Profile Photo', *Blog.Twitter.Com*, 2017. https://blog.twitter.com/en_us/topics/product/2017/rethinking-our-default-profile-photo.html.
15   Ibid., 155.
16   Ibid.
17   Lydia O'Connor, and Daniel Marans, 'Here are 13 Examples of Donald Trump Being Racist', *Huffpost UK*, 2016. https://www.huffingtonpost.co.uk/entry/donald-trump-racist-examples_n_56d47177e4b03260bf777e83?ri18n=true.
18   Matt Baume, 'Donald Trump's 8 Worst Attacks on the LGBTQ+ Community', *Them*, 2020. https://www.them.us/story/donald-trump-worst-lgbtq-attacks.
19   Jacob Henry, 'White Conservative Politician Sends Tweet Claiming to be Black Gay Obama Support', *Metro*, 2020. https://metro.co.uk/2020/11/11/white-conservative-politician-sends-tweet-claiming-to-be-black-gay-obama-supporter-13577157/.
20   Kai Baldwin, 'Virtual Avatars: Trans Experiences of Ideal Selves Through Gaming', *Markets, Globalization & Development Review* 3, no. 3 (2019).
21   Ibid., 8.
22   Ibid., 10.
23   A fantasy race in the World of Warcraft universe.
24   Ibid., 12.
25   Ibid.
26   Ibid., 16.
27   Ibid., 4.
28   James Chen, 'The Vtuber Takeover of 2020', *Polygon*, 2020. https://www.polygon.com/2020/11/30/21726800/hololive-vtuber-projekt-melody-kizuna-ai-calliope-mori-vshojo-youtube-earnings.
29   Minoru Hirota, 'Bācharu-ka suru hito no sonzai. VTuber no koshikata, yukusue', *Yuriika. Uta to hyōron, tokushū bācharu YouTuber* 07 (2018): 45–52.
30   Patricia Hernandez, 'Why Pokimane's Vtubing Twitch Stream Has Everyone Talking', *Polygon*, 2020. https://www.polygon.com/2020/9/14/21436437/pokimane-imane-anys-twitch-vtubing-vtuber-anime-livestream-mainstream-popularity.
31   Chen, 'The Vtuber Takeover of 2020', 2020.

Chapter 4

1. Brittany Bennet, '7 Ways Older Millennials Text Differently Than Younger Millennials. 2018'. https://www.bustle.com/p/7-ways-older-millennials-text-differently-than-younger-millennials-8539988 (Accessed 10 April 2022).
2. Michael Beißwenger, and Steffen Pappert, 'How to be Polite with Emojis: A Pragmatic Analysis of Face Work Strategies in an Online Learning Environment', *European Journal of Applied Linguistics* 7, no. 2 (2019): 225–54.
3. Jieun Kiaer, *Translingual Words: An East Asian Lexical Encounter with English* (London: Routledge, 2019), 42.
4. Ibid.
5. Penelope Eckert, 'Three Waves of Variation Study: The Emergence of Meaning in the Study of Sociolinguistic Variation', *Annual Review of Anthropology* 41, no. 1 (2012): 87–100.
6. Jieun Kiaer, personal interviews, 2016.
7. See for example Maekawa, 2004 for Japanese; Smith and Clark, 1993 for English; Mozziconacci, 2001 for Dutch.
8. Danielle N. Gunraj, April M. Drumm-Hewitt, Erica M. Dashow, Sri Siddhi N. Upadhyay and Celia M. Klin, 'Texting Insincerely: The Role of the Period in Text Messaging', *Computers in Human Behavior* 55 (2016): 1067–75.
9. S. Han, *Mobile Instant Messaging in Korean: Linguistic Variations Among Patterns*, Unpublished Mst dissertation, University of Oxford, 2017.
10. Gunraj et al., 'Texting Insincerely', 2016.

Chapter 5

1. See Jieun Kiaer, *Pragmatic Particles: Findings from Asian Languages*. Bloomsbury Studies in Theoretical Linguistics (London: Bloomsbury, 2021) for a discussion of the sensitivity of particles to sociocultural factors in Korean.
2. See Jieun Kiaer, *The History of English Loanwords in Korean*. LINCOM Studies in English Linguistics; 19 (Muenchen: Lincom, 2014) for a discussion of English loanwords in Korean.
3. See Kiaer, *Translingual Words*.
4. https://unicode.org/emoji/proposals.html.
5. Quoted from the Dumpling Emoji Project website: https://www.dumplingemoji.com/.
6. Damian Radcliffe and Hadil Abuhmaid, *Social Media In The Middle East: 2019 In Review*, 2020. https://scholarsbank.uoregon.edu/xmlui/bitstream/handle/1794/25119/social_media_middle_east_2019.pdf?sequence=3.

7   Judith Vonberg, 'Teen Behind Hijab Emoji: "I Wanted an Emoji of Me"', *CNN*, 2017. https://edition.cnn.com/2017/07/18/europe/hijab-emoji-teenager/index.html.
8   At an even more local level, Yao Sun's (forthcoming) *Consuming and Destigmatising Osaka-ben: A Study on Language Commodification and Language Ideology* discusses the example of a set of stickers on Line, based on a person from Kansai (a westerly region of Japan that includes Osaka, Kyoto and Kobe) who came to Tokyo all alone and started to use an even stronger Kansai dialect than would even be used in Kansai in order to avoid being washed away in the wave of city life. Examples like this show that the demand for representation reaches even further than the national level, as even in a country like Japan that is comparatively over-represented in the standard emoji collection, there are still those who wish to show their local heritage.
9   'Emoji Encoding Principles', *Unicode*. http://www.unicode.org/emoji/principles.html (Accessed 27 April 2021).
10 Mark Davis and Peter Edberg, 'Unicode Technical Report #51: Unicode Emoji', *Unicode*, 2015. https://www.unicode.org/reports/tr51/tr51-3-archive.html#Gender.
11 Philip Seargeant, *The Emoji Revolution: How Technology is Shaping the Future of Communication* (Cambridge, 2019), 139.
12 Ibid.
13 Davis and Edberg, 'Unicode Technical Report #51'.
14 'Yellow Emojis Not Neutral Symbols of Identity', *The University of Edinburgh*, 2021. https://www.ed.ac.uk/news/2021/yellow-emojis-not-neutral-identity-symbols?utm_campaign=cam_news2021&utm_content=1625059634&utm_medium=social&utm_source=facebook&fbclid=IwAR39NuEH25-FilFHogcUigpMTtBAUWha_i93y70j6aLp89Vjk62j7V24i6U.
15 Zara Rahman, 'The Problem with Emoji Skin Tones That No One Talks About', *The Daily Dot*, 2018. https://www.dailydot.com/irl/skin-tone-emoji/.
16 Ibid.
17 Ibid.
18 Paige Tutt, 'Apple's New Diverse Emoji Are Even More Problematic Than Before', https://www.washingtonpost.com/posteverything/wp/2015/04/10/how-apples-new-multicultural-emojis-are-more-racist-than-before/?noredirect=on, 2015. https://www.washingtonpost.com/posteverything/wp/2015/04/10/how-apples-new-multicultural-emojis-are-more-racist-than-before/?noredirect=on.
19 'Emoji Encoding Principles', *Unicode*. http://www.unicode.org/emoji/principles.html (Accessed 27 April 2021).
20 *Have You Ever Heard of the 'Emoji Commission'?*. Video. DW Documentary, 2020. https://www.youtube.com/watch?v=Fr9L27V337E [21:00].
21 Arielle Pardes, 'Don't See Yourself on Your Emoji Keyboard? She Can Help', *Wired*, 2019. https://www.wired.com/story/jenny-8-lee-picture-character/.
22 Ibid.

23 Paul Hunt, 'World Emoji Day 2021: How Emoji Can Help Create a More Empathetic World, for All of Us 🫶'. *Adobe Blog*, 2021. https://blog.adobe.com/en/publish/2021/07/15/global-emoji-trend-report-2021.

24 Simon Kemp, 'Digital 2016: Global Digital Overview', *DataReportal*, 2016. https://datareportal.com/reports/digital-2016-global-digital-overview (Accessed 8 February 2022).

25 Marcel Danesi, *The Semiotics of Emoji: The Rise of Visual Language in the Age of the Internet* (Bloomsbury Publishing, 2017).

26 Ibid., 23.

27 Ibid.

28 Ibid.

29 Paul D. Hunt, 'What Will It Take to Create a More Inclusive Future for Emoji?' *Adobe Blog*, 2021. https://blog.adobe.com/en/publish/2021/04/15/towards-diverse-inclusive-future-for-emoji-uk.

30 See Delfina Utomo, '6 Singapore Emojis We Wish Existed', *Time Out Singapore*. Time Out, 12 May 2020. https://www.timeout.com/singapore/things-to-do/singapore-emojis-we-wish-existed; Helena Wasserman, '12 African Emoji We Would like to See - Including Proper Sandals and Pap', *Business Insider*, 2018. https://www.businessinsider.co.za/african-emoji-we-would-like-to-see-2018-9.

31 Rebecca Ratcliffe, 'New Emoji Set Aims to Shatter Image of Africa as Zone of Famine and War', *The Guardian*, 18 November 2019. https://www.theguardian.com/global-development/2019/nov/18/new-emoji-set-aims-to-shatter-image-of-africa-as-zone-of-famine-and-war.

32 Giovanni Torre, 'The New Indigenous Emojis Coming to Your Smartphone Screen', *National Indigenous Times 2*, 26 February 2022. https://nit.com.au/26-02-2022/2734/the-new-indigenous-emojis-coming-to-your-smartphone-screen.

33 Liz Stinson, 'Finland Just Designed the Most Finnish Emoji Ever', *Wired*, 5 November 2015. https://www.wired.com/2015/11/finland-national-emoji/.

34 Alexander Wong, 'Twitter Releases Special Emoji for Malaysia's Merdeka Celebration', *Tech-Gadgets*, 27 April 2021. https://www.malaymail.com/news/tech-gadgets/2021/08/27/twitter-releases-special-emoji-for-malaysias-merdeka-celebration/2000833; Monrawee Ampolpittayanant, 'Celebrating Thailand's National Day with Thai-Themed Emoji', *Twitter Blog*, 5 December 2019. https://blog.twitter.com/en_sea/topics/events/2019/Celebrating-thailand-national-day-with-thai-themed-emoji.

Chapter 6

1 Daria Marmer, 'These Emojis Can Increase Click-Through Rates, According to New Data', *Hubspot*, 2018. https://blog.hubspot.com/marketing/best-emojis.

2 Owen Churches, Mike Nicholls, Myra Thiessen, Mark Kohler, and Hannah Keage, 'Emoticons in Mind: An Event-Related Potential Study', *Social Neuroscience* 9, no. 2 (2014): 196–202.
3 Lydia Kraus, Robert Schmidt, Marcel Walch, Florian Schaub, and Sebastian Möller, 'On the Use of Emojis in Mobile Authentication', in *IFIP International Conference on ICT Systems Security and Privacy Protection*, 265–80 (Cham: Springer, 2017).
4 'Emoji Marketing: How to Use Emoticons to Significantly Increase Your Conversions', *Neil Patel*. https://neilpatel.com/blog/emoji-marketing-how-to-use-emoticons-to-increase-your-conversions/ (Accessed 21 April 2022).
5 '30 Statistics About Using Emojis for Businesses', *The Pipeline*. https://blog.zoominfo.com/emoji-statistics-for-businesses/ (Accessed 27 April 2022).
6 'Emoji and Burger King Team for Anti-Bullying Campaign', *License Global*, 2019. https://www.licenseglobal.com/character/emoji-and-burger-king-team-anti-bullying-campaign?elq_mid=2613&elq_cid=3939780.
7 Keith Broni, 'China's Annual Emoji Censorship', *Emojipedia*, 2021. https://blog.emojipedia.org/chinas-annual-emoji-censorship/.
8 Cheryl The, 'China Blocked Candle and Cake Emojis from Weibo in Order to Censor Anniversary Commemorations of the Tiananmen Square Massacre', *Insider*, 2021. https://www.insider.com/chinese-censors-blocked-candle-emojis-anniversary-tiananmen-massacre-2021-6.
9 Jeremy Burge, 'Samsung Puts Japan Back on the Map', *Emojipedia*, 2017. https://blog.emojipedia.org/samsung-puts-japan-back-on-the-map/.
10 View the stickers here: https://tinyurl.com/emojispeak6a
11 Kim Soyeong, '오조오억-허버허버'가 왜 남혐이냐, 뜻도 모르면서'…논란 Ing', *Money Today*, 2021. https://news.mt.co.kr/mtview.php?no=2021042211464429191.
12 'Misogynistic Attacks on Archer', *The Korea Times*, 2021. https://www.koreatimes.co.kr/www/opinion/2021/08/137_313178.html.
13 'Sexual Solicitation'. *Facebook*. https://www.facebook.com/communitystandards/sexual_solicitation (Accessed 23 April 2022).
14 Eric Goldman, 'Emojis and the Law', *Washington Law Review* 93 (2018): 1244.
15 'The Role of Emoji in New York City Sexual Harassment', *Phillips & Associates*, 2019. https://www.newyorkemploymentattorney-blog.com/the-role-of-emoji-in-new-york-city-sexual-harassment/.
16 Darlene Murdoch v. Medjet Assistance LLC and Roy Berger, 2:2016cv00779, (US District Court for the Northern District of Alabama 2018).
17 Erica N. Stewart V. Tarold Durham and Belhaven University, 3:2016cv00744, (US District Court for the Southern District of Mississippi 2016).
18 'XXX Show Intention to Rent Apartment, Says Judge', *Perma.Cc*, 2022. https://perma.cc/3APF-AQ6V.
19 Ibid.
20 Ibid.

21 Goldman, 'Emojis and the Law', 1268.
22 Justin Jouvenal, 'A 12-Year-Old Girl is Facing Criminal Charges for Using Certain Emoji. She's Not Alone', *The Washington Post*, 2016. http://adam.curry.com/art/1456703641_HbNrBjzX.html.
23 Chris Matyszczyk, 'Teen Arrested After Alleged Facebook Emoji Threats', *CNET*, 2015. https://www.cnet.com/culture/teen-arrested-after-alleged-facebook-emoji-threats/.
24 Jouvenal, 'A 12-Year-Old Girl Is Facing', 2015.
25 Goldman, 'Emojis and the Law', 1259.
26 Ibid., 1271.

Chapter 7

1 Unicode, *Emoji Frequency*. 2022 [online]. https://home.unicode.org/emoji/emoji-frequency/.
2 Paul Ekman, *Emotions Revealed: Understanding Faces and Feelings* (United Kingdom: Orion, 2012).
3 Harold G. Johnson, Paul Ekman and Wallace V. Friesen. 'Communicative Body Movements: American Emblems' (1975): 335–54.
4 H. K. Kabali, M. M. Irigoyen, R. Nunez-Davis, J. G. Budacki, S. H. Mohanty, K. P. Leister, and R. L. Bonner, Jr, 'Exposure and Use of Mobile Media Devices by Young Children', *Pediatrics* 136, no. 6 (2015): 1044–50. https://doi.org/10.1542/peds.2015-2151.
5 Common Sense Media, *The Common Sense Census: Media Use by Kids Age Zero to Eight* (V Rideout – San Francisco, CA: Common Sense Media, 2017). https://www.commonsensemedia.org/sites/default/files/research/report/csm_zerotoeight_fullreport_release_2.pdf.
6 Ofcom, 'Children and Parents: Media Use and Attitudes Report 2019', *Making Sense of Media*, 2020. https://www.ofcom.org.uk/__data/assets/pdf_file/0023/190616/children-media-use-attitudes-2019-report.pdf.
7 J. Fane, C. MacDougall, J. Jovanovic, G. Redmond and L. Gibbs, 'Exploring the Use of Emoji as a Visual Research Method for Eliciting Young Children's Voices in Childhood Research', *Early Child Development and Care* 188, no. 3 (2018): 359–74. DOI: 10.1080/03004430.2016.1219730.
8 Hye Young Han, Eun Sil Park, and Hye Jung Shin, 'Effect of Group Intervention Using Emoticons on Emotional Empathy and Conversational Function of School-Age Children with Intellectual Disabilities1', *Journal of Speech* 30, no. 2 (2021): 9–20.

9 Ho Kim, 'A Study on the Use of Communication Functions in Mobile Messenger Emoticons-Focus on Line Messenger', *The Journal of the Korea Contents Association* 17, no. 9 (2017): 184–91.
10 Ibid.

Chapter 8

1 S. G. Hong, 'A Study on the Characteristics of Emoticon Usage of Socially Distant Users in CMC', Unpublished master's thesis, Yonsei University, Seoul, Korea, 2020.
2 M. Beißwenger and S. Pappert, 'How to Be Polite with Emojis: A Pragmatic Analysis of Face Work Strategies in an Online Learning Environment', *European Journal of Applied Linguistics* 7, no. 2 (2019): 225–54. https://doi.org/10.1515/eujal-2019-0003.
3 M. Iqbal, 'Snapchat Revenue and Usage Statistics (2022), *BusinessofApps*, 2002a. https://www.businessofapps.com/data/snapchat-statistics/; M. Iqbal, 'TikTok Revenue and Usage Statistics (2022), *BusinessofApps*, 2022b. https://www.businessofapps.com/data/tik-tok-statistics/.
4 V. Petrock, 'A Look at Gen Z's Preferred Social Platforms', *Insider Intelligence*, 2021. https://www.emarketer.com/content/gen-z-preferred-social-platforms.
5 Insider Intelligence, 'Snapchat Global Usage Statistics, Trends, and Forecast', *Insider Intelligence*, 2022. https://www.insiderintelligence.com/insights/snapchat-user-statistics/#:~:text=Snapchat's%20user%20demographics&text=TikTok%20will%20overtake%20Snapchat%20among,TikTok%20among%20total%20Gen%20Zers.
6 P. Suciu, 'Generation Divide: Different Age Groups Use Emojis Differently and That Isn't Likely Going to Change', *Forbes*, 2021. https://www.forbes.com/sites/petersuciu/2021/08/24/generation-divide-different-age-groups-use-emojis-differently-and-that-isnt-likely-going-to-change/?sh=39ded3465357.
7 S. Sanjay, 'Why Does Gen Z Use Emojis So Weirdly?' *Vice*, 2020. https://www.vice.com/en/article/7kpngb/gen-z-young-people-use-emojis-differently-than-millennials.
8 K. Yurieff, 'Sorry, Millennials: The Face with Tears of Joy Emoji Isn't Cool Anymore', *CNN Business*, 2021. https://edition.cnn.com/2021/02/14/tech/crying-laughing-emoji-gen-z/index.html.
9 See Alecia Wolf ('Emotional Expression Online: Gender Differences in Emoticon Use', *Cyberpsychology & Behavior* 3, no. 5 (2000): 827–33) for a detailed discussion.
10 Wolf, 'Emotional Expression Online'.
11 Marília Prada, David L. Rodrigues, Margarida V. Garrido, Diniz Lopes, Bernardo Cavalheiro, and Rui Gaspar, 'Motives, Frequency and Attitudes Toward Emoji and Emoticon Use', *Telematics and Informatics* 35, no. 7 (2018): 1925–34.

12 Anna Oleszkiewicz, Maciej Karwowski, Katarzyna Pisanski, Piotr Sorokowski, Boaz Sobrado, and Agnieszka Sorokowska, 'Who Uses Emoticons? Data from 86 702 Facebook Users', *Personality and Individual Differences* 119 (2017): 289–95.
13 Z. Chen, X. Lu, S. Shen, W. Ai, X. Liu, and Q. Mei, 'Through a Gender Lens: An Empirical Study of Emoji Usage over Large-Scale Android Users', *CoRR*. vol. abs/1705.05546 (2017).
14 Stella Ting-Toomey, and Tenzin Dorjee, *Communicating Across Cultures*, 2nd ed. (Guilford Publications, 2018), 243.
15 M. Koziol, 'Emoji: SwiftKey Report Shows Australia Is 'The Land of Vice and Indulgence', *The Sydney Morning Herald*, 2015. https://www.smh.com.au/lifestyle/emoji-swiftkey-report-shows-australia-is-the-land-of-vice-and-indulgence-20150422-1mqg83.html.
16 A. Rawlings, 'Why Emoji Mean Different Things in Different Cultures', *BBC*, 2018. https://www.bbc.com/future/article/20181211-why-emoji-mean-different-things-in-different-cultures.
17 K. Broni, 'China's Annual Emoji Censorship', *Emojipedia*, 2021. https://blog.emojipedia.org/chinas-annual-emoji-censorship/.
18 M. Shibata, 'The Middle Finger Emoji Could Land You in Jail in the UAE', *Vice*, 2015. https://www.vice.com/en/article/ypw9mw/the-middle-finger-emoji-could-land-you-in-jail-in-the-uae.
19 T. Nasrallah, 'Sending Red Heart Emojis on WhatsApp 'Can Land User in Jail' in Saudi Arabia', *Gulf News*, 2022. https://gulfnews.com/world/gulf/saudi/sending-red-heart-emojis-on-whatsapp-can-land-user-in-jail-in-saudi-arabia-1.85676931.
20 E. Izadi, 'Indonesia Wants to Banish "Gay" Emoji', *The Washington Post*, 2016. https://www.washingtonpost.com/news/worldviews/wp/2016/02/13/indonesia-wants-to-banish-gay-emoji/.
21 R. Schraer, 'The Russians Using Emojis to Evade Censors', *BBC*, 2022. https://www.bbc.com/news/60649725.
22 AFP, 'Milk Tea Alliance: Twitter Creates Emoji for Pro-Democracy Activists', *BBC*, 2021. https://www.bbc.com/news/world-asia-56676144.

Chapter 9

1 Based on my forthcoming work: Jieun Kiaer, *The Languague of Hallyu*.
2 Michael Beißwenger, and Steffen Pappert, 'How to Be Polite with Emojis: A Pragmatic Analysis of Face Work Strategies in an Online Learning Environment', *European Journal of Applied Linguistics* 7, no. 2 (2019): 225–54.
3 Ho-min Sohn, *The Korean Language*, Cambridge Language Surveys (Cambridge: Cambridge University Press, 1999), 408.

4 Jieun Kiaer, *Pragmatic Particles: Findings from Asian Languages*. Bloomsbury Studies in Theoretical Linguistics (London, 2021).
5 Jungbok Lee, *Sahoicek sothongmang (SNS)uy ene mwunhw yenkwu (A Study on Linguistic Culture Through SNS)* (Sotong, 2017).
6 Seonhwa Kim, 'Tongsin eneey nathanan chengsonyentuluy mwuncang congkyel pangsik yenkwu (A Study on Adolescents' Sentence Concluding Styles in Mobile Language: Focusing on Twitter Users)' (Master's Thesis, *Hankwuk Kyowen Tayhakkyo Tayhakwen*, 2013).
7 Sangyeop Han, *Mobile Instant Messaging in Korean: Linguistic Variations Among Patterns* (unpublished Mst dissertation, University of Oxford, 2017).
8 Danielle N. Gunraj, April M. Drumm-Hewitt, Erica M. Dashow, Sri Siddhi N. Upadhyay, and Celia M. Klin. 'Texting Insincerely: The Role of the Period in Text Messaging', *Computers in Human Behavior* 55 (2016): 1067–75.
9 The data was collected in December 2016., and January and March of 2017 in Gangseo District, Seoul. The data used for this chapter was originally collected and reported in Han. *Mobile Instant Messaging in Korean*; and Jieun Kiaer and Sangyeop Han, 'Multi-modal Endings in Korean Instant Messaging: The Case of Korean Youth', presented at the *29th Association of Korean Studies at Europe* (AKSE) Conference, Rome, 11–14 April 2019.
10 This finding is in line with Lee, *Sahoicek sothongmang (SNS)uy ene mwunhw yenkwu*.
11 Gretchen McCulloch, *Because Internet: Understanding How Language Is Changing* (London: Random House, 2019), 127.
12 Ibid., 133.
13 Ezra Marcus, 'Tone Is Hard to Grasp Online. Can Tone Indicators Help?', *The New York Times*, 2020.
14 Ibid.
15 'All the Tone Tags I'm Aware of and Their Meanings', *Tone Tags*. https://tonetags.carrd.co/#masterlist (Accessed 27 April 2022).
16 B. Muliadi, 'What the Rise of TikTok Says About Generation Z', [online] *Forbes*, 2020. https://www.forbes.com/sites/forbestechcouncil/2020/07/07/what-the-rise-of-tiktok-says-about-generation-z/> (Accessed 8 June 2022).
17 Mansoor Iqbal, 'Tiktok Revenue and Usage Statistics (2022)', *Business of Apps*, 11 November 2022. https://www.businessofapps.com/data/tik-tok-statistics/.
18 See all of Tiktok's secret emojis here: https://emojipedia.org/tiktok/show_all/
19 A. Turner, 'How to Unlock TikTok's Secret Emoji Codes', [online] *Mashable*, 2021. https://mashable.com/article/how-to-unlock-tiktok-secret-emoji-codes (Accessed 8 June 2022).
20 Ibid.
21 T. Francis and F. Hoefel, '"True Gen": Generation Z and Its Implications for Companies', [online] *McKinsey*, 2018. https://www.mckinsey.com/~/media/McKinsey/Industries/Consumer%20Packaged%20Goods/Our%20Insights/True

%20Gen%20Generation%20Z%20and%20its%20implications%20for%20companies/Generation-Z-and-its-implication-for-companies.pdf (Accessed 8 June 2022).

22 Matthew Guschwan, 'New Media: Online Fandom', *Soccer & Society* 17, no. 3 (2016): 351–71, 351.

23 J. Johnson, 'North Korea's Kim Flashes K-pop "Finger Hearts" Gesture in Bid to Soften Image, Photos Show', [online] *The Japan Times*, 2018. https://www.japantimes.co.jp/news/2018/09/23/asia-pacific/north-koreas-kim-flashes-k-pop-finger-hearts-gesture-bid-soften-image-photos-show/ (Accessed 10 September 2022).

24 'Are Idols Aware of the Emojis we use to Represent Them', *Reddit*, 2021. https://www.reddit.com/r/kpopthoughts/comments/kv0910/are_idols_aware_of_the_emojis_we_use_to_represent/.

25 A character who initially acts cold or hostile, but gradually shows a warmer side as one gets closer to them.

Bibliography

'012486, 1010235, 이 숫자의 뜻을 아십니까? . . . [독자사연] 삐삐(Beeper)의 추억 [Do You Know What These Numbers Mean?; 012486, 1010235 . . . [Letters to the Editor] A Memoir of Bbibbi(Beeper); Own Translation]'. 풀무원의 '아주 사적인' 이야기 *[Pulmuone's 'Very Private' Stories; Own Translation]*, 2011. http://blo.pulmuone.com/1488

'30 Statistics About Using Emojis for Businesses'. *The Pipeline*. https://blog.zoominfo.com/emoji-statistics-for-businesses/ (Accessed 27 April 2022).

'All the Tone Tags I'm Aware of and Their Meanings'. *Tone Tags*. https://tonetags.carrd.co/#masterlist (Accessed 27 April 2022).

'Apple Ios 4.0'. *Emojipedia*. https://emojipedia.org/apple/ios-4.0/ (Accessed 23 April 2021).

'Are Idols Aware of the Emojis We Use to Represent Them'. *Reddit*, 2021. https://www.reddit.com/r/kpopthoughts/comments/kv0910/are_idols_aware_of_the_emojis_we_use_to_represent/.

'Are There Any Emojis to Identify the BTS Members with, Like on Twitter?'. *Quora*, 2019. https://www.quora.com/Are-there-any-emojis-to-identify-the-BTS-members-with-like-on-Twitter

'Emoji and Burger King Team for Anti-Bullying Campaign'. *License Global*, 2019. https://www.licenseglobal.com/character/emoji-and-burger-king-team-anti-bullying-campaign?elq_mid=2613&elq_cid=3939780.

'Emoji Encoding Principles'. *Unicode*. http://www.unicode.org/emoji/principles.html (Accessed 27 April 2021).

'Emoji Marketing: How to Use Emoticons to Significantly Increase Your Conversions'. *Neil Patel*. https://neilpatel.com/blog/emoji-marketing-how-to-use-emoticons-to-increase-your-conversions/ (Accessed 21 April 2022).

'emoticon, n'. *OED Online*. March 2022. Oxford University Press. https://www.oed.com/view/Entry/249618?redirectedFrom=emoticon (Accessed 26 April 2022).

'How GFRIEND Express Their Teamwork. Even the Emoji Are in Displayed Fandom Colo'. *Reddit*, 2021. https://www.reddit.com/r/GFRIEND/comments/nil11q/how_gfriend_express_their_teamwork_even_the_emoji/.

'Insider Tips: How to Text Like a Korean In 2022'. *Lingua Asia*, 2021. https://linguasia.com/korean-texting.

'Misogynistic Attacks on Archer'. *The Korea Times*, 2021. https://www.koreatimes.co.kr/www/opinion/2021/08/137_313178.html'.

'Rethinking Our Default Profile Photo'. *Blog.Twitter.Com*, 2017. https://blog.twitter.com/en_us/topics/product/2017/rethinking-our-default-profile-photo.html.

'Sexual Solicitation'. *Facebook*. https://www.facebook.com/communitystandards/sexual_solicitation (Accessed 23 April 2022).

'Show Intention to Rent Apartment, Says Judge'. *Perma.Cc*, 2022. https://perma.cc/3APF-AQ6V.

'The Role of Emoji in New York City Sexual Harassment'. *Phillips & Associates*, 2019. https://www.newyorkemploymentattorney-blog.com/the-role-of-emoji-in-new-york-city-sexual-harassment/.

'Yellow Emojis Not Neutral Symbols of Identity'. *The University of Edinburgh*, 2021. https://www.ed.ac.uk/news/2021/yellow-emojis-not-neutral-identity-symbols?utm_campaign=cam_news2021&utm_content=1625059634&utm_medium=social&utm_source=facebook&fbclid=IwAR39NuEH25-FilFHogcUigpMTtBAUWha_i93y70j6aLp89Vjk62j7V24i6U.

Ampolpittayanant, Monrawee. 'Celebrating Thailand's National Day with Thai-Themed Emoji'. *Twitter Blog*, 5 December 2019. https://blog.twitter.com/en_sea/topics/events/2019/Celebrating-thailand-national-day-with-thai-themed-emoji.

Baldwin, Kai. 'Virtual Avatars: Trans Experiences of Ideal Selves Through Gaming'. *Markets, Globalization & Development Review* 3, no. 3 (2019): 1–20.

Baume, Matt. 'Donald Trump's 8 Worst Attacks On The LGBTQ+ Community'. *Them*, 2020. https://www.them.us/story/donald-trump-worst-lgbtq-attacks.

Beißwenger, Michael, and Steffen Pappert. 'How to Be Polite with Emojis: A Pragmatic Analysis of Face Work Strategies in an Online Learning Environment'. *European Journal of Applied Linguistics* 7, no. 2 (2019): 225–54.

Bellis, Mary. 'Arpanet: The World's First Internet'. *Thoughtco*, 2018. https://www.thoughtco.com/arpanet-the-worlds-first-internet-4072558.

Bennet, B. '7 Ways Older Millennials Text Differently Than Younger Millennials'. 2018. https://www.bustle.com/p/7-ways-older-millennials-text-differently-than-younger-millennials-8539988 (Accessed 10 April 2022).

Broni, Keith. 'China's Annual Emoji Censorship'. *Emojipedia*, 2021. https://blog.emojipedia.org/chinas-annual-emoji-censorship/.

Burge, Jeremy. 'Samsung Puts Japan Back on the Map'. *Emojipedia*, 2017. https://blog.emojipedia.org/samsung-puts-japan-back-on-the-map/.

Canagarajah, A. Suresh, ed. *Literacy as Translingual Practice: Between Communities and Classrooms*. Routledge, 2013.

Chen, James. 'The Vtuber Takeover of 2020'. *Polygon*, 2020. https://www.polygon.com/2020/11/30/21726800/hololive-vtuber-projekt-melody-kizuna-ai-calliope-mori-vshojo-youtube-earnings.

Chen, Zhenpeng, Xuan Lu, Sheng Shen, Wei Ai, Xuanzhe Liu, and Qiaozhu Mei. 'Through a Gender Lens: An Empirical Study of Emoji Usage Over Large-Scale Android Users'. *arXiv preprint arXiv:1705.05546* (2017).

Cheng, L., 2017. ¿ *Digo lo que Siento y Siento lo que digo?: una Aproximación Transcultural al Uso de los Emoticonos y Emojis en los Mensajes en CMC*. 199–217.

Churches, Owen, Mike Nicholls, Myra Thiessen, Mark Kohler, and Hannah Keage. 'Emoticons in Mind: An Event-Related Potential Study'. *Social Neuroscience* 9, no. 2 (2014): 196–202.

Common Sense Media. *The Common Sense Census: Media Use by Kids Age Zero to Eight*. V Rideout - San Francisco, CA: Common Sense Media, 2017.

Creese, Angela, and Adrian Blackledge. 'Translanguaging and Identity in Educational Settings'. *Annual Review of Applied Linguistics* 35 (2015): 20–35.

Danesi, Marcel. *The Semiotics of Emoji: The Rise of Visual Language in the Age of the Internet*. Bloomsbury Publishing, 2017.

Darlene Murdoch v. Medjet Assistance LLC and Roy Berger, 2:2016cv00779, (US District Court for the Northern District of Alabama 2018).

Davis & Edberg. 'Unicode Technical Report no.51'. 2015.

Davis, Mark and Ned Holbrook. 2022. 'Unicode® Technical Standard #51'. *Unicode.org*. http://www.unicode.org/reports/tr51/#Introduction (Accessed 16 January 2022).

Dawkins, Richard, and Ward Lalla. *The God Delusion*. Boston: Houghton Mifflin Company, 2006.

Ekman, P. *Emotions Revealed: Understanding Faces and Feelings*. New York: Henry Holt. 2004.

Erica N. Stewart V. Tarold Durham and Belhaven University, 3:2016cv00744 (US District Court for the Southern District of Mississippi 2016).

Evans, Vyvyan. *The Emoji Code: How Smiley Faces, Love Hearts and Thumbs Up Are Changing the Way We Communicate*. Michael O'Mara Books, 2017.

Fane, Jennifer, Colin MacDougall, Jessie Jovanovic, Gerry Redmond, and Lisa Gibbs. 'Exploring the Use of Emoji as a Visual Research Method for Eliciting Young Children's Voices in Childhood Research'. *Early Child Development and Care* 188, no. 3 (2018): 359–374.

García, Ofelia, and Wei Li. *Translanguaging : Language, Bilingualism and Education*. Basingstoke: Palgrave Macmillan, 2014.

Gim, C. 카카오톡, 말하는 이모티콘 출시. *Asia Economy Daily*, 2012. http://www.asiae.co.kr/news/view.htm?idxno=2012081610260446783 (Accessed 18 April 2022).

Goldman, Eric. 'Emojis and the Law'. *Washington Law Review* 93 (2018): 1244.

Grice, Herbert P. 'Logic and Conversation'. In *Speech Acts*, ed. Peter Cole and Jerry L. Morgan, 41–58. Boston: Brill, 1975.

Gunraj, Danielle N., April M. Drumm-Hewitt, Erica M. Dashow, Sri Siddhi N. Upadhyay, and Celia M. Klin. 'Texting Insincerely: The Role of the Period in Text Messaging'. *Computers in Human Behavior* 55 (2016): 1067–75.

Guschwan, Matthew. 'New Media: Online Fandom'. *Soccer & Society* 17, no. 3 (2016): 351–371.

Han, Hye Young, Eun Sil Park, and Hye Jung Shin. 'Effect of Group Intervention Using Emoticons on Emotional Empathy and Conversational Function of School-Age Children with Intellectual Disabilities1'. *Journal of Speech* 30, no. 2 (2021): 009–020.

Han, S. *Mobile Instant Messaging in Korean: Linguistic Variations Among Patterns*, unpublished Mst dissertation, University of Oxford, 2017.

Have You Ever Heard of the 'Emoji Commission'? Video. DW Documentary, 2020.

Henry, Jacob. 'White Conservative Politician Sends Tweet Claiming to Be Black Gay Obama Support'. *Metro*, 2020. https://metro.co.uk/2020/11/11/white-conservative-politician-sends-tweet-claiming-to-be-black-gay-obama-supporter-13577157/.

Hernandez, Patricia. 'Why Pokimane'S Vtubing Twitch Stream Has Everyone Talking'. *Polygon*, 2020. https://www.polygon.com/2020/9/14/21436437/pokimane-imane-anys-twitch-vtubing-vtuber-anime-livestream-mainstream-popularity.

Hirota, Minoru. 'Bācharu-ka suru hito no sonzai. VTuber no koshikata, yukusue'. *Yuriika. Uta to hyōron, tokushū bācharu YouTuber* 07 (2018): 45–52.

Hong, S. G. 'A Study on the Characteristics of Emoticon Usage of Socially Distant Users in CMC'. Unpublished master's thesis, Yonsei University, Seoul, Korea. 2020.

Hua, Zhu, Emi Otsuji, and Alastair Pennycook. 'Multilingual, Multisensory and Multimodal Repertoires in Corner Shops, Streets and Markets: Introduction'. *Social Semiotics* 27, no. 4 (2017): 383–393.

Hua, Zhu, Li Wei, and Agnieszka Lyons. 'Polish Shop (Ping) as Translanguaging Space'. *Social Semiotics* 27, no. 4 (2017): 411–433.

Hunt, Paul. 'World Emoji Day 2021: How Emoji Can Help Create a More Empathetic World, for All of Us'. *Adobe Blog*, 2021. https://blog.adobe.com/en/publish/2021/07/15/global-emoji-trend-report-2021.

Hunt, Paul D. 'What Will It Take to Create a More Inclusive Future for Emoji?' *Adobe Blog*, 2021. https://blog.adobe.com/en/publish/2021/04/15/towards-diverse-inclusive-future-for-emoji-uk.

Iqbal, Mansoor. 'Tiktok Revenue and Usage Statistics (2022)'. *Business of Apps*, 11 November 2022. https://www.businessofapps.com/data/tik-tok-statistics/.

Jouvenal, Justin. 'A 12-Year-Old Girl Is Facing Criminal Charges for Using Certain Emoji. She's Not Alone'. *The Washington Post*, 2016. http://adam.curry.com/art/1456703641_HbNrBjzX.html.

Kabali, Hilda K., Matilde M. Irigoyen, Rosemary Nunez-Davis, Jennifer G. Budacki, Sweta H. Mohanty, Kristin P. Leister, and Robert L. Bonner. 'Exposure and Use of Mobile Media Devices by Young Children'. *Pediatrics* 136, no. 6 (2015): 1044–1050.

Kavanagh, Barry. 'Emoticons as a Medium for Channeling Politeness Within American and Japanese Online Blogging Communities'. *Language & Communication* 48 (2016): 53–65.

Kemp, Simon. 'Digital 2016: Global Digital Overview'. *DataReportal*. 2016. https://datareportal.com/reports/digital-2016-global-digital-overview (Accessed 8 February 2022).

Kiaer and Han. 'Multi-Modal Endings in Korean Instant Messaging: The Case of Korean Youth'. Presented at the 29thAssociation of Korean Studies at Europe (AKSE) Conference, Rome, 11–14 April, 2019.

Kiaer, Jieun. *Language Stylistics*. Forthcoming.

Kiaer, Jieun. *Learning Beyond Words*. Forthcoming.

Kiaer, Jieun. *The Routledge Course in Korean Translation*. London: Routledge. 2017.

Kiaer, Jieun. *Translingual Words : An East Asian Lexical Encounter with English*. London: Routledge, 2019, 42.

Kiaer, Jieun, and Loli Kim. *Understanding Korean Film: A Cross-Cultural Perspective*. London: Routledge, 2021.

Kiaer, Jieun, M. J. Park, N. Choi and D. Driggs. 'The Roles of Age, Gender and Setting in Korean Half-Talk Shift', 담화와인지 26, no. 3 (2019): 279–308.

Kim, Ho. 'A Study on the Use of Communication Functions in Mobile Messenger Emoticons-Focus on Line Messenger'. *The Journal of the Korea Contents Association* 17, no. 9 (2017): 184–91.

Kim, M. H. 'A Study on Emoticon Use of Situational Context: Focused on Relative Importance and the Level of Closeness of Conversation'. Unpublished master's thesis, Hongik University, Seoul, Korea.

Kim, Seonhwa. 'Tongsin eneey nathanan chengsonyentuluy mwuncang congkyel pangsik yenkwu (A Study on Adolescents' Sentence Concluding Styles in Mobile Language: Focusing on Twitter Users)'. Master's Thesis, *Hankwuk Kyowen Tayhakkyo Tayhakwen*, 2013.

Kraus, Lydia, Robert Schmidt, Marcel Walch, Florian Schaub, and Sebastian Möller. 'On the Use of Emojis in Mobile Authentication'. *IFIP International Conference on ICT Systems Security and Privacy Protection*, 265–80. Cham: Springer, 2017.

Kwon, Hee Jin, Zhou Yu, and Jeong Yun Heo. 'The Influence of Psychological Distance on Emoticons' Usage Behavior'. *Design Convergence Study* 17, no. 1 (2018): 47–62.

Lee, Jungbok. *Sahoicek sothongmang (SNS)uy ene mwunhw yenkwu (A Study on Linguistic Culture Through SNS)*. Sotong, 2017.

Marcus, Ezra. 'Tone Is Hard to Grasp Online. Can Tone Indicators Help?'. *The New York Times*, 2020.

Marmer, Daria. 'These Emojis Can Increase Click-Through Rates, According To New Data'. *Hubspot*, 2018. https://blog.hubspot.com/marketing/best-emojis.

Matyszczyk, Chris. 'Teen Arrested After Alleged Facebook Emoji Threats'. *CNET*, 2015. https://www.cnet.com/culture/teen-arrested-after-alleged-facebook-emoji-threats/.

McCulloch, Gretchen. *Because Internet: Understanding How Language is Changing*. Random House, 2019.

Merriam-Webster.com Dictionary, s.v. 'Avatar'. https://www.merriam-webster.com/dictionary/avatar (Accessed 27 April 2022).

Nowak, Kristine L., and Christian Rauh. 'The Influence of the Avatar on Online Perceptions of Anthropomorphism, Androgyny, Credibility, Homophily, and Attraction'. *Journal of Computer-Mediated Communication* 11, no. 1 (2005): 153–178.

A. 2011. 012486, 1010235, 이 숫자의 뜻을 아십니까? ....[독자사연] 삐삐(beeper)의 추억 [Do you know what these numbers mean?; 012486, 1010235 . . . [Letters to the Editor] A memoir of Bbibbi(beeper); own translation]. 풀무원의 '아주 사적인'

이야기 *[Pulmuone's 'very private' stories; own translation]*. http://blog.pulmuone.com/1488 (Accessed 17 April 2022).

O'Connor, Lydia, and Daniel Marans. 'Here Are 13 Examples of Donald Trump Being Racist'. *Huffpost UK*, 2016. https://www.huffingtonpost.co.uk/entry/donald-trump-racist-examples_n_56d47177e4b03260bf777e83?ri18n=true.

Ofcom. *Children And Parents: Media Use And Attitudes Report 2019*. Making Sense Of Media, 2020. https://www.ofcom.org.uk/__data/assets/pdf_file/0023/190616/children-media-use-attitudes-2019-report.pdf.

Oleszkiewicz, Anna, Maciej Karwowski, Katarzyna Pisanski, Piotr Sorokowski, Boaz Sobrado, and Agnieszka Sorokowska. 'Who Uses Emoticons? Data from 86 702 Facebook Users'. *Personality and individual differences* 119 (2017): 289–295.

Otheguy, Ricardo, Ofelia García, and Wallis Reid. 'Clarifying Translanguaging and Deconstructing Named Languages: A Perspective From Linguistics'. *Applied Linguistics Review* 6, no. 3 (2015): 281–307.

Otsuji, Emi, and Alastair Pennycook. 'Metrolingualism: Fixity, Fluidity and Language in Flux'. *International journal of multilingualism* 7, no. 3 (2010): 240–254.

Pardes, Arielle. 'Don'T See Yourself on Your Emoji Keyboard? She Can Help'. *Wired*, 2019. https://www.wired.com/story/jenny-8-lee-picture-character/.

Pardes, Arielle. 'The Wired Guide to Emoji'. *Wired*, 2018. https://www.wired.com/story/guide-emoji (Accessed 20 February 2022).

Potts, Christopher. *The Logic of Conventional Implicatures*. Oxford: Oxford University Press, 2005.

Prada, Marília, David L. Rodrigues, Margarida V. Garrido, Diniz Lopes, Bernardo Cavalheiro, and Rui Gaspar. 'Motives, Frequency and Attitudes Toward Emoji and Emoticon Use'. *Telematics and Informatics* 35, no. 7 (2018): 1925–34.

Prensky, Marc. 'Digital Natives, Digital Immigrants Part 2: Do They Really Think Differently?'. *On the Horizon* (2001).

Radcliffe, Damian, and Hadil Abuhmaid. *Social Media in the Middle East: 2019 In Review*, 2019. https://scholarsbank.uoregon.edu/xmlui/bitstream/handle/1794/25119/social_media_middle_east_2019.pdf?sequence=3.

Rahman, Zara. 'The Problem With Emoji Skin Tones That No One Talks About'. *The Daily Dot*, 2018. https://www.dailydot.com/irl/skin-tone-emoji/.

Ratcliffe, Rebecca. 'New Emoji Set Aims to Shatter Image of Africa as Zone of Famine and War'. *The Guardian*, 18 November 2019. https://www.theguardian.com/global-development/2019/nov/18/new-emoji-set-aims-to-shatter-image-of-africa-as-zone-of-famine-and-war.

Rouse, Margaret. 'What Is Paging? A Definition from WhatIs.com'. *SearchMobile Computing, TechTarget*. 2007. http://searchmobilecomputing.techtarget.com/definition/pager (Accessed 7 December 2021).

Ruiz, Michelle. '2019 was the Year of the Celebrity Notes App Statement'. *Vogue*, 2019. https://www.vogue.com/article/best-celebrity-notes-app-statements-2019.

Seargeant, Philip. *The Emoji Revolution: How Technology Is Shaping the Future of Communication*. Cambridge, 2019, 139.
Silver, Laura. 'Smartphone Ownership is Growing Rapidly Around the World, but Not Always Equally'. *Pew Research Center*. 2022. https://www.pewresearch.org/global/2019/02/05/smartphone-ownership-is-growing-rapidly-around-the-world-but-not-always-equally/ (Accessed 15 February 2022).
Sohn, Ho-min. *The Korean Language*. Cambridge Language Surveys. Cambridge: Cambridge University Press, 1999, 408.
Soyeong, Kim. '오조오억-허버허버'가 왜 남혐이냐, 뜻도 모르면서"…논란 Ing'. *Money Today*, 2021. https://news.mt.co.kr/mtview.php?no=2021042211464429191.
Spencer, Caleb. 'Coronavirus: Digital Poverty "A Threat To Children In Care"'. *BBC News*, 2020. https://www.bbc.co.uk/news/uk-wales-52654426.
Statista. 'Smartphone Users 2026'. 2022. https://www.statista.com/statistics/330695/number-of-smartphone-users-worldwide/ (Accessed 26 January 2022).
Stinson, Liz. 'Finland Just Designed the Most Finnish Emoji Ever'. *Wired*, 5 November 2015. https://www.wired.com/2015/11/finland-national-emoji/.
The, Cheryl. 'China Blocked Candle and Cake Emojis From Weibo in Order to Censor Anniversary Commemorations of the Tiananmen Square Massacre'. *Insider*, 2021. https://www.insider.com/chinese-censors-blocked-candle-emojis-anniversary-tiananmen-massacre-2021-6.
Torre, Giovanni. 'The New Indigenous Emojis Coming to Your Smartphone Screen'. *National Indigenous Times 2*, 26 February 2022. https://nit.com.au/26-02-2022/2734/the-new-indigenous-emojis-coming-to-your-smartphone-screen.
Tutt, Paige. 'Apple's New Diverse Emoji are Even More Problematic Than Before'. 2015. https://www.washingtonpost.com/posteverything/wp/2015/04/10/how-apples-new-multicultural-emojis-are-more-racist-than-before/?noredirect=on.
Utomo, Delfina. '6 Singapore Emojis We Wish Existed'. *Time Out Singapore*. Time Out, 12 May 2020. https://www.timeout.com/singapore/things-to-do/singapore-emojis-we-wish-existed.
Vonberg, Judith. 'Teen Behind Hijab Emoji: "I Wanted An Emoji of Me"'. *CNN*, 2017. https://edition.cnn.com/2017/07/18/europe/hijab-emoji-teenager/index.html.
Wasserman, Helena. '12 African Emoji We Would like to See - Including Proper Sandals and Pap'. *Business Insider*, 2018. https://www.businessinsider.co.za/african-emoji-we-would-like-to-see-2018-9.
Wei, Li. 'Moment Analysis and Translanguaging Space: Discursive Construction of Identities by Multilingual Chinese Youth in Britain'. *Journal of Pragmatics* 43, no. 5 (2011): 1222–1235.
Wilkinson, Rachel. 'The Father of the Emoticon Chases His Great White Whale'. *Narratively*. 2022. https://narratively.com/the-father-of-the-emoticon-chases-his-great-white-whale/ (Accessed 26 April 2022).
Wolf, Alecia. 'Emotional Expression Online: Gender Differences in Emoticon Use'. *Cyberpsychology & behavior* 3, no. 5 (2000): 827–833.

Wong, Alexander. 'Twitter Releases Special Emoji for Malaysia's Merdeka Celebration'. *Tech-Gadgets*, 27 April 2021. https://www.malaymail.com/news/tech-gadgets/2021/08/27/twitter-releases-special-emoji-for-malaysias-merdeka-celebration/2000833.

Yeon, Jaehoon, and Lucien Brown. *Korean: A Comprehensive Grammar*. London: Routledge, 2013.

Zappavigna, Michele. *Discourse of Twitter and Social Media: How We Use Language to Create Affiliation on the Web*. Vol. 6. A&C Black, 2012.

정, 윤희. '카카오톡 이모티콘, 다날 휴대폰결제로 산다'. *Zdnet.co.kr*. 2022. http://www.zdnet.co.kr/news/news_view.asp?artice_id=20111215104248&lo=zv41 (Accessed 26 April 2022).

Index

Page numbers in *italics* indicate figures in the text and references following "n" refer endnotes.

Adobe Global Emoji Trend Report, 2021   83
Advanced Research Projects Agency (ARPAnet)   36
affectionate emojis   133–5, *134*
affordability   3, 15, 140
Ai, Kizuna   41
American-dominated Unicode Consortium   74
angry emoji   108
animojis   12, 43
anti-bullying emojis   95
Apple emoji keyboard   20, 72, 137
Apple's emoji designs   20
Apple's 'generic' emojis   78
Arab cultural symbols   75
Arabic speakers   142
Article 19 of the United Nations Universal Declaration of Human Rights   70
Asian-style emoticons   18
at-issue (inherently lexical) meaning   16
aubergine emoji   34
avatars   23, 27, 36–43, 82, 166, 167, 175

Baldwin, Kai   40, 41
bastard   16
Because Internet (McCullough)   23
Bitmoji   27
Black emojis   79
Black Lives Matter (BLM) movement   13, 96
blue heart emoji   99, 137, 160
bomb and explosion emojis   93
borderless communication   49–51
Breazeal, Cynthia   105
broken heart emoji   93
Browning, Dean   39

Buddhist group chat conversation   157, *158*
'Bulletproof Boy Scouts' (BTS) emoji   160–2
Bump, Phillip   39

cake emoji   96
California-based Unicode Consortium   72
candle-related emojis   97, 99
capitalism   15
Carlos, John   35
censorship   95–8
central data systems   24
Chen, James   40
Cher   93
'childish' tone of emojis   93
children and emojis   112–13
China
  characters as emojis   18, 86
  demographic diversity   82
  Douyin emojis   86–7, *87*
  emojis and interpretations   20, *20*, 114, *114*
  emojis in work-related messages   123
  open mouth and cold sweat emoji   88
  red rose emoji   ix, 121–3, *123*
  smirking face emoji   88, 89
  sun and coffee emojis   123, *123*
  Unicode emojis   88
  WeChat emojis   83–5
  winking face emoji   88
Chinese Communist Party (CCP)   96
Chinese-style punctuation   51
Chinese viral expression   84
CMC, *see* computer-mediated communication (CMC)
colourful conversations   51–3, *52*, *53*

colour of emojis   3
commitment (inherently pragmatic) meaning   16
communication mismatches   55
communities of practice   54
competence, emoji   54-5
computer-mediated communication (CMC)   9-11, 28, 30, 58, 172, 173
Confetti effect   52, *52*
cool emoji   83
Covid-19 pandemic   viii, 35
creativity   24
cross-cultural emoji misunderstandings   5
crossed flags emoji   97
cultural diversity   4
customizable emojis   81, 82, *82*

Daily Lives of High School Boys   164
Danesi, Marcel   23, 88
darker or lighter skin-toned emojis   79
Dawkins, Richard   22
demographic diversity, China   82
digital divide   15
digital natives   25
DOCOMO Japanese mobile carrier   19
'doge' meme   32
doggy head emoji   132
Douyin emojis   86-7, *87*
Dumpling Emoji Project   73, 74

easy-to-use nature of emojis   1
Eiffel Tower emoji   69
Ekman, Paul   109, 110, 116
Ekman's six basic emotions   110, 116
Emoji 1.0   72
emoji-branded plush toys   95
The Emoji Code (Evans)   23
Emojics blog   93
'Emoji Encoding Principles'   80
emoji ethics   37-9
emoji keyboard   1, 9, 12, 18, 20, 26, 31, 72, 81, 86, 87, 96, 97, 133, 137, 160, 161, 169, 172, 175
emoji lexicon   71, 72
emoji linguistics   173-6
emoji literacy   14
emoji motivations

selection and frequency   45
solidarity   46, 48
speed   46-7
style   46-8
thumbs-up emoji   46
emoji native   14-15
Emojipedia   34, 93
emoji politeness   130
emoji protests   96
emoji reactions   91
The Emoji Revolution (Seargeant)   23
emojis of protest   143
emoji speak   2, 4, 30, 43, 45, 49, 55, 57, 63, 106, 107, 121, 126, 169, 170, 172, 173
    alternative authority   13-14
    for Black Lives Matter (BLM) movement   13
    constant acquisition   12
    dynamism   12
    emoji words   11
    grassroots movement   13
    intentions and impact   11
    leaders of   13-14
    letter words   11
    multiculturalism   13
    multi-modal resources   11
    mutual comprehension   13
    'newspeak'   8, 11
    and punctuation   17, *17*
    regional variation   13
    on smartphone screen   11
    with Ukraine   13
emoji stylistics
    happy emotions   151
    linguistic phenomenon   151
    punctuation markers   152
    wrong emoji usage   151
'Emoodji' app   113
emoticons/emotion icon   7, 12, 18-19, *19*, 24, 32, 50, 61, 62, 87, 116, 118, 130, 145, 147, 152
English-style punctuation   51
etymology   7, 66-8
Evans, Vyvyan   23
eye-catching emoji   1

Facebook Messenger   ix, 10, 26, 27, 107, 174

face-to-face silences   46
face with medical mask emoji   34, 35, *35*, 84
face with rolling eyes emoji   114
face with tears of joy emoji   30, *31*, 113
facial expression symbol   67
Fahlman, Scott   18
'fairy comment'   33, *33*
falafel emoji   75
fashionable emojis   54
Fate/stay night meme   165
'faulty comparison' criterion   69
female emojis   76
'finger-heart' gesture   160, *161*
folded hands emoji   145
food and drink emojis
    Central and South American   73
    dango   73
    emoji lexicon   71, 72
    fast-food items   72
    Japanese cuisine   73
    kamaboko   73
    Middle Eastern-inspired items   73
    narutomaki   73
    oden   73
    US-style junk foods   72
forms and meanings of emoji   2
French speakers   142
friend emojis   26
'friendzone' emoji   137
frowny sign   18
full-stops   58, 59

gay-themed emojis   142
gender dysphoria   40
gender-neutral emojis   76
general emoji etiquette   121–2
generic yellow emoji   77, *78*, 79
Gen Z   26, 128
    TikTok users   156–7
    tone indicators   154
GFRIEND fandom   159, 160
Gibson, William   37
Goldman, Eric   102, 103
Google Jamboard   65, *66*
Google's Emoji Kitchen app   81
Google Translate   141
grammar rules in mobile languaging   58
Graphics Interchange Format (GIFs)   22

Greek letters   19
grinning face with smiling eyes emoji   111, *111*
GroupLens   111
Guazzelli, Michael   154
Gunraj, Danielle N.   57, 59

'Haha' reaction   92
hand gestures   122
handwritten communication   12
heart emojis   108, 121, 135, 136
hijab emoji   75
Huang, Eddie   74
hugging emojis   85
human emotions by emojis   76, 77
    angry emoji   108
    autocorrect function   109
    bodily expressions   107
    emotional intelligence   110, 112
    facial expressions   106
    happiness and *kawaii*   107
    heart emojis   108
    physical gestures   106
    reacting through emoji   106–7
    six core emotions   109–112, *111*
    tone indicators   107–8

idiolects   53–4, 65
image macros   21–2
Indigemoji   89
'in-message' emojis   31
innocuous emojis   98
Inside Out (2015)   109
Instagram   26, 107
intergenerational communication   55–7
internet poverty   15
interpersonal relations   5
interpreted emojis   10
intimacy   129–30
iPhone 3G   19
iPhone 13 models   24
iPhone Notes app   24

Jackson, Peter   22
Jamboard workshop   125–6
Japanese carrier images   77
Japanese etymology   67
Japanese mobile phones   19–20
Japanese-style emoticon   50

Japanese Vtuber fandoms 166–7
jjalbang ix, 53, 117, *117*, 118

KakaoTalk 26, 53, 58, 65, 87, 88, 98, 115, 117, 123, 130
kanji characters 67
Kawaii emojis 115–18, *116, 117*
keyboard symbols 18
Kim Jong-un, North Korean president 160
Korea, *see also* South Korea
   emoji stylistics 150–1
   intergenerational communication 55, 56
   Jamboard workshop 125–6
   jjalbang ix, 53, 117, *117*, 118
   KakaoTalk 26, 53, 58, 65, 87, 88, 98, 115, 117, 123, 130
   non-verbal expressions 144
   popular culture fandoms 145
   smiley and sad face emoticons 144
   smiling eyes emoticon 61
   speech and gesture styles 150, 151
   squiggle 61, 62
   vowel combinations 145
K-pop fandoms 48
   BTS emoji 160–2
   EXO 160–2
   reaction images 162–4, *163*
   on Twitter/internet forums 159
Kraus, Lydia 94

Language Online (Barton and Lee) 28
laugh-cry emojis 132
laughing emoji 92
law and emojis 100–3, *101, 103*
Line app 115, 117
Line messaging application 142
linguistic practices 2, 4
LinkedIn ix, 37, 94
little yellow faces 67
Liu Xiaobo 96
The Lord of the Rings trilogy (Tolkien) 22

McCullough, Gretchen 23
McGill, Andrew 79
mailbox emojis 69
Manga and Anime fandoms 164–6
Marcus, Ezra 154

Marília, Prada 130, 131
marketing, emojis 93–5
mathematical language 18
meaning most emoji 33–4
melon-eating emoji 84
memes 22, 31, 32
memojis 43, 82
message exchanges 52, *53*
MeToo movement 35
middle finger emoji 142
Milk Tea Alliance movement 35
misuse/absence of emoji 54
Moon Jae-in, South Korean president 160
Moore, Lisa 80
More than Polite 150
multilingual communication 50

'namaste' emoji 145
negative emotions 61
'Newspeak' (Orwell) 8, 11, 169
non-verbal gestures 3
non-verbal signs 9
notes app apology 24
Nyanners 42

OED definition 8, 9, 18–19
Olympic torch emojis 96
one's emojing style 12
online banking 28
online fan communities 158–60
online meme generators 31
online messaging features 9
online messenger programs 29
online-only business 27–8
online shopping 28
open mouth and cold sweat emoji 88
Oruchuban Ebichu 163
Orwell, George 11, 169, 170
orz 86

Patel, Neil 94
Pavliscak, Pamela 109, 110
PayPal 97
people hugging emoji 85
personified character emojis 118
phone call 'app' 29
pictorial resources 8
Picture Character 8, 80

picture words   9
Pierre   137
pinched fingers emoji   75, *75*
pink flower emoji   135
Pokimane   42
politeness of emoji   56, 124–6, *125*
poorly placed emoji, consequences   92
post-pandemic world, emojis   173
Potts, Christopher   16
prescriptive grammar   59
pre-set emojis   3, 23
proprietary emojis   94
prune prevention   118
punctuation   57–60, 63

'quit smoking'   83

raised fist with dark skin tone emoji   35
Ramadan emoji   75
real image sticker pack   116, *116*
realistic emojis
    Apple's 'generic' emojis   78
    AR Emoji feature   82
    Black emojis   79
    customizable emojis   81, 82, *82*
    darker or lighter skin-toned
        emojis   79
    female emojis   76
    gender-neutral emojis   76
    generic yellow emoji   77, *78*, 79
    global 'language' of emojis   81
    human emojis   76, 77
    Japanese carrier images   77
    light-skinned emoji   79
    official design guidelines   76
    person wearing turban   78, *78*
    racial representation   77
    transgender flag emoji   80
    Unicode's design guidelines   76
    zero width joiner   78
real-life gestures emoji   96
*Reclaiming Conversation: The Power
    of Talk in a Digital Age*
        (Turkle)   112
Reddit   162
red heart emoji   137, 142
red rose emoji   ix, 121–3, *123*

'safe' emojis   122, 128, *129*, 138–9, *139*

Samsung   97
sarcasm   154
Seargeant, Philip   23
'selection factor for exclusion'   69
The Semiotics of Emoji (Danesi)   23, 88
sensitivity
    age and hierarchy   126–9, *129*
    cross-cultural sensitivity   141–3
    cross-gender emojing   132
    emoji politeness   124–6, *125*
    folded hands emoji   145
    gender differences   130–1
    general emoji etiquette   121–2
    group chat matters   140–1
    individual matters   139–40
    intimacy   129–30
    'namaste' emoji   145
    poo emoji   122
    safe emojis   122
    smiling emojis   143–5
    static and geometric emojis   124
    studying emojis   122
    tears of joy emoji   145
    U+1F3E9 emoji   146
sentence-final punctuation   60
sentence-initial punctuation   60
sexual emojis/emoji strings   98
Shigetaka Kurita   19
shy emoji   85
single-emoji reactions   92
skewered dumplings   73
smiley face emojis   x, 18, 61, 132, 143–5
smiling happy face emoji   113
smirking face emoji   88, 89
Smith, Tommie   35
Snapchat   26–7, 128
social movements   98–9
social networking services (SNS)   26
SoftBank's emoji system   19
sound and moving images   8–9
soundmojis   43
sound words   9
South Korea
    affectionate emojis   133–5, *134*
    emoji for women   130
    emoji stylistics   150–1
    face with tears of joy emoji   130
    folded hands emoji   130
    LINE   21

loudly crying face emoji   130
prescriptive grammar   59
Samsung   97
speech and gesture styles   150–1
Spanish intergenerational communication   55, 56
stickers   21
straightforward emojis   127
Strengthening Effective Language of Feelings in Education (SELFIE project)   113
studying emojis   122
stylistics   5
Suk, Jeannie   71

'tailor-made' mobile languaging styles   59
Taiwanese flag emoji   97
tears emotions   61
tears of joy emoji   145
Tencent emoji   83, 84
text speak   24
'Three S' model   4
thumbs-up emoji   34, 46, 142, 171
TikTok   23, 24, 33, 128, 156–7
To emoji   9
Tokyo Tower emoji   69
Tolkien   22
tone indicators   153–4
tone tags   153–4
transgender flag emoji   80
translanguaging   49, 50
'Truck-kun' meme   165
Turkle, Sherry   112
Tutt, Paige   79
Twitter   24, 32, 35, 37, 38, 143
   top 10 emojis   47, *47*
Twitter account @Emoji Mashup Bot   81
Twitter Public Policy   36

U+1F3E9 emoji   146
Uglow, Tea   80

unamused face emoji   114
Unicode Consortium   33–4, 67–70, 74, 75, 80
Unicode emojis   19–21, 23, 60, 67–71, 73, 74, 76, 82, 83, 86–8, 111, 157
   on iOS 4   78, *77*
upside down face emoji   34

verbal expressives   16
video games   39–40
virtual avatar   41
virtual communication   60–2
virtual immigration   10
virtual interactions   106
virtual reality (VR)   23
vision for the future   5
visual communication   9
Voting membership   69
VRChat   37
vtuber phenomenon   41–3

The Washington Post (Tutt)   79
water pistol emoji   103
Web 2.0   10, 24, 28–9, *29*
Web 3.0   10, 24, 30
websites   20
WeChat   ix, 20, 21, 26, *83*, 83–5, *85*, 99, 115, 123, 127, 142
   custom sticker   *155*, 155–6
Weibo   83, 96, 99, 142
WhatsApp   107, 127, 142
winking face emoji   88, 149, 153
World of Warcraft avatar   40
writing hand emoji   157, *157*

Yamato, Ami   41
yellow ribbon emoji   98, 99

Zoom and Teams   10
ZoomInfo   94

www.ingramcontent.com/pod-product-compliance
Lightning Source LLC
Chambersburg PA
CBHW052113300426
44116CB00010B/1650